Faith, Hope and Educat

Aspects of Research at the National Centre for Christian Education
Liverpool Hope University 2008-15

Edited by Andrew B. Morris

Liverpool Hope University Press

Faith, Hope and Educational Research:
Aspects of Research at the National Centre for Christian Education
Liverpool Hope University 2008-15
Edited by Andrew B. Morris

This book first published 2016

Liverpool Hope University Press
Taggart Avenue, Hope Park, Liverpool L16 9JD

British Library Cataloguing in Publication Data
A catalogue record for this book is available from the British Library

ISBN 978-1-898749-14-1

Contents

Acknowledgements

This book comprises a selection of edited research projects produced by, or under the umbrella of, the National Centre for Christian Education (NCfCE) at Liverpool Hope University between 2008 and 2015. Elements of one report, commissioned by NCfCE and completed in 2012, have subsequently been published in 2014 in the journal Research Papers in Education.

May I record my thanks to all those who have generously allowed me to make use of their research, as well as those many individuals within Liverpool Hope University, especially Bill Chambers, Liz Gayton, Bart McGettrick and Kenneth Newport (who facilitated publication of this book), all of whom have, over a number of years, encouraged and supported the promotion, development and continued existence of the National Centre for Christian Education.

Much of the Centre's funding is derived from commissioned projects to provide Continuing Professional Development courses/conferences for Catholic and Anglican dioceses, and develop teaching materials for use in Initial Teacher Education programmes. Additionally, it has received a variety of commissions to evaluate large-scale projects funded by national and international charitable bodies.

However, it is most important to express my sincere thanks for the financial support of the Theodore Trust and, in particular, the considerable generosity of the Jerusalem Trust, both of whom have provided funds to enable the Centre's on-going work of teaching and research and, in the case of the Jerusalem Trust, the publication of the fruits of that research.

Andrew B. Morris - Editor

Preface

The National Centre for Christian Education at Liverpool Hope University - initially known as the Centre for Christian Education - was established in 2006 by Professor John Sullivan. Its primary purpose was providing programmes of Continuing Professional Development (CPD) for Christian educators in schools, local authorities, colleges and dioceses. At that time there were few Higher Education Institutes in England offering a comprehensive range of Christian CPD courses. Of those working in this field the most notable, in addition to the National Centre for Christian Education at Hope, include The Maryvale Institute in Birmingham, St. Mary's University College, Twickenham and, until its closure in 2015, Heythrop College in London.

Today, while continuing to offer programmes of Christian professional development, the Centre promotes high quality research in Christian Education: work that is chiefly carried out through commissioning (and commissioned) empirical research, and supervising doctoral and masters level students. Currently, it is one of only four designated centres for Christian Education Research in the United Kingdom. The other three are the North of England Institute for Christian Education at Durham University, the Centre for Catholic Education at the Institute of Education in London and the National Institute for Christian Education Research at Christ Church Canterbury University. In addition, there is a large body of quantitative research into religion and values carried out at Warwick University by Professor Leslie Francis under the auspices of its Religions and Education Research Unit.

This book is concerned with the outcomes of the research programme at Liverpool Hope's National Centre for Christian Education from 2008-2015. It seeks to both provide an overview of research undertaken by staff and students working within the Centre and to encourage others to build on the foundations it has laid in this academic area. To that end, it is hoped that a second volume may be published in due course.

After briefly explaining the background to the Centre's genesis, its development and the range of its current programme, the book describes ten pieces of research grouped under two main headings. In the first there are edited versions of four case studies taken from PhD and EdD theses concerned with specific values and attitudes in Catholic sector schools. The second, larger, section comprises six projects describing research into different aspects of engagement and performance in the mission of a variety of Christian schools.

Combining disparate research into a single manuscript has necessitated some adaption of the various original stylistic formats to ensure some consistency in their presentation in this book. Consequently, I have kept, as far as possible, the authors individual writing styles but have adopted a number of relatively small but idiosyncratic variations on those usually employed in doctoral theses such as Harvard, Chicago, MHRA etc. I trust they will not irritate the general reader, particularly professionals in the field, or detract from the contents of the individual contributions.

Andrew B. Morris - Editor

Contributor Profiles

Geraldine (Gerry) Bradbury

Gerry is a former primary school teacher and headteacher. She subsequently worked as a Diocesan Officer, Deputy Director of Schools and finally as Director of Schools in the Diocese of Salford before starting a well-earned retirement in 2011. Among other things, she has been involved in the development and delivery of a leadership training programme, first within the Diocese and subsequently for the North West Training Partnership of Catholic dioceses. The success and value of the programme has been recognised nationally and is being developed for use in a number of Catholic and Anglican dioceses in England.

Currently, she is a consultant with the National Centre for Christian Education at Liverpool Hope University contributing, from time to time where her schedule allows, to its extensive CPD programme. In addition, she has worked for the Catholic Education Service helping develop its Headteacher Succession Planning programme, while at the same time undertaking professional doctoral studies, looking at the evolution of the Catholic educational system in England.

Alison Clark

After successfully completing her doctoral research at Liverpool Hope University in 2015, Alison established herself as independent 'Values Consultant and Trainer' (www.valuesreflection.com). She was formerly a member of the Faculty of Education at Liverpool Hope, lecturing in Teacher Education with responsibility as Head of Year 3. In addition, she lectured in Religious Education and Professional Studies at undergraduate and PGCE level. Before her appointment at Liverpool Hope, she worked in secondary and primary schools, as a teacher and manager of Religious Education, PSHE and Citizenship, and was Head of the School of Humanities in a Further education College.

Her Master's degree was in Theology, with a focus on peace movements in the 20th century while her research interests working within in the 'National Centre for Christian Education' at Hope were concerned with values in education, with an emphasis on faith-based schools. She has collaborated with colleagues at Christ Church Canterbury University on materials for training teachers relating to the ethos of faith-based schools, the results of which are distributed nationally. A further interest is global learning, including the eco-schools agenda and human rights. She led the non-credit bearing enhancement course, the 'Anglican Teaching Certificate', at Hope from 2009-2014 and co-delivered Continuous Professional Development (CPD) for school teachers on Global Learning. She is a undertakes research for the Hope's Centre for Education Policy Analysis and is a member of the Chartered Management Institute.

Fiona Dineen is a committed and practicing Catholic. She is a native of Limerick, Ireland where she attended Catholic primary and secondary schools and, subsequently, a Catholic College of Education. She has been professionally involved in Catholic education for ten years. Her initial training was as a teacher in the Primary sector. She has taught in a number of primary schools, is a teacher in a Catholic primary school and part-time lecturer in Religious Education at Mary Immaculate College, and is currently seconded by her school to the Catholic Diocese of Limerick as Diocesan Advisor for Religious Education at the Primary level. She is particularly interested in the on-going professional development of primary educators and, as one element of her Diocesan role provides in-service training in both Arts and Religious Education. Fiona's research interests also include education policy and practice in the Primary Sector, sacramental preparation, and the emerging models for exploring ethos and identity in Catholic schools. She successfully completed doctoral studies at Liverpool Hope University at the end of 2014, graduating in July 2015.

After successfully completing his BA (Hons) undergraduate degree at Chester University, **Mark Dumican's** first career was as a Systems Analyst before he considered, but initially rejected, the idea of teaching. However, his Christian faith, idealism and interest in 'making a difference' in the world soon determined his eventual career path within the teaching profession. He enrolled at Manchester University and completed a Post Graduate Certificate Education, and has subsequently been awarded an MSc in Education Management at Liverpool Hope University, a National Professional Qualification for Headship at The National College for School Leadership before successfully completing an MEd degree, again at Liverpool Hope University.

He has worked in the teaching profession for twenty years, during which he spent two as a classroom teacher, a further two as deputy head of Computing, four years as Head of Computing, two years as an Assistant Headteacher, ten years as a Deputy Headteacher and for the last two years as the (very honoured and proud) Headteacher of St Edmund Arrowsmith Catholic High School in Wigan. When he was teaching GCSE and A Level computing in 2002 he completed the computing industry examinations and became a Microsoft Office Specialist (MOS) Master. At that time he also produced a computing resource for schools entitled 'Bridging the Gap', (which can still be purchased from Amazon!).

Alan Flintham was, for 15 years, Headteacher of a secondary school serving a socially challenging urban area of North Nottinghamshire, until retiring on age-related grounds in 2005. He has worked as a self-employed Education Consultant and Associate Research Fellow in the Centre for Christian Education at Liverpool Hope University and until very recently, was a non-stipendiary priest in the Derby Diocese of the Church of England.

As a Research Associate of the National College for Leadership of Schools and Children's Services, he has published 'Reservoirs of Hope: spiritual and moral leadership in headteachers', 'When Reservoirs Run Dry: why some headteachers leave headship early', and most recently 'What's Good About Leading Schools in Challenging Circumstances'. His work is featured as a chapter in *Passionate Leadership in Education*, edited by Brent Davies and Tim Brighouse (Sage, 2008) and its development resulted in the award of a PhD from the University of Liverpool in 2009. He is the author of *'Reservoirs of Hope: sustaining sacred and secular spirituality in school leaders'* (Cambridge Scholars Publishing, 2010).

He has been rapporteur and facilitator for National College Leading Practice Seminars on 'Leadership and Spirituality' and 'Leading Schools of a Religious Character'. He was awarded a Churchill Travelling Fellowship to visit Australia in 2005 to study how school principals are sustained and supported in that country, which has led to further on-going research into the impact of personal faith on school leadership, from a variety of faith perspectives both sacred and secular, in the UK and in Australia. He has been involved in the setting up and evaluation of a recently developed peer support scheme for Nottinghamshire headteachers, and has significant experience of mentoring and supporting both newly qualified and experienced colleagues from all phases and social contexts of schools.

Ray Godfrey is a free-lance research consultant working with the Liverpool Hope University Centre for Christian Education. He was formerly Reader in Educational Statistics at Canterbury Christ Church University and the Open University. He is an epistemologist, with degrees in Latin, Greek, ancient history and philosophy; mathematics; the philosophy and psychology of education; and statistics. He spent thirteen years teaching mostly maths and some religious education in a number of comprehensive schools before moving into the tertiary education sector.

He has carried out, collaborated in, or supported research projects in a wide range of fields, including: moral values and beliefs of pupils in French and English schools; river pollution; the early mathematical development of children in England, Slovenia and five other countries; the long term consequences of permanent exclusion from primary schools; permanent exclusion of ethnic minority pupils from schools and the coding of ethnicities in school returns to DfES; progression of pupils in maths, science and English through Year 7; Special Educational Needs; teaching foreign languages in primary schools; preparing mentally ill students for further education; and the effects of ageing on elite athletic performance.

In addition to publications connected with these projects, he has written on: the philosophies of John White, Democritus and Russell; effect-size and meta-analysis; the role of research compared with professional experience; and misinterpretation of the difference between qualitative and quantitative research.

Elizabeth (Beth) Green – see Director Profiles

Jonathan Lawford has taught in the secondary sector for twenty-seven years in five different Catholic schools. He has worked in a variety of roles including Head of Year, Head of Department, Assistant Head teacher, Deputy Head teacher and Head of School. He has spent the last 17 years on the Leadership Team of three schools. His teaching specialism is Religious Education which he has taught across the full secondary range of pupils aged 11+ (Year 7) through to 18-19 year olds taking Advanced Level courses in Year 13.

He has two Bachelor Degrees - from The University of Newcastle upon Tyne and from the University of Louvain - a Post Graduate Certificate in Education and a Postgraduate Diploma in Christian Education from the University of Liverpool. He is currently working on a thesis for a Professional Doctorate in Education at Liverpool Hope University. His specialist area of research is Parental Involvement in Faith schools. He has spoken at a number of national conferences on this theme.

Jonathan holds the National Professional Qualification for Headship and is a designated Specialist Leader in Education by the National College for Teaching and Leadership. He has extensive experience supporting other schools in the North West of England developing both leadership and teaching and learning strategies. Also he is a trained coach and facilitator in the Improving and Outstanding Teacher programmes. The quality assurance of schools and diagnostic reviewing are a particular interest to him and he has reviewed school performance with several of Her Majesty's Inspectors of Schools in different parts of the country. In addition he has led a variety of professional development sessions on school improvement. In his spare time he is currently learning Italian and how the play the Guitalele - with mixed success.

David Moore was an experienced teacher and Headteacher before leaving the profession to become an Anglican Parish Priest, first in Brixton and, later, in the St Paul's district of Bristol.

He has been an 'Attached Inspector' to Her Majesty's Inspectorate for local authority inspection of Haringey and Brent schools with a specific responsibility to pioneer work meetings with community and parents and has served in the role of HMI for 24 years.
As one of Her Majesty's Inspectors of Schools he has held national responsibility for Behaviour and Discipline, Bullying, Attendance, EWS, aspects of ethnicity, been responsible for policy and development in the areas of Pupil Referral Units, Learning Mentors, Learning Support Centres, Pupil, Parent Support Workers, Managed Transfers of Pupils and Money Following the Child.

He was responsible for changes to exclusion procedures, behaviour and attendance strategies, and for developing Excellence in Cities Programmes, Behaviour Improvement Programmes, Secondary School Social Emotional Aspects of Learning (SEAL), alternative education paths for disaffected students and anti-bullying strategies. He has appeared before the Education Select Committee on three occasions to give evidence and advice and was the professional advisor to Sir Alan Steer's working group on behaviour in schools. He was also Assistant Divisional Manager Northern region with particular responsibility for the Greater Manchester Local Authorities and Learning and development of HMI colleagues within the region and for all new HMI nationally.

He was awarded an honorary doctorate for services to education by University College Lincoln in 2008 and awarded Commander of the British Empire (CBE) in January 2010 and is currently working as independent education consultant with the Centre for Christian

Education at Liverpool Hope University as well as providing In-service training for local authorities and inspection organisations.

Andrew B Morris – see Director Profiles

Columb Waters

Columb Waters is a retired Headteacher of a Catholic middle school in the Archdiocese of Birmingham and a former diocesan Religious Education inspector and school governor. He has worked as a teacher in London and, having obtained a headship, gained wide experience of school development and re-organisation in a Local Authority who changed from a two to a three tier system of education and back again. Following his early retirement he moved to Liverpool where he is currently an EdD student at Liverpool Hope University.

He taught in five different Catholic State schools over a period of thirty three years until his retirement in 2004. These schools included secondary, primary and middle schools and each was situated in two dioceses in four different local authorities. He held a variety of posts from probationary teacher to head teacher. His main teaching subject was RE which he taught at all levels including A Level. He trained as a diocesan Ofsted inspector in the Westminster and Birmingham dioceses where he undertook these inspections. He has also served as a governor in a number of Catholic schools. In 2003 Archbishop Vincent Nichols granted him the '*Ubi Caritas*' award for services to the Birmingham diocese.

He has a B.Ed. (Hons) in Religious Education from London University and an M.A. in the Philosophy of Education from The London Institute of Education for which he was awarded a Distinction. His dissertation was on Moral Education. In July 2014 he was awarded a Professional Doctorate in Education by Liverpool Hope University. His thesis was on the values of Catholic secondary school students. His main academic interests are theology, philosophy and educational management. He is married with three adult children and a committed Catholic who until moving to a new parish was heavily involved in various parish ministries and a vice- chair of the parish pastoral council. For now he is enjoying retirement until the next challenge.

Director Profiles

John Sullivan: Director 2006-2007

John Sullivan has been Professor of Christian Education at Liverpool Hope University since March 2002 and a member of the Department of Theology, Philosophy & Religious Studies. His experience includes more than twenty years in Catholic secondary schools and tertiary colleges as teacher and senior manager, including time as Vice Principal and Headteacher and also as Chief Inspector in a London borough, with oversight of 100 schools and colleges.

John moved into higher education in 1994, providing in-service training, consultancy and teaching Master's courses in Catholic educational leadership. For five years he directed a Master's programme in Catholic School Leadership while at St Mary's University College,

Twickenham, winning an award from the USA National Catholic Educational Association in 2001 for "an outstanding contribution to Catholic teacher formation and development."

John has published seven books and more than 70 chapters and articles (in the UK, Ireland, USA, Europe and Australia) on aspects of religion and education. His latest books are *Learning the Language of Faith* (Chelmsford: Matthew James Publishing, 2010), *Communicating Faith* (Washington, DC: The Catholic University of America Press, 2011) and, co-edited with Stephen McKinney, *Education in a Catholic Perspective* (Ashgate, 2013).

He is frequently invited as keynote speaker at local, national and international conferences on aspects of mission into practice in Christian education. He has a special interest in exploring the match between purposes, contexts and approaches at all levels of Christian education and also in analysing the factors than inhibit and enhance the effective communication of faith. He is a member of the editorial team for *International Studies in Catholic Education*, an editorial adviser for *Journal of Religious Education*, a consultant for Liverpool Hope University's Centre for Christian Education and a member of the Advisory Board for the Irish Centre for Religious Education.

Andrew Morris: Director 2007-12

Andrew was born in 1946 in Birmingham. He was educated at St. Philip's Grammar School and trained as a teacher at Loughborough Teacher Training College from 1964-67. He has spent forty years working in Catholic education in a variety of teaching, leadership, administrative and governance roles. He has been awarded a Certificate of Education, a Diploma of Loughborough College, has four degrees, including a PhD and an honorary BA.

He is a former secondary school Headteacher and Deputy Director of Schools in the Archdiocese of Birmingham. He has been an external examiner for PGCE students in at York St. John University. He has worked as a consultant to the Catholic Education Service and also in collaboration with the Office for Standards in Education to publish a number of papers on the academic standards and attainment in Catholic schools in England.

He was seconded for a period of five years from the Archdiocese of Birmingham to Liverpool Hope in October 2007 as Senior Research Fellow and Director of the (then) Centre for Christian Education. Following that secondment and his retirement from the Diocesan Schools Commission he was appointed Course Director of Post Graduate Research at the Maryvale Institute in Birmingham from 2013-15. He remains an Associate Maryvale Institute, of the National Centre for Christian Education and is also an Associate Member of the National Institute for Christian Education Research at Canterbury Christ Church University.

His academic specialism is in the field of faith-based education and school leadership. He has over thirty articles published in academic journals (with more forthcoming), is an established author, book and peer article reviewer, provides educational training and other support for

Catholic and Anglican dioceses, is an international conference speaker and advisor to Institutes of Higher Education, Local Authorities, other providers of Schools, the Catholic Education Service and various Catholic and Anglican Dioceses. He has prepared employment and other quasi-legal documentation for the CES, Catholic dioceses and local authorities, and has been the lead liaison officer for the Catholic sector in three Local Authority reorganisation schemes, Coventry, Oxfordshire and Warwickshire.

He is the author of '*Fifty Years On: The Case for Catholic Schools*'; '*Re-Imagining Christian Education for the 21st Century*' and '*Catholic Schools in a Plural Society: Collected Papers and Essays 1994-2012*' published by Matthew James (in 2008, 2013 and 2014 respectively) and also '*Catholic Education: Universal Principles, Locally Applied*' published by Cambridge Scholars Press in 2012. He has six entries in '*Encyclopaedia of Christian Education*' published in 2015 by Rowman & Littlefield Publishing.

Elizabeth Green: Director 2012-15
Elizabeth (Beth) Green is an experienced educational practitioner, having taught history and led pastoral teams in private and state funded church schools in the United Kingdom before obtaining an MA in Educational Management at Kings College London. She holds the Hans Prize in Education from King's College London and is a Fellow of the Higher Education Academy. She completed her DPhil in Education at Green Templeton College, Oxford before taking up a post as an Associate Research Fellow in the Centre for Christian Education at Liverpool Hope University and taught on the undergraduate and post-graduate courses in the Education Faculty in 2009. She was appointed Director of the National Centre for Christian Education (NCfCE) in 2012.

Beth has expertise in social theory, school ethos and school leadership and management and has been identified as a national leader in the field empirical work in Christian Education in the UK by the Church of England and by the Evangelical Alliance. She has an international profile regularly publishing in high impact journals, consulting and engaging in research collaborations across Europe and Australia and is the author of *Mapping the Field: A review of the current research evidence on the impact of schools with a Christian ethos (2009)*, published by Theos, the public theology think tank based in London.

She worked on an international collaboration with Calvin College (USA), Canterbury Christ Church University (UK) and the Anglican Diocese of Sydney (AU) designing a distinctively Christian approach to teaching and learning called What If Learning (WIL) and she led on the methodology for a major study investigating the influence of WIL on the practices of teachers in Christian schools.

In January 2015 she was appointed Director of Cardus Education, part of the Canadian research and educational institution which, rooted in Judeo-Christian social thinking, seeks to enrich and challenge public debate for the common good, as its Director of Education. She is also the Canadian regional editor for the recently launched International Journal of Christianity and Education.

Ros Stuart-Buttle: Director March 2015 to date

Following the Beth Green's move to Canada, Ros Stuart-Buttle, a Theology and Education specialist was appointed Director in March 2015 of the renamed Centre - now known as the Centre for Christian Education and Pastoral Theology.

She began professional life over thirty-five years ago teaching Humanities and Religious Education across a number of primary and secondary schools before moving into a diocesan education and adult adviser role. This was subsequently followed by six years as Director of Educational Outreach at Ushaw Seminary. Since 2002, she has been working in higher education, with a particular interest in and passion for adult learning and continuing professional development in faith and theology for Christian teachers and lay ministers.

Living in the United States from 1996-2000 gave Ros the opportunity to complete her postgraduate studies in Catholic theology and also introduced her to online theological education. Returning back to the UK, she completed a PhD with the University of Liverpool which explored adult theological education and new learning technologies. Much of her work since then has focused in this direction, particularly her building of a successful national programme of online adult theological education for the Catholic Bishops' Conference alongside her consultancy, research and publications in the field, both nationally and internationally. Ros was re-appointed to Liverpool Hope University in September 2011, having taught there previously from 2002-2004. She teaches undergraduate and post-graduate courses for the Faculties of Education as well as Arts and Humanities. She is the course leader for the university's church certificate courses which offer both Catholic and Anglican studies to serving and prospective teachers in church schools. She currently supervises and examines at both postgraduate taught and doctoral level and is about to launch a new Masters programme in Christian Education and Leadership from January 2016.

Ros is a Fellow of the Higher Education Academy and a longstanding and much respected Board member of the Bishops' Conference of England and Wales Catholic Certificate in Religious Studies. She is Foundation Governor at a leading north-west Catholic high school academy and frequently receives requests to speak at conferences and church events about faith, theology and education. Her recent publications include a monograph *Virtual Theology, Faith and Adult Education: An Interruptive Pedagogy* (2013) Cambridge Scholars Publishing. She has book chapters on 'Does Religious Education Matter?' and 'What Do Teachers Think?' in: Shanahan, *Does RE Matter?* (forthcoming) Ashgate, and a chapter entitled 'Communicating Faith and Online Learning', in: J. Sullivan (2011) *Communicating Faith*, Catholic University of America Press. In addition to a her journal articles Ros' current writing projects include joint editorship of a volume of essays on Faith, Formation and Education to be published in 2016, and a chapter for another edited collection reflecting on changes and challenges in Catholic Education since 1965 to the present day.

As its most recent Director, Ros looks forward to continuing the work of her predecessors in enabling people to come together to journey in rich conversation about Christian faith, ministry and learning.

The National Centre for Christian Education at Liverpool Hope University: Its Background and History

Andrew B. Morris

Background – Religion in Contemporary Society

In recent years a variety of commentators from both religious and secular perspectives have publicly argued that our society is becoming increasingly hostile to religious faith and its expression in public life and its promotion of education (see, for example, Weller et al., 2001; Grace, 2003; Nichols, 2005, 2006; Davies, 2013; Gove, 2015; Moore, 2015). That antipathy is evident within national politics. For example, the Liberal Democrat Party election manifesto of 2010 and Green Party education policies of 2014 (re-stated in their 2015 election manifesto), albeit in differing ways, proposed particularly hostile measures to the well-being of Church schools.[1] Such antipathy presents a major issue for the 36% of all primary and 16% of all secondary schools in England and Wales that are defined by Government as having a religious character (Department for Education, 2013).

The overall size of this sector in England hides subtle differences that affect the manifestation of religious character in the various maintained religious schools through elements of their curriculum, pupil intake, patterns of employment and the ethos schools strive to create. The vast majority belong either to the Church of England or Roman Catholic Church, but there are also a small number provided by minority Christian denominations, some Jewish, Muslim and Sikh schools, together with a few joint ventures by different Christian denominations working together in a variety of partnerships.

For those concerned to promote the Church sector, its purposes and contribution to the common good can no longer be taken 'as read' but needs, once again, to be effectively articulated to the wider society. In particular, school leaders at all levels, including classroom teachers, middle and senior managers, as well as governors and administrators, need to be helped and encouraged to develop a more confident engagement with, and proclamation of, the Christian faith at their work in their schools and in the increasing number of newly created Academies. How such a need can be met is more problematical as there are few Higher Education institutions that are in a position to meet the increasing demand for professional help and support that such individuals require once they leave formal higher education, and to support and encourage doctoral level empirical research in the area. Liverpool Hope University, has attempted to take up this challenge.

---

[1] The 2010 Liberal Democrat manifesto (p.37) proposed to abolish longstanding legislation allowing school governors to give preference in admissions to baptised Catholic children and preference in employment to practicing Catholic teachers. The Green Party education policy document of 2014 proposed that, if in a position to do so, the party would not allow any state maintained school to be run by a religious organisation (ED 176), in effect proposing to abolish or nationalise all existing schools with a religious character, currently representing just over one-fifth of the maintained sector. A slightly more nuanced statement, but intended to have the same effect, was included in its 2015 election manifesto proposed to "phase out state funding for schools run by religious organisations" (p. 37).

History of Liverpool Hope University

Hope is one of the newer English universities but can trace its history back over a century and a half ago, when the Church of England Diocese of Chester and the Roman Catholic Sisters of Notre Dame established separate teacher education Colleges for women. These Colleges (St. Katharine's, established in 1844 and Notre Dame, established in 1856) were in Warrington and Liverpool City Centre respectively. They were supplemented on Merseyside when a second Catholic teacher education College, Christ's College, situated adjacent to St. Katharine's, admitted its first students in 1965.

In 1980 the three colleges joined in an ecumenical federation under the holding title of Liverpool Institute of Higher Education (LIHE). The late Archbishop Derek Worlock and late Bishop David Sheppard wrote of this as being "a sign of hope" and part of their wider ecumenical vision for the city. In time, the Governing Council established a working party to consider how a fully integrated college could be constituted with a new title and in 1995 a new Instrument and Articles of Government established a single, unified, ecumenical university, and a new name - Liverpool Hope - which better reflected its role and mission. A Company Limited by Guarantee and registered as a Charity was formed.

Its status of a fully accredited institution of the University of Liverpool had been achieved in 1994 which gave full responsibility to the college for the quality and standards of its course provision and provided recognition of its academic standing. In 1998, the Accreditation Agreement with the University of Liverpool extended to cover taught postgraduate awards and in 2002 Liverpool Hope University College gained taught degree awarding powers.

Approval by the Privy Council of the title Liverpool Hope University came in 2005, with the granting of Research Degree Awarding Powers (RDAP) followed four years later, in 2009. Its self-proclaimed mission as the 'only ecumenical university in Europe' highlights a Christian Foundation which strives:

- to provide opportunities for the well-rounded personal development of Christians and students from other faiths and beliefs, educating the whole person in mind, body and spirit, irrespective of age, social or ethnic origins or physical capacity, including in particular those who might otherwise not have had an opportunity to enter higher education;
- to be a national provider of a wide range of high quality programmes responsive to the needs of students, including the education, training and professional development of teachers for Church and state schools;
- to sustain an academic community enriched by Christian values and worship, which supports teaching and learning, scholarship and research, encourages the understanding of Christian and other faiths and beliefs and promotes religious and social harmony;
- to contribute to the educational, religious, cultural, social and economic life of Liverpool, Merseyside, the North-West and beyond.

Establishing a Centre for Christian Education at Hope

Reflecting Hope's Christian identity in its founding charter, and almost unique commitment to sustaining and strengthening that identity and purpose (Glanzer, 2008) the University established a Centre for Christian Education (CfCE) under the Directorship of Professor John Sullivan in 2006 with additional financial support from a number of educational and philanthropic charitable trusts.

Under Professor Sullivan's leadership, and building on the lengthy record of service provided by Hope University in the area of initial and in-service provision for teachers in schools for church and state, the major focus of the Centre's activity was as a consultancy providing professional development courses integrating theological, spiritual, educational and leadership perspectives in support of forms of Christian education that are distinctive (in witnessing to and inviting discipleship), inclusive and effective.

He wanted to provide opportunities for personal renewal of teachers (and other adults) working in and for church schools, to enhance their sense of vocation and facilitate their mutual support by helping bridge the gaps that often developed between the established Christian churches and the schools they provided. In addition to that initial vision, however, he foresaw, and hoped, that the Centre would facilitate and generate scholarly and professional material – books, chapters, articles – that would contribute towards keeping alive and credible the vision of forms of Christian education that invite, convey and model Christian faith integrated fully into professional teaching and leadership – at that time a relatively neglected field of academic study in the UK – and, in addition, expressed the hope that it would develop into a Centre of national significance.

Over subsequent years those two wishes were realised, with its research profile expanded and the Centre being subsequently re-branded as the National Centre for Christian Education during the tenure of his immediate successor Dr Andrew Morris, following his secondment to Liverpool Hope from the Archdiocese of Birmingham Schools Commission as a Senior Research Fellow in 2007, and that of Dr Elizabeth Green who became Director in 2012 at the conclusion of Dr Morris' secondment. Following Dr Green's appointment at the start of 2015 as Director of Cardus Education, part of the Canadian research and educational institution, Dr Ros Stuart-Buttle became the fourth, and is the current, Director of the National Centre for Christian Education at Liverpool Hope University, now located within the Theology Department of the Arts and Humanities Faculty.

The National Centre for Christian Education (NCfCE)

While the original purposes of the Centre, as set out by Professor John Sullivan in 2005/2006 remained, during the directorships of Dr Morris and Dr Green, its activities broadened in terms of the quantity and variety of work being commissioned and in the external grants it was able to attract to support the increased activity,[2] including individual research projects

---

[2] Between 2007 and the end of 2012 the Centre had attracted some £400,000 to support its activities from grants, INSET income and commissioned research projects.

with both internal and external students undertaking PhD and EdD programmes at the University.

The Centre's consultancy work with schools, colleges, HEIs, and dioceses in different parts of the country was expanded, providing In-Service Training (in various forms) for schools in Merseyside, Blackburn and the Midlands; for the Catholic dioceses of Southwark, Arundel & Brighton, Nottingham and Birmingham; and providing training and accreditation support for the North East and North West consortium of Catholic dioceses and the Church of England dioceses of Coventry and Oxford for their respective leadership development programmes.

Renamed as the National Centre for Christian Education in 2010 it was a central agency in the development of formal links between the Liverpool Hope and Canterbury Christ Church Universities to take forward the Transforming Lives Project designed to have a direct impact upon the preparation of students for their future teaching careers, as well as in helping to develop materials that can be used in much wider contexts both in the UK and abroad (see, Clark, 2013).

Within Hope, it initiated developments to make more explicit the University's commitment to promoting a greater understanding of the role of Christian education in a secular world, including the development of two separate Post-Graduate Certificates, one in Christian Education Leadership, the other in Christian Chaplaincy. Both certificates have been developed to be taken as stand-alone qualifications (60 credits) or as one element part of an MA in Theology & Religious Studies or in Education. In addition, it sought to help Hope staff and undergraduates working within the Education Faculty, as well as individual schools, colleges and dioceses, to become more able and confident in articulating, leading and promoting a Christian educative mission in society.

To that end, and in response to development of the University's research culture, the Centre became one focus of increased research activity within the Education Faculty,[3] first with members of staff who had been encouraged to undertake studies leading towards a PhD and later recruiting a number of outside students seeking doctoral qualifications at Hope. It also came to play a major role in the development of, and recruitment of students to, a new professional doctorate programme. As its scope and areas of research activities broadened it has been able to attract additional external funding to support its central role in Masters and Doctoral Programmes in Education and its close working and structural relationship with the Directorate of Continuing Professional Development.

It hosted its first annual Conference in July 2012 exploring the opportunities and dilemmas facing Christian education and debating what it might offer the diverse, pluralistic society of 21st Century England, which led to the publication of some of the conference papers (Morris,

---

[3] The stated purposes of the University in proposing and , subsequently, securing the secondment of Dr Andrew Morris to Hope as Senior Research Fellow and Director of the (then) Centre for Christian Education included the requirement that he should help develop colleagues' research expertise within the Education Faculty, enhance its research capacity and support post-graduate student research.

2012). A second conference, organised in collaboration venture with Christchurch Canterbury University and hosted in Canterbury was held the following year.

Christian Education Research Focus
In addition to the work outlined above, the Centre developed a programme of empirical research, focusing on mechanisms that help create a Christian school/college community and an associated supportive ethos and the relationships between Christian ethos, Christian leadership and institutional effectiveness.

In February 2010 the Education Faculty extended its post-graduate provision with the introduction of a part-time professional doctorate; a popular route for many educators wishing to combine research with professional practice. The submission for validation of the programme and the subsequent advertising documents stated that Liverpool Hope could make a significant contribution to the policy and praxis of education and training through the Doctor of Education (EdD) programme by focusing on professionally grounded scholarship and a series of core values embedded in Hope's Christian character. The programme was based on the premise that the qualities of a person with such a degree lay within the personal and professional lives of candidates and, consequently, focused on improved professional practice and personal growth.

It was argued that its coherence was to be found in the lived experience of the individual student and in the ways in which they built her/his own learning through reflection and practice. The significance of the inter-disciplinary nature of the first cohort of students accepted on to the programme in October 2010 was, at least in part, concerned with their abilities to share their own professional practices across the cohort; experiences that could be developed alongside supervisors with the skills and abilities to engage in a developmental process of learning, practice and reflection.

To facilitate this approach, students were expected to form a relationship with the National Centre for Christian Education or one of the other four designated research centres established within the Faculty. This enabled the generic research content associated with taught element of the programme to be firmly rooted within one of the research centres which, in turn, provided students with subject area expertise as they prepared their research projects and appropriate supervision during the research phase of their studies.

At the beginning of the 2012-13 academic year there were, in total, some eighteen members of Hope staff and post-graduate doctoral students – both EdD and PhD - attached to, and working within NCfCE. Their research interests covered such broad areas as:
- Christian Leadership;
- Teachers and Teaching in Catholic Schools
- School Ethos and Engagement in Catholic and CofE schools/academies
- Christian School Effectiveness;
- The Efficacy and Impact of Values Education;

- Developing and Sustaining Christian Culture/Charism in Schools;
- Christian Schooling and Community Cohesion;
- The Differential Impact on Students of a Catholic School Ethos;
- Transmission of Faith and Culture in Christian Schools;
- Developing Young Children's Spirituality;
- Parental Influences on Pupils in Christian Schools;
- Promoting Catholic Education in Jordan/Mauritius;
- Church Responses to the Academy Programme
- The Christian Character of Joint Church Academies
- The History of Catholic Teacher Organisations

By the end of the 2014-15 academic year some of those research projects have been successfully completed or are nearing completion; some are on-going but still some way from completion. A small number of students, for a variety of personal and professional reasons,[4] have withdrawn from their studies.

References

Clark, A. (2013) Transforming Lives, in: Morris A. B. (ed) Re-Imagining Christian Education for the 21st Century, Chelmsford, Matthew James Publishing.

Davies, M. (2013) Christian England at an End, homily given at the Northern Catholic Conference Liverpool Hope University, 9th June.

Department for Education (2013) Schools, Pupils and Their Characteristics: January 2013, table 2c, state-funded primary and secondary schools - number of schools by their status and religious character, London, Department for Education.

Glanzer, P. L. (2008) Searching for the Soul of English Universities: An exploration and analysis of Christian Higher Education in England, British Journal of Educational Studies, 56. 2. 163-183.

Gove, M. (2015) In Defence of Christianity, http://www.spectator.co.uk/features/9487882/in-defence-of-christianity [Accessed 4.04.2015]

Grace, G. (2003) Educational Studies and Faith-Based Schooling: moving from prejudice to evidence-based argument, British Journal of Educational Studies, 51. 2. 149-167.

Moore, C. (2015) Muslim Faith Schools Must Be Scrutinised More Than Christian Ones, Daily Telegraph, 14th December, p.19.

Nichols, V. (2005) Proclaiming the Faith in a Pluralist Society, University of Wales Public Lecture, Tuesday 6th December.

Nichols, V. (2006) Why I Keep Faith in Our Schools, Birmingham Post, 13th April.

Weller, P., Feldman, A. & Purdam, K. (2001) Religious Discrimination in England & Wales, London, Home Office Research, Development and Statistics Directorate.

---

[4] For example, illness; taking up a new post in another institution; changes in the student's supervisory team; financial constraints.

Part 2: Values and Attitudes in Catholic Schools: Four Case Studies

Three of the four papers that comprise this section are taken from professional doctoral (EdD) theses; the final paper from a doctoral (PhD) thesis. All four are case studies concerned, in slightly different ways, with the values and attitudes that characterise the respective Catholic institutions involved in the research.

Columb Waters is a committed and practising Catholic with considerable teaching experience in the state maintained Catholic sector. Within the context of the current, so called, 'faith school debate', he examines three specific connected criticisms made by detractors of Catholic schools - that they foster intolerance in their students, they fail to promote community cohesion and, by giving preference to baptised Catholic pupils, they segregate children on religious grounds so causing societal fragmentation.

Undertaken in a large Catholic secondary school, the main element of Columb's research was a series of semi-structured individual interviews with forty Year 10 and 11 students. He triangulated the data from his pupil sample with semi-structured individual interviews with staff, a school document survey and formal and informal observations of staff and pupil behaviour in the school.

While accepting the limitations of findings from a single case study, he feels able to conclude that these three specific criticisms against maintained Catholic schools cannot be substantiated, at least in so far as this sample group of forty students is concerned. His found the students to be tolerant, open to others, able to mix well with others and had a sense of belonging to a number of different communities, illustrated, he argued, by their commitment to the values of equality, respect, fairness, anti-discrimination, anti-prejudice, anti-racism and other spiritual, moral and religious values.

The context for **Alison Clark's** doctoral thesis derived from her personal interest in the ways in which schools promoted their values together with her observation of a resurgence in the number of values education programmes designed for community schools, and prominence that, so called, 'faith schools' gave to the development of the [religious] character of their pupils.

She argues that while all teachers are expected to promote the spiritual, moral and physical development of young people during their time in school, the processes adopted may vary depending on the view of education which underpins the *raison d'être* of a particular school. That pupils should achieve the highest possible levels of academic attainment is a goal common to all schools, as is the recognition that the school's environment provides a context for pupils' social development, which includes, either explicitly or implicitly, some specific values. It is expected that teachers will reflect professional values in their conduct, and school governors expect them to endorse the mission, ethos and educational aims of the school to which they are appointed.

The purpose of her research was to explore, using a case study design, how teachers in one maintained 11-18 Catholic secondary school engaged with, and reacted to, the school's expressed values and its Catholic ethos. The school in question is located on the outskirts of a small market town in England and the research took place during the academic year 2012-2013. There were approximately 1200 students on roll at the time from a wide variety of socio-economic backgrounds, sixty-two per cent of whom were baptised Catholics.

She had two main aims:
- To explore the role of an aspirational ethos with a focus on Five Core Values established by those with the legal responsibility for 'preserving and developing'[1] the school's religious character (i.e. Honourable Purpose, Respect, Compassion, Co-operation and Stewardship).
- To listen to and engage with the perspectives of teachers on: the values of the school, and values and the role of the teacher in student formation.

These aims generated the following research questions:
- How do the Five Core Values influence the day-to-day activities, choices and behaviours in the school?
- How do the Five Core Values impact upon the roles and work of teachers?

The extract from her thesis concentrates upon the second of those research questions.

She found that while the Five Core Values espoused by the school influenced both its day-to-day activities and had an impact on how teachers understood their respective roles in the school, its specific religious character provided a challenge for many of them. In adapting their professional lives to that context they drew on their experiences in other, often very different, schools in developing and adapting to the expectations they, and the school hierarchy, made upon them.

The prominence given within the school to the Five Core Values contributed more to the teachers than simply their understanding of the agency of their role. They contributed to the generally held perception of the school as being an inclusive community, and were seen by many teachers as providing the 'glue' that held it together.

Mark Dumican's research is also concerned with pupil values. He argues that the values, attitudes and beliefs which faith school graduates will be encouraged to acquire during their years of formal education will differ in schools from the various faith traditions within the English system. However, he goes further, arguing that variations will occur in schools within

---

[1] Education Act 2002, s.12.2; School Governance (Constitution) Regulations 2007, r.8.

the same faith tradition, since the specific culture within each educational establishment, the makeup of teacher and student bodies and the social context in which they operate will inevitably lead to different outcomes.[2]

He uses a sample of 15 and 16 year old pupils attending a Catholic Secondary School in the North West of England having a total of 1224 pupils on its roll of which 98.7% are baptised Catholics. As part the school's self-evaluation process, pupils are asked to 'self-identify' the character of their religious adherence using established research categories (see Francis, L. J., 2002). In the year group (Yr.11; n = 242) from which his sample is taken (n = 40), nine percent categorised themselves as 'practising', forty-one per cent as 'sliding', forty-five percent as 'lapsed' and five per cent as 'non-Catholic' – very similar to the school as a whole.[3] In academic terms the Key Stage 2 scores of the school intake aged 11 is slightly above the national average and the percentage of pupils eligible for free school meals some 4% below. Its socio-economic profile places it in the middle of the local authority range.

His research is rooted in debates about the effects, or otherwise, of schools with a religious character on the values and attitudes of their pupils. The first of two extracts taken from his work explores the cultural impact, if any, of the triumvirate of parish, school and home on pupils' religiosity and their own understanding of what it means to be a young Catholic person. The second, using an expanded version of Francis' typologies, explores the extent to which pupils identify their contribution to supporting the school's defined religious character and how they view the practice of their faith within the parish and school settings.

Bearing in mind the circumstances of the school and the catchment that it serves, he is wary of extrapolating from his case study to the wider community of Catholic schools.

The limitations of a single case-study are also acknowledged by **Jonathan Lawford** in his currently on-going study of the nature and character of parental involvement in a Catholic Secondary School. The context for his research is evidence that 'good pupil outcomes' are likely to be positively associated with 'good parental involvement' in their children's education and, secondly, the paucity of empirical studies of this possible phenomenon in respect of the Catholic sector.

In the light of official Church documents emphasising the prime role of parents in the education of their children (Code of Canon Law, Can. 796, §1; Gravissimum Educationis 1967, §6), he is particularly interested in whether the religious character of the school, which governors and senior staff are under a legal requirement to 'preserve and develop' (School Governance (Constitution) Regulations 2007, r. 8) is reflected in the way parents understand and involve themselves in one school's educational enterprise.

---

[2] Mark recognises that this observation would also apply to secular schools but it is schools with a religious character, in this case Catholic, which provides the context for his research.

[3] Of the 1224 pupils on the school roll, 11% categorised themselves as 'practising', 42% as 'sliding', 41% as 'lapsed' and 6% as 'non-Catholic'.

He notes the term 'parental involvement' can have, in the school context, at least two different meanings; 'spontaneously occurring parental involvement' and 'attempts to intervene to enhance such involvement' (Desforges & Abouchaar, 2003, p. 84). Spontaneous involvement is more likely to be initiated by parents, while intervention, of various kinds, is likely to be initiated by the school.

Bearing those distinctions in mind, Jonathan's pilot study uses semi-structured interviews with a small number of parents (n = 24) to explore the hypothesis that in a Catholic Secondary school, deemed outstanding by Ofsted and Diocesan authorities, the joint religious enterprise of parents and school in educating children will be a prominent feature underpinning both types of parental involvement.

Among other findings, this study suggests that parents in the sample of academically high attaining children[4] are more likely help with them with their homework and talk with them about their school work at home. Within the family, their religious faith was often the subject of discussion and they were more likely than not to cite the Catholic character of the school as a major reason for choosing it for their children. They were less likely to contact school or meet formally with staff. Those parents in the sample whose children have comparatively lower levels of academic attainment were more reluctant to be involved with homework – possibly because of a lack of confidence - and were more likely to be involved in intervention strategies initiated by the school. Matters of faith were not a high priority for them.

References

Code of Canon Law Annotated (2004) Montréal, Wilson & Lafleur Limitée, p. 618.

Gravissimum Educationis [Declaration on Christian Education] (1977), in: Franchi, L. (2007) An Anthology of Catholic Teaching on Education, Hounslow, Scepter UK Ltd., pp. 107-120

Desforges C. with Abouchaar A (2003) The Impact of Parental Involvement, Parental Support and Family Education on Pupil Achievement and Adjustment, DfES Research Report 433, Nottingham, Department for Education & Skills.

School Governance (Constitution) Regulations (2007), London, Department for Education.

---

[4] As defined by their academic progress during ages 11 to 16 and their performance in public examinations taken at age 16+.

Catholic Secondary School Students and their Values

Columb Waters

Editor's Note:
There are two main elements described in Columb's professional doctoral thesis, for which he awarded an EdD in June 2014. While his primary concern was with the values held by students, he also interviewed teaching and non-teaching staff, surveyed school documentation and undertook both formal and informal observations for the purpose of triangulation and validation of his findings. This extract is taken, mainly, from chapter six of the thesis, concerned with data derived from student interviews.

Introduction

This research addresses three criticisms of so called 'faith schools'; that they cause their pupils to become intolerant of others; that they segregate them from those holding different world views leading to fragmentation in society; and, consequently, they do not make a positive contribution to promoting community cohesion. These criticisms have been articulated in their strongest form by Hirst (1985) and Lord Dormand of Easington (Hansard, 1991). Both imply a logical necessity between faith schools and these negative results (Thiessen, 2001, p.36) but, if true, all faith schools would have to be shown to have these results (Short, 2002, p.563). These assertions, however, are theoretical rather than empirically based. For such criticism to be valid, even if formulated less strongly, they need a level of evidential support which seems to be lacking in regard to these three criticisms. Their underlying rationale seems to be 'contact hypothesis' which assumes that mixing children of diverse faiths, ethnicities and backgrounds will automatically produce harmonious communities and promote community cohesion. However, there is evidence of widespread racial abuse, bullying and violence in schools which do not have a religious character (McDonald et al., 1989, p.391; Troyna & Hatcher, 1992). Such research suggests the 'contact hypothesis' may not survive empirical investigation.

There has been a number of other criticisms made of schools with a religious character[1] but they are not the focus of this study. I am concerned solely with the three criticisms noted above and am not aware of any empirical research in this specific area though, of course, other research based in Catholic schools is related to these issues.[2] I hope, therefore, that by undertaking research of the criticisms articulated by Hirst and Lord Dumond (among others), I will add to the corpus of 'evidence-based argument' (Grace, 2003) that already exists in the field of Catholic education.

While I acknowledge my findings are from a small sample group in a single Catholic secondary school I will argue that, if the claimed detrimental characteristics are not in evidence among the vast majority of students in what can be shown to be an archetypical

---

[1] See, for example, Judge, H. (2001); Thiessen, E. J. (2001); Hand, M. (2003); Marples (2005); Allen & West, (2009); Osler, (2007, 2010).

[2] See, for example, Grace, 2002; O'Keefe & Zipfel, 2007; Casson, 2013.

Catholic school, it is reasonable to suggest that such institutions do not necessarily promote anti-social attitudes and values. On the contrary, should my research findings provide evidence that, after four years of Catholic secondary school, students are neither intolerant of, nor segregated from, others, such an education cannot be said to necessarily promote fragmentation in society. If my data show the students in this particular school make a positive contribution to community cohesion, I can argue there can be little justification in questioning the continued presence of Catholic secondary schools in the dual system of schools (those with and without a religious character) that has existed in England since the 1870 Education Act and was re-affirmed in the 1944 Education Act (Morris, 2008, p.33).

The overall findings of this research, I believe, support the views of those who claim what is important in educating children is not the setting in which the children receive their education, but the content (see, for example, Pring, 2007; Alexander, 2007; Reich, 2007; Levinson, 2007; Short, 2002). A curriculum that promotes tolerance, anti-racism, equality, inclusion, mutual respect and good citizenship is possible in both faith schools and non-religious ones. Further, such a curriculum is essential because these desirable outcomes will not happen by accident and, I maintain, a choice for parents of different types school is the most appropriate arrangement for a pluralistic, multicultural, multi-faith and inclusive society.

Research Methods

Using, primarily, semi-structured interviews with a sample of students (n = 40) the thesis seeks to answer the question, 'What values do students profess to hold after spending three or four years in a Catholic secondary school?' While their declared attitudes and values are the main focus of the research, my findings are preliminary and provisional because of limitations of interviews as a research method, in particular drawing conclusions based on data derived from a single method. To test the validity of the student data, therefore, staff completed a questionnaire; a sample, including the School Based Police Officer, were interviewed (n = 9); school documentation was analysed and the general day to day life of the school observed. The student interviews concentrated on the themes of family, friends, school, religion, morality, citizenship and service to others. Their responses identify four important overarching values, family, friends, school or education, and religion. In practice, values are not separated out discretely and conveniently under these themes and so there is overlapping and connections between categories within the different themes. So, for example, the value of respecting others in school is the same as respecting others in the community under the theme of citizenship.

Summary of Main Findings

While there was general agreement within the sample individual students differed in the emphasis they placed upon on the various areas.[3] They greatly valued belonging and a sense of community, which is found especially in the themes of family, friends and the school. In these three, especially, the values of trust, support, loyalty, companionship, emotional

---

[3] These differences and nuances are described in the next section – Student Interviews: Details [Ed].

security, self-esteem and social life were evidenced. There is some evidence they valued belonging to other communities whether local, regional, national or international and, for some, the parish is an important community to which they feel an affiliation.

Equality and fairness were mentioned often and included anti-racism, anti-discrimination, anti-prejudice, openness to others, learning from others and inclusion. The students believe that we should not make distinctions based on ethnicity, religion, special needs or gender. Closely allied to equality is respect in all its dimensions. This includes respect for self, family, teachers, others, the school building and equipment, other religions and ethnic groups, laws, lawful authority, and democracy. The school gives great importance to teaching the Catholic faith and nurturing belief, prayer life and spirituality. For some students all of these values are important, but the commitment of others is variable. Some who do not attend church still believe in God and prayer, continue to call themselves Catholics, and most seem to accept at least some of the school's Christian teaching. This was seen especially in their commitment to treating others as they would like to be treated in all sorts of situations. Some went further and quoted part of the Great Commandment to love your neighbour. This principle was evidenced in their compassion, concern and support for those who were suffering and in need. The students have a developed sense of right and wrong and this, together with their religious principles, underpins and provides a rationale for many of their other values. For example, they think it wrong to steal, bully others, risk one's health unnecessarily or break promises. Many would not lie on principle but others adopt a situation-dependent approach to truth telling.[4] Education is extremely important to all the students and involved a cluster of other values such as ambition, individual responsibility, self-discipline, hard work, good, behaviour, forgiveness, preparation for adult life, and citizenship.

Student Interviews - Details[5]

Theme 1 - Family
All of the students, with the exception of two where we ran out of time, were asked towards the end of their interviews to state the two or three most important values in their lives. Twenty-eight out of the thirty-eight placed the family in this group, and all forty said during the interview that their families were 'very important'. As they explained their reasons for rating their families so highly, a cluster of other values emerged around this key value.

Reliability
The students stated that they could depend on their families absolutely. Many of them used the phrase 'they're always there for me.' One student replied, 'friends come and go but

---

[4] There was a difference in the responses to truth telling to teachers in school and to parents outside school. Twenty-two students state they would not lie to teachers, but thirteen would do so depending on the situation; eighteen would not lie to parents, but seventeen would in certain circumstances.

[5] When quoting from the students' interviews 4G or B represents student number 4 girl or boy. All year 10 students will be identified with a number 10 following the gender identification e.g. 28B10 represents student number 28, a boy in year 10. If there is no number after the G or B they are students in year 11.

family doesn't so they're very important' (23G). This gave them complete security that, even if everyone else let them down, their family would never do so.

Emotional Security
A number of the students spoke specifically about emotional security though only one phrased this value in these precise words. Others spoke of being close to their families or loving or caring for them. One student stated, 'they are very important to me because I love them and they love me back' (37B10).

Support and Trust
Most of the students referred to the total support they received from their families in helping them when things went wrong, or to sort out problems or worries, or with school work. They also received encouragement to work hard and with their future career ambitions. Associated with the last value was that of trust. This has two aspects or dimensions. First many of them believed that they could confide their problems in their families. Second they trusted that their families would be able to suggest solutions to resolve problems and issues.

> *'We're a really close family and we've always been there for each other. Like if I've got any problems, the first thing I do is tell them all about it as soon as I get home from school. So how has your day been and stuff and I always tell them the truth, and she [mum] always like...if I've got any like problems, or I'm upset about anything, she'll get it sorted out straight away.'* (S13G)

Companionship
A number of the students mentioned being close to their families and this already contains the notion of enjoying each other's company, but a minority of students mentioned this specifically. One student said family 'is important like because I do a lot of stuff with my family... go out for like meals and like shopping and all that.' (6G)

Belonging
None of the students used the phrase 'belonging to the family', but we can see contained in the emergence of all of the above values the notion of belonging. The students describe feeling completely secure, trusted, loved and cared for and comfortable with each other. As one student said the family was important because, 'they're my family.' (4G)

Theme 2 - Friends

Friendship
The other theme that appeared most (twenty-one times) in the responses of the thirty-eight students who, towards the end of their interview, were asked to name their top two or three values was friendship. Nearly all of the students said during the interview that friends were very important to them. The exception was a student who claimed not to have any close friends but 'just friends' in school. He did have friends out of school but not school friends. In this regard he was the exception. All the others had close friends at school and met up,

most of them frequently, out of school apart from one student who lived a greater distance than the others from the school. An examination of the expression 'close friends' reveals some important student values; the first of these is belonging.

Belonging and Loyalty
The number of close friends each student had varied from 'three really close friends' (25G10) at one end of the continuum to 'a massive group' (3G). Whether the groups were large or small, there was a strong sense of belonging. It would seem that belonging to the group gives them emotional security and a feeling that people cared about them. It also made them feel accepted and not an outsider or a loner. The fact that others valued their friendship enhanced their self-esteem.

Another value associated with belonging is loyalty. This is demonstrated most by two groups, one who have been together since joining primary school aged four years (13G), and a second who have been together since Year 7 (14G). Others might not have been formed as long, but all seem tightly knit, as was evident when discussing belonging. The student interviews also demonstrated that students valued their social life.

Social Life
Friendship groups extended to out of school. The favourite group activities outside school were: shopping, going to the cinema, the park, and bowling or for a meal, visiting each other's houses and 'talking for ages' (11G). Some students played football and rugby in the park, while others pursued individual interests and played for sports teams such as football, rugby, volley ball and athletics, or they went to the gym or swimming and other clubs provided by the council or private businesses, or they belonged to local choir groups. Their social activities show that they feel at home in their local area and appreciate the way, for example, the park is maintained. Another value that emerged from the students' discussions was openness to others.

Openness to Others, Equality and Respect
Out of school, either because they lived in the same area or went to the same clubs or choir groups, the vast majority of the students interviewed said that they had also made friends with students who did not attend the school and who were non-Catholic. These students agreed that they got on well with students from other schools, had no problems mixing with them and treated them exactly the same as their school friends. One claimed that they did not feel any 'barrier' (31B10) between them. One student said, "I've met one of my best friends from there [sports club]" (S13G). Three pupils gave a more unusual reply. Whereas many indicated that they didn't bring religion into their friendships with people outside school, these three said that they did discuss their religion with them; for example, one stated:

> *'We get on well because I think they're interested sometimes to hear about Catholicism and they always think it is strange and that we're really serious but it's good to hear what they have to say and they like what I have to say.'* (S27G)

In all three cases it was a genuine exchange of information. Interestingly one of these three students mentioned that none of these non-Catholic friends has 'ever been bothered by the fact that we go to a Catholic school, anything like that' (9G). Openness to others meant treating them equally and with respect. A typical response was 'treat others like you'd like to be treated' (37B10). In each of the following themes it will become clear that equality is one of the students' strongest values.

Mutual Trust and Support
These values seem to underpin much of the students' discussions. One student said that 'we tell each other things and like talk about school and stuff like that' (31B10). Two students said that they talked about their families with their friends, not necessarily about problems in the families. Two other students did mention that some of their friends were finding it difficult to cope with family break up. In addition, the fact that the groups spoke about being close and that they meet so frequently out of school, almost every weekend for some groups, that it is not unusual to meet in each other's houses, and that for many of the students, family and friends are their top two values, all lead me to the conclusion that there is a great deal of trust and mutual support between them. If I am correct in this, trust also entails the value of confidentiality.

Theme 3 - School
The students develop their values in school in the context of the ethos of that school. So listening to them describe their school is a good place to start to understand what is important to them. These are some of the frequent comments that they made: the school is Catholic, friendly, warm, safe, a good school, a good place, a nice place to be, enjoyable, a place where people help each other, where people are listened to, a happy place, lots of different clubs for everyone to get involved in and where the pupils are well behaved.

Here, by way of examples, are three direct responses that the students gave when asked to say something about their school. It is 'Welcoming, safe, friendly, very well educated, happy, busy, lots of people' (7G). 'It's a Catholic school ......it's got really good teachers, really good pupils. Really like it' (21 G). 'The behaviour's really good and the teaching's really good' (22G).

These and similar comments tell us about the students' values and what is important to them. A number of students mentioned that it was a Catholic school, and this has a very important influence on all their values, but I will discuss that in the theme of religion. To return to the other values portrayed above, I begin with the value respect.

Respect - for teachers
The respect for the teachers is based on a number of factors. First nearly all the students spoke appreciatively about the quality of the teaching and the lessons. One student summed this up by claiming that the teaching was 'extremely good' (25G10). There was one student who complained about the teaching of just one teacher but he was very much the exception.

The second reason why the students trusted the teachers was their absolute trust and confidence that the teachers would help them to achieve the very best grades possible in their forthcoming GCSE exams. As one student said the teachers 'have quite high standards to get us the best grades possible in all the subjects' (5B).

The third reason given for their respect of the teachers and that was their willingness to give up their own time, either at lunch time or after school, to explain things to the students. One boy stated, 'Say if you still didn't get it after the lesson, then like your teacher would come back to you and say do you still understand that, and if you need to, like come back to me at dinner hour [or] after school' (31B10). In the interest of validity, I should note that one student said that 'some' rather than all, and another three students stated that 'most' rather than all, teachers were supportive. The vast majority of students found all the teachers supportive.

A fourth reason for the students' respect is the teachers' pastoral care of the students. The students felt that they could approach them confidentially about any problem, even one that was not a school problem but a concern about something out of school. One boy said that the teachers will help with school work, 'but not just that…say…something's happening outside of school or anything like that, they'll offer you support and help you through that and stuff like that' (33B10). One example of this is that if bullying on Facebook occurs outside school, it is dealt with by the school. A final reason that the students respect the teachers is because the respect is reciprocal, and they feel that the teachers respect them. As one girl stated, 'Students have like a lot of respect for teachers and vice versa as well' (24G). I will now move to the next dimension of respect.

Respect - for other students and self-respect
A second dimension of the value of respect is respect for the other students and self-respect. Most of the students were unable to give a good account of the school mission statement even though they admitted being told about it on a number of occasions. However, one thing that many of them could recall is that it refers to respecting oneself and others. As one girl replied, 'it means like you've got to have respect for other people and yourself' (24G).

Respect - for the school buildings and equipment
The final dimension of respect was respect for the building and equipment. This is really another aspect of respecting the other teachers and pupils. Each student has a responsibility to look after these things so that others can benefit from using them. In fact there is very little vandalism or graffiti and, when there is any, it is dealt with strictly by the teachers. One value that the students raised spontaneously when discussing respect for the school and the equipment was gratitude. The students really appreciated the school facilities and the buildings. One student said, 'we're lucky to have some of the stuff that we have… so we should look after it' (6G).

It is possible to conclude from the interviews and the data above that the value of respect in all its dimensions is a very strong feature both for the students and the teachers.

Ambition and success
Nearly all pupils mentioned (of their own volition) that it was a good school, not just in the sense of a good place to be, but having a good reputation for high achievement, especially for high GCSE and vocational exam results. These are seen as the passport to achieving places in 6th Form Colleges that will put them on the path to good careers, either through university or other forms of training. Thus they have high aspirations for their future careers though some are still undecided about this and are concentrating on first getting into college and then university. Others had clearer career aims; for example, four wanted to be doctors, three teachers, two photographers, two midwifes. Others wanted to become an architect, a psychologist, a lawyer, a chiropractor, a policeman, a pastor in a Christian church, a professional sports person and, reflecting the fact that the school has a specialism in music and technology, three wanted to be graphic designers, one wanted to be a classical singer, and finally another hoped to become an actor.

Individual responsibility and self-discipline
The students realise that they have to take responsibility for their own learning. They accept that they need to be organised, to work hard and meet their homework deadlines. As one boy said, 'lots of the teachers help you with what you need. I mean of course when it comes to exams and things, they don't help you too much, because you have to be independent and work to your best ability' (32B10). The students accept the fact that they will get detention if they fail to meet deadlines, and enough students talked about doing their homework and handing it in on time to conclude that most students have a good work ethic.

Clustering around these values of individual responsibility and self-discipline are other values such as hard work, patience, good organisation and study skills, and the value of putting off short term goals and gratification for long term ones.

Good behaviour
The students value good behaviour because it ensures that the lessons are not disrupted, and it allows them to learn and do well at their work. One girl replied when asked if the students are well behaved: 'Yes, in umm in like my lessons, if they get told off, they just stop because everyone wants to learn at this age and do well in their GCSEs and that' (24G). Another reason students value good behaviour is that there is very little bullying, so they feel safe and secure and can therefore enjoy school. Of course it is to be expected that in a large school there will be a small minority of students who do misbehave. One boy explained that the good behaviour was underpinned by their religion. He said:

> *'I think personally [this is] because of our spiritual side to the school, and because faith is encouraged quite a lot. I think that's what sort of makes us want to do better, and want us to be good pupils and well behaved.'* (32B10)

Fairness
When the students were asked if the system of rewards and punishments was fair, nearly all the students agreed that it was. One girl simply stated, 'Yes, if you do something wrong then

you get punished. If you do something right then you get rewarded' (8G). Although most students said that the reward system was fair, there were a few who queried this. Two complained that the "naughty" students who improved were given more rewards than those who were consistently good.

Another student thought that the lower ability students were rewarded more, while yet another student thought the opposite and that the clever students received more rewards than the average student, and finally one student complained of favouritism. We can conclude that all the students thought it was important that there should be fairness in the school's punishment and reward system. This raises another important value in connection with punishment, namely forgiveness.

Forgiveness
The students are almost unanimous that once a student has done wrong and completed their punishment, the teachers and the school forgive them and that the teachers do not hold any grudges against them. One student thought that forgiveness is what the school is about, 'just forgiving everyone, like maybe the teachers forgiving pupils and pupils forgiving each other maybe for something they've done to each other' (14G). I now turn to the value of education.

Education
The implication of all the students' responses is that education is a key value. All of the students, with the exception of two where we ran out of time, were asked towards the end of their interviews to state the two or three most important values in their lives. Fourteen put education in the top three, and two more placed it in fourth place. One said:

> *'I'd put them [friends] second but if you put your friends before education you're not going to get that far, so umm education's worth more than friends but family's more important than education because they're the one who's give you the education and sent you to an education.'* (16G)

Community and sense of belonging
As one examines the student values under this theme of the school, one begins to get a real sense of the ethos of the school. As we have seen, the students said it was a good place to be, warm, friendly, safe and enjoyable. Everyone is respected and supports each other so that nobody is left behind. Students are generally well behaved and are treated fairly, despite a small number of students disagreeing about the allocation of rewards, and forgiveness is a strong feature of the school.

Very positive relationships have been developed, and staff and students are united in the aim that the students should become the best that they can be. In short, one could describe the ethos as very positive. One could also say that the school formed a strong community. To use some of the key phrases in the DCSF'S (2007) definition of community cohesion which we quoted earlier, there is 'a common vision and sense of belonging…similar life opportunities are available to all…and positive relationships exist and continue to be developed' (ibid, p.3).

Pride

Implicit in many of the students' responses is their pride in their school community and in themselves. Pride can become a vice when it is excessive but can also be a virtue; for example, soldiers are often said to be proud of their regiment. If we refer back to the students' quotations at the start of this theme, the school, it seems that they are very proud of their school and its good teachers, well-behaved pupils, high educational achievements and friendly ethos. They imply that they are also proud to be members of this school. This is a good basis for the values of self-esteem and self-respect. One student, when asked about her motivation to get good exam results, said, 'I want to do it for myself, I want to like be proud of myself and having good results' (13G).

Theme 4 - Religion

Catholic faith

There is the recognition by the students that the Catholic faith is a key value and influences much of school life, including an emphasis on RE, assemblies, class prayers, masses, moral education and religious feasts such as Christmas and Easter and the provision of a school chaplain. Perhaps more significant is the importance placed by the students themselves on faith in their daily lives. The first aspect is evidenced by the fact that when the students were asked at the start of the interview to talk about their school, fourteen (nearly 39%) referred to its Catholicism or the faith. There is evidence for the second aspect, which I describe as personal commitment, in the fact that when thirty-eight of the students were asked to state their top two or three values, nine (nearly 24%) included the faith. The students' religious values are evidenced in their religious practice, in their belief in God, in their views on prayer and in the spirituality which is implicit in these values.

One indicator of their faith commitment is religious practice. The student interviews revealed that the number who attend Church every Sunday is 14; those who attend once or twice a month is 4; the number who attend occasionally or rarely for special occasions is 13; and finally 8 students said that they did not attend at all. (One student is not a Catholic and is not included in these numbers.) A few showed exceptional commitment, including one who, apart from regular attendance, is very involved in her parish as a Eucharistic minister and a reader, and is also involved in parish social activities.

An interesting point to arise in this analysis is that in nearly every case where students attend Church, whether regularly, occasionally or rarely, they are accompanied by at least one other family member, by which I include grandparents. This would indicate that for these students at least the family plays an important part in nurturing the faith. Three members of the student sample belonged to an impact group, and there are approximately 34 members of this group in the whole school. Their aim is to make the church and liturgies more relevant and appealing to more young people. They meet at one of the local parishes on a rota basis on a Sunday once or twice a month and invite other young people to the meeting. This is a little more evidence of some of the students' commitment to the Catholic faith. But others might still think that the numbers attending church regularly is low. However Church attendance is only one of the criteria for commitment to Catholicism. Nearly all the students who do not attend still identify themselves as Catholic. Only one student said that she did not believe in God, because she believed that if there were a God he would not allow all the evil in the world (7G). Others expressed varying levels of belief in God and some argued that they did not think it necessary to attend church. Others said believing in God and praying were what was important.

Given the students' variable personal commitment to the faith it is difficult to assess how much they feel they belong to the local, national or international Catholic communities outside of school. All I can say is that it seems likely to be on a continuum, starting from those who feel a strong sense of belonging, to those who feel little or no identification with them. Mass in school was voluntary except on two occasions in the year. On these occasions everyone just accepted this as part of being a Catholic school, but it would have more significance for some than others. As one student said, 'we don't hate them or anything. They're just there, masses' (23G). Another criterion of faith and belief is the students' involvement in prayer, which also provides evidence of their spirituality. It is recognised that spirituality is a contested concept and is used widely including in the concept of secular spirituality (Van Ness, 1996; de Souza, 2006). Here I am using it to refer to religious spirituality (Sheldrake, 2007).

Prayer and spirituality
There are a number of dimensions to prayer. Two of these are prayer in school and secondly prayer on one's own. The students said that they prayed in school three or four times each day. Everyone treated prayers respectfully whether they attend church or not. One girl said, 'it's just like a time that everyone prays…..no-one talks when there's a prayer' (19G).

Thirty-two were asked if they found prayers in school helpful. There were a variety of responses, which were mostly positive. These could be placed into two sections, though with slight reservations which I will explain later. The first reflects a view of God as a dispenser of help and gifts; for example, he reassures, motivates, relieves stress and helps with problems. One example of this group is a girl who said, 'Yes, if I'm like stressed and it's good before exams as well, we always say a prayer then, so that helps' (23G). The second group of responses reflected a more mature view of prayer as developing a relationship with God. One student stated simply, 'Because it means something to be in contact with God' (8G). My reservations about dividing the responses in this way is that one can have a relationship with God and still ask for things and vice versa, so my twofold division is simply about emphasis. Overall the students said that they found praying in school was helpful, and their responses showed that students valued prayer and spirituality. Three students said that they were not helpful.

The majority of the sample (38) was then asked if they prayed on their own apart from school prayers, and only six replied in the negative. The other thirty-two had a variable commitment to prayer, with some praying every night at home or when they were at church, and others just occasionally, for example, if they or one of their families were ill. Two students found

21

praying on their own more helpful than praying in school. Praying for others is an indication of the value of compassion and concern for others which is one of the values associated with spirituality and to which I now turn.

Compassion and concern for others
Thirty of the students were asked if it served any purpose to pray for others when there was a local, national or global tragedy. One student replied negatively because despite praying to eliminate poverty this still exists. Another said only sometimes, because prayer at other times remains unanswered. A third thought that as a result of the prayers God might inspire a person to give practical help but that people should help others anyway, without the need to pray. But the majority thought that it was good to pray at these times. One girl said, 'when they see people praying for them, I think that it gives them hope, and belief that they can like come out of a bad situation and carry on with their lives' (36G10). I would suggest that many of the students' responses demonstrate some level of belief and faith in God and also of spirituality and compassion.

Respect for other religions, equality and love of neighbour
Part of a commitment to faith and belief is an appreciation of other people's religion. When thirty of the students were asked to name a religion other than Catholicism, all could name at least one, and seventeen could name three or more, including other Christian denominations. The most frequently mentioned ones were Judaism, Hinduism, Sikhism and Islam. All of the students said that they learned about them in RE in Years 7 and 8, and one remembered visiting a synagogue with the school. As they were now in Years 10 and 11, they had forgotten or at least could not recall much of what they had learned, and their knowledge of other religions was limited. However, when all but one of the forty students were asked how should people of other religions be treated, the responses were unanimously positive. The students' commitment to the values of respect and equality which they demonstrated in the previous theme again was evident, and two also provided evidence of a commitment to the Golden Rule and love of your neighbour. Another said that we are all made in the image of God (33B10).

All of the students said that people of other religions should be treated exactly the same as one would treat those who were fellow Catholics and that is because essentially all human beings are the same, and all should be treated fairly and equally. Another described other religions as simply other routes to the same God (24G). Another student said that everyone has the right to choose their own religion (22G).

Theme 5 - Morality
The first key moral value that I researched with the students was truthfulness. I would remind the reader that I am using a rational paradigm in my research, which intuitionists, who believe that morality is largely intuitive and innate with rationality playing a much smaller role (see Haidt, 2006; 2013), would question. First the following scenario was presented to three of them. 'Suppose someone asks a friend to tell the teacher that he is sick so that he can truant from school, what do you think the friend should do?' I then changed the wording for

the remaining thirty-six students to 'your friend' and 'what would you do?' as this is the more important question for the research. (One student was not asked this question.) I give a summary below of the students' responses to this and a second scenario, which I will explain later before forming some conclusions about the data.

Truthfulness
Of the thirty-nine students asked the question in either format their replies fell into two categories. The first group of twenty-two said that they would not lie to the teacher for a variety of reasons, such as: they thought lying was wrong, they did not want to get into trouble themselves, it was not their responsibility and that education was important so their friend should be in school. Only two of this group said simply that they did not want to lie; as one student said, 'No…. because they need to be in school and it's lying' (26G10). The second smaller group of thirteen students said that they would lie to the teacher depending on the situation, although most said that they did not like lying. Most of these would only lie for a best or a close friend. As one girl said, 'If it was my best friend, I'd probably just tell the teacher that she's sick' (38G10). Of the remaining four students, two said they would say nothing and two were not sure what they would do.

In order to examine the students' commitment to truthfulness further, a second scenario was presented to them. It was: 'Suppose a friend wanted to go out and he/she said I am telling my mum I haven't got any homework, will you back me up? What would you do?' (The scenario was sometimes phrased differently but it remained essentially the same question.) Again there was a range of responses that could be divided into two groups. The first consisted of eighteen of the forty students who would not lie to the parent for a variety of reasons. Some just thought lying was wrong; others did not want to get involved. The second group was made up of seventeen students who would lie to the parent depending on the situation. Some would not tell a lie to the parent over a serious matter but did not think missing homework that important and would 'tell like a bit of a lie to help your friend' (36G10). Another student called lies in these situations 'white lies' (20G). Among the remaining five students, there were two who were unsure what they would do and three whose responses were unclear.

In conclusion I think it would be correct to say simply that all the students know that lying is wrong and none like lying. But there was a difference in the responses to truth telling to teachers in school and to parents outside of school. (22 would not lie to teachers, but 13 would depending on the situation: 18 would not lie to parents, but 17 would in certain circumstances). So while some students would not lie, others would do so depending on the circumstances. I now turn to discuss the value of honesty.

Honesty
This value was examined under two further scenarios. In the first the students were asked. 'If they saw someone in front of them drop a £20 note, what they would do?' All of the students except one said they would pick it up and return it to the owner. They gave a number of different reasons for this. These were: they wouldn't like it to happen to them, the person might really need that money for food, it's the right thing to do, and if you do not give it back

it is stealing. One student replied that she would give it back 'because I've been brought up to think it really' (24G). This is a reminder that values are not just developed in School but also in the home. Finally, there was one student who said honestly that he would keep it even though he knew that he should not do so.

The second scenario presented to the students was, 'What would they do if they were shopping with a friend who pushed a jumper into their bag and told them to walk out with it?' It is true to say that almost all of the students reacted with shock even at this suggestion, and all forty said they would put the jumper back and refuse to shoplift. The main reasons given were that it was stealing and they were not thieves, it was not right, and again the feeling of guilt they would have if they did. Some students thought that it would be unfair on the shopkeepers, others that it was a criminal offence and they did not want to break the law, and three students gave reasons based on the bible. Finally, another student said she would not shoplift, 'Because well it's breaking the law isn't it, stealing and I'm a Catholic as well, and it's against the ten commandments isn't it, don't steal' (15G).

We can conclude this section on honesty by stating that if the views expressed to me by the students are accurate then they display a commitment to honesty. The next value under the theme of morality that I wish to discuss is the students' general attitude to bullying, which, in this case, can be described best as being one which is clearly and firmly opposed.

Anti-bullying
The students' interviews showed that bullying in the school is rare. Fourteen of them said that they were unaware of any incidents, one had been bullied in school, and three had a friend who had been. The remaining twenty-two students had either witnessed some name calling in school or had heard about it. All agreed that the school dealt well with any incidents and stopped them immediately, even if it was a case of online bullying that occurred out of school. Teachers were always ready to listen to students who reported incidents and in addition prefects were available to help students. All of the students considered it to be wrong and used words such as disgusting, appalling, horrible, totally wrong, unfair and hurtful. They found it hard to understand why anyone would bully another person, but a number thought that it was because of the bully's own insecurities and problems although they added that this did not excuse it. The discussions revealed a compassion for people who are bullied. The students argued that no one should harm another person's happiness and self-esteem and claimed everyone should feel welcome in the school community and be treated equally and fairly. Two students said that they would support the person being bullied by saying 'something and stop it' (22G).

Equality
This is the next value I want to discuss further under the theme of morality. Some of the students were asked two questions. First, thirty-nine of them were asked how, in their opinion, we should treat people with special needs, i.e. those with either physical or learning disabilities. The responses were nearly all very similar. They believe that people with special needs should be treated the same as anyone else, except that they should receive extra support

to cope with their disabilities. They should be treated fairly, without discrimination and they should not be made to feel that people look down on them or pity them. As one student said, 'well obviously they're going to need extra help than someone who doesn't have special needs...but they certainly shouldn't be called or abused for it....they're still in the image of God, so why shouldn't we like help them?' (33B10). One unusual response was from a student who agreed that special needs children should receive equal opportunities but was just a little concerned that if the teachers needed more time to explain subjects to those with learning difficulties it 'might hold me back' (9G). This was an exceptional view and does not change the overwhelming consensus that special needs students should be treated equally.

The second question that thirty-eight of the students were asked in relation to equality was should boys and girls receive exactly the same education and job opportunities. The responses were unanimously in favour of equality. They argued that the genders were equal, to treat them differently would be unfair and discriminatory, and that both are entitled to equal rights. One boy commented, 'it's like sexist not to have women on equal pay and it's offensive to them. They don't think they can do a suitable job, same job' (28B10).

Keeping promises
Twenty-six students were asked, if they had promised to go and see their sick grandmother on Saturday at 3pm and, afterwards, friends invited them out at the same time, what would they do? They all said that they would keep their promise and see their grandmother because family was more important than friends, and they could see their friends anytime but, as their gran was ill, her future was uncertain. One student said her grandmother would appreciate her more than her friends and another that she would need the company. From these answers, it was unclear if they would keep their promise because they thought that this was the right thing to do, or because of their commitment to family, or because of both of these reasons. So I changed the question to a general one and asked twelve students, if you made a promise to meet someone, for example to go to a match or to help them with a computer, and in the meantime you received a better offer, what would you do? Ten of the students said that they would keep their promise, for a variety of reasons. They thought it was right to keep to the first arrangement otherwise it would be unfair, selfish or disrespectful. As one student stated, 'I think it's unfair...if I have said that I am going out with them to cancel like my plans with them, just for some other people' (36G10).

One said that he would try to keep his promise, and one was unsure what he would do. I think that there is good evidence in the students' responses, particularly to the second format, that the students do value promise keeping. In addition, in discussing the first question format, there is more evidence of a strong commitment to the value of family that we have seen under the theme of the family.

Health and healthy living
This is a wide area, so I focussed on the students views on drugs, alcohol and tobacco. All of the students were aware of the dangers of these substances. One student informed me that there were posters all over the school warning them about their consequences and outside

speakers visited the school to warn them of their possible side effects. It is possible to summarise their views as follows. They all thought that drugs apart from prescription ones were bad for your health and in addition were illegal, and none of them agreed with their use. One of them argued that drugs 'mess up your body and your brain and your thinking and they can have an effect on you and on other people' (5B). The majority of the students also thought that smoking was bad for health; two of them stressed this because of family illness in one case and a family death caused by smoking in the other. Despite this seven students thought that, though it was wrong and they had no wish to smoke, if adults wished to smoke, it should be left up to their personal choice.

All of the students are aware of the dangers of heavy drinking and the bad consequences that drunken behaviour can have on others, including drink driving, which can cause serious accidents and even fatalities. But they are very relaxed about these dangers, and the unanimous view among the students is that drinking in moderation is acceptable. This view was expressed by a student who said, 'Alcohol I don't think is too bad because I think the majority of the country drink alcohol, and like people do get drunk, and get like bad situations come out of it, but it can be done in moderation' (20G). The same student did warn that underage drinking can be dangerous for another reason, because it can be secret drinking and their parents might not know where they are. Students were divided about underage drinking. All thought drinking at a very young age was bad for your health, but some thought that, for those aged 16 years and above, drinking in sensible amounts at a party or a glass of champagne at a special occasion, e.g. a wedding, was acceptable. Others argued that young people should not drink below the legal age; as one student stated, 'It's wrong because of the law and you don't want to disrespect the law. You should always follow it' (25G10).

It is clear from the students' discussions that they think that drugs and tobacco can cause greater harm to health than alcohol, which they think is only bad for health if taken in excess and not in moderation. The discussion also revealed a commitment to health and a healthy life style. Incidentally, this discussion also revealed a commitment to the values of moderation and respect for the law.

Theme 6 - Citizenship
The first value that I want to examine in this theme is anti-racism.

Anti-racism (equality, fairness, anti-discrimination, anti-prejudice and respect for others)
Despite the fact that the school and its immediate neighbourhood is, as we have already noted, almost entirely mono-cultural, all the students could describe a racist incident, although none of those interviewed had personal experience of being abused racially. Any incidents that have occurred in school are extremely rare and usually involve name calling. One student said that he had come across 'racist views' in school but said, 'It isn't active in our school towards pupils' (39B). One student equated it with bullying and argued that it could lead to violence and prevent community cohesion (18G).

26

All of the students condemned racism in the strongest terms. They used words and phrases such as: wrong, bad, low, unfair, disgusting, disrespecting God's creation, we're all made in God's image, disrespectful, unacceptable, should not be tolerated, horrible, wrong in every way, hurtful, demeaning, discriminating, not nice, damaging to peoples' confidence and making people feel inferior. One student expressed her views on equality and discrimination by saying, 'discriminating against people because of like their race and their colour....it's completely wrong. Because they're exactly the same as my race...They don't need to be treated differently.' (23G). One student described racism as 'being prejudiced towards a different race...it's wrong because you shouldn't judge people at all but you shouldn't especially judge them on I think like when you don't know anything about them.' (27G). The discussion with the students about racism revealed that they are committed to a cluster of values around the central value of anti-racism which include equality and fairness, anti-discrimination, anti-prejudice and respect for others.

Openness to immigrants (fairness, equality, anti-discrimination and inclusiveness)
Thirty-nine of the students were asked their opinions about allowing immigrants to enter England. Those who made a distinction all said that asylum seekers and refugees should be allowed to enter the country. In respect of economic immigrants, twenty-nine said that all legal immigrants who were prepared to work for a living should be allowed into the country but gave a variety of reasons.

Some said that they themselves have freedom of movement to go and work in other countries, so immigrants should enjoy this same right. One student quoted the example of her grandfather who had emigrated to Australia. Others thought that England would benefit from the culture of other countries which the immigrants brought with them, e.g. new ideas in fashion, food and music. Others said that England would benefit from the skills that some of them brought with them, for example immigrant doctors. Others said that we are helping to give the immigrants a better quality of life. One student said, 'It creates multiculturalism, which I think is a good thing for any country...It introduces different ideas and different personalities into like a local community' (28B10).

Another six agreed that they should be allowed into England but have added other conditions that could be resolved. But another four students stated conditions which are or could be regarded as discriminatory. The first of these would accept immigrants provided this did not prevent him from finding work himself. This seems to imply that he regards immigrants as a threat to employment and a group to blame if he is unemployed. This view was stated more clearly by another pupil who thought that unemployed English people should get priority over immigrants when applying for jobs. The first student implies some discrimination against immigrants and the second student's condition is clearly discriminatory because it would mean that immigrants were not treated equally.

The remaining two students objected to immigrants being allowed to settle permanently in England. One of these said immigrants should be allowed in on a temporary basis, but after they have had time to improve their economic status, they should return and help to improve their own country. The second student argued that immigrants make the unemployment situation in England worse. She said:

'If they want a better life I understand why they come here, but on the other hand like...I wish they didn't because I'd rather it just be English people in an English country. Because there's so many people unemployed and I think if like people from different countries weren't here, there'd be a lot less and it would be beneficial for us.' (13G)

The last two views are discriminatory, anti-immigration, anti-equality and prejudicial, especially in the case of the last student and are definitely the exception to the overwhelming majority opinion. In total, thirty-seven of the students would agree to immigrants being allowed into this country permanently albeit eight of these did place conditions on this, and two of the conditions were discriminatory. If I am correct, this demonstrates that the majority of the students do possess the value of openness to the immigrant. This value involves other values such as treating immigrants equally, fairly and without discrimination or prejudice once they have gained legal entry. The next value that I examined with the students was that of democracy.

Democracy
The students had learned about Parliament and to a lesser extent Local Government in Key Stage 3 in geography and history lessons. So we focussed our discussions on Parliament. Some of them had a good knowledge of Parliament, the party system and the roles of Ministers, others at the other end of the continuum could remember very little. Some students mentioned that the school had organised a mock election in school at the 2010 UK Elections, and the students had to take on the roles of the main political parties, make up policies and speak about them before the votes were taken. So they knew that Parliament was important and governed the country though many were unclear about the details. One aspect of democracy they were all familiar with was voting.

In addition to their experience of the mock election, pupils vote for form captains and representatives on the school council. Most of the students take these votes seriously and think that they are beneficial to those standing for election and for the student voters. One student stated, 'I think it teaches you ....how to be like responsible for people and not just yourself' (6G). Others said those who vote also benefit because it gives them a voice in school affairs.

The students' commitment to a democratic voting system is demonstrated by the fact that all of the thirty-five students who were asked said that they would vote when legally entitled to. Four mentioned the fact that the suffragettes had fought so hard to get women the vote that they felt that they would be betraying them if they failed to vote. One student said that he did not want to take the right to vote for granted because this right was denied to some people in other countries, another that he wanted to make a difference, and another group of students said that if they did not vote, they would have no right to criticise the government.

Respect for, and obedience to, the laws of the country
These are two important values for citizens. The students were unanimous that we should respect the laws of the country by obeying them. They argued that laws are essential for order and safety in society otherwise there would be chaos.

One student stated, 'they give justice. They give fairness, safety and…it would be morally correct thing to do, it gives us guidance' (39B). One student raised the possibility of a conflict between personal convictions and the law. She said that she would obey all laws, 'unless I absolutely disagreed with it so much that I just couldn't follow it' (14G). This introduced the distinction between moral laws and legal laws, but there was no time to pursue it. A number of the students gave the simple reason for obeying the law that they did not want to go to prison. All were respecters of the law and wished to live as law abiding citizens.

Respect for the police and authority.
Laws themselves will not protect society unless there is an authority to enforce it. There is in fact an elaborate justice system to do this, but for most students their experience of this will be restricted to their knowledge of the Police. This research was undertaken when the national media carried stories of the two policewomen murdered in Greater Manchester on 18th September 2012. This highlighted the dangerous job the police had, and two students directly referred to the incident in the interviews.

All of the students recognised and respected the role of the police and the authority vested in them. The consensus was that they were doing a difficult job in the interest of everyone. Despite this overwhelming support for the police, two students commented that they would obey the Police and treat them fairly but would only respect the ones who treated them with respect. One of these students referenced the police shooting of Mark Duggan in Tottenham on 4th August 2011, which sparked the London riots of that month, as an example when she thought that the police did not show respect (8G). Even allowing for these two caveats the students demonstrated respect for the police and their authority and the importance of obeying them.

The next group of citizenship values were demonstrated by the students while discussing the London Olympic and Paralympic Games of 2010.

National pride
The students were almost unanimous in judging that England had excelled in hosting these Games. They thought that they had been very beneficial to England. They had increased England's international reputation and helped it to publicise itself favourably to the world, attract tourists into the country and boost the economy.

More importantly the Games promoted a greater sense of national pride and community. This pride was evident in the following student response: 'The way in which our country were able to host it, …gave me a sense of pride and a sense of patriotism…It made me proud to feel British' (32B10).

Community and sense of belonging
This pride in England promoted a new sense of community and belonging. The students talked of bringing everyone together and spoke of 'our country' (36G10). These values were evidenced by one student who said, 'It gave us…a huge sense of community' (25G10).

World community
Two students extended the notion of national to international community. One said, 'I think we just learned to get on better and to…respect people more, like the different countries and … show that we're all one world' (27G).

Learning from other cultures
Several students said that the Games were a good opportunity to learn from other nationalities and cultures. For example, 'People of different cultures…were brought together, so we learnt more about different cultures and each other' (20G).

Equality and fairness
The students have already demonstrated a commitment to these values when discussing other themes. There is evidence of a substantial commitment to them also in the discussion on the Games in relation to the number of international visitors. A number of them said that we should treat people from other countries 'the same as people from our country' (30G10). These values were also raised in relation to the paralympians. One student said that they were inspirational, that they had given everyone a wider perspective on people with special needs in general and that they should be treated fairly. There were three exceptions to the majority opinion of the Games. One thought that they were a waste of money, another that they were boring and a third said that she did not watch them.

Sport
Though the students value sport highly, only a minority of students actually stated that the Games could inspire young people to take up sport.

Theme 7 - Service to Others

Charity
In the school service to others takes the form of helping different charities. Each Year Group vote on an annual basis for a charity of their choice and throughout the year they raise money through selling cakes, sweets, raffle tickets and running other events for that charity. In addition the school is twinned with a school in South Africa. The school sends money to the African school to improve facilities, and it also sponsors teachers so that they can visit the African school. The school also has a junior branch of the Catholic international charitable organisation, the St. Vincent de Paul Society. This group raises funds for other charities during the year. It is clear that charities play a big part in the life of the school.

It is important to note that although the school does contribute to Catholic charities such as the Catholic Agency for Overseas Development (CAFOD) and The Good Shepherd, the students may choose any charity that their Year Group wishes to support. For example, they have contributed to the local hospice and the local cancer hospital, and the twinned school is not a Catholic school. All of the thirty-nine students that I asked were unanimous that many forms of local, national and global charities were important. Four students qualified their support. One said charities should account for how the money is spent and another stated we should only give to reputable charities. Two other students claimed we should not give money to those who choose to live on benefit or to those who are homeless through their own fault, for example because of drug abuse.

The students' understanding of charity seems to be best understood in the Christian meaning of the word love or *agapē* as 'caring for others' (Hunter, 1965, p.60). 'Others' here means everyone.

Discussion

I tested the validity of my data derived from student interviews by the triangulation outlined above (see research methods). The process showed a high degree of symmetry and agreement between the data sets with only two minor discrepancies. First the staff and the document survey emphasised the importance of the Mission Statement, but most of the students could only describe it in general terms. This may simply be a matter of the language used. Second the staff and both Ofsted and the Diocesan Inspection reported prayerful and religious assemblies, whereas the ones that I observed, though containing a religious theme and a prayer, also contained a lot of announcements. This may have been inevitable at the start of a new school year. I will argue that these two minor discrepancies do not affect the research conclusions significantly. Consequently, it is reasonable to remove the 'provisional and preliminary' status that I attributed to the student data and present them as the final answer to the main research question, namely, 'What values do students profess after spending three or four years in a Catholic Secondary School?'

Reliability, emotional security, support, trust, companionship and belonging present a very positive picture of the students' family life. If I am correct, this is valid for the majority of the students. However, being at a Catholic school does not make the students immune from the problems and difficulties affecting families today including family breakdown. Despite this, it remained true for all forty students that, however the family unit was composed, it remained very important to them. Similar findings are reported by O'Keefe & Zipfel (2007, p.118)[6] and by Osler & Starkey (2005, pp.99-100) in their research in Catholic and secular schools respectively, so I am not claiming that all of the values reported here in my research are necessarily exclusive to Catholic students.

Responses to interviews under the general theme of 'school' indicate that my sample valued respect, ambition, individual responsibility and self-discipline, success, good behaviour,

---

[6] Their sample comprised 72% baptised Catholics, 14% other Christians, 3% Muslim, 1% other religions, 5% no religion and 4% unknown in a total of sixteen Catholic schools – fifteen secondary and one Sixth Form College

fairness, forgiveness, education, community, and a sense of belonging and pride. These resonate with other recent research in three Catholic schools which found that the students and staff identified four main values: friendliness, respect, discipline and trust that animated the schools' Catholic ethos (Casson, 2013, p.37). Casson also found a strong sense of community, but questioned the extent to which it could be described as Catholic (pp.122-3). Grace (2002, pp.232-3) found that the students appreciated the quality of the teaching in four of the five Catholic schools in his survey where there was an atmosphere of forgiveness and justice - though some students dissented from that view. O'Keefe and Zipfel (2007) found, perhaps unsurprisingly, that ninety-six per cent of their student sample wanted to do well in school and succeed in later life. Of more significance was the eighty-one per cent who considered school important and sixty-one per cent who liked being in a Catholic school (p.102) while seventy-two per cent preferred being in a school with clear rules and where good behaviour is required (p.104).[7]

Most students had some but varying degree of commitment to the values of faith and belief, prayer and spirituality. From the data about religious practice, I concluded that their sense of community and belonging to the Catholic community outside of school varied. Nearly all of the students thought it was helpful to pray for others in times of tragedy, illustrating compassion and concern for others. When the students spoke about people of other faiths, they demonstrated again their commitment to fairness, equality and respect. Most went beyond mere toleration of difference to argue that others should be treated in the same way as their co-religionists. In support of their argument, two students quoted the Christian commandment to love your neighbour as yourself.

In respect of their religious practice, there are similarities between my research findings and those of other authors researching in Catholic schools. Flynn (1993) noted a decline in youth mass attendance (p.413). Casson (2011) found a low regular Sunday mass attendance by the students and, felt able on that basis to identify eight types, including a group who did not believe in God but regarded themselves as Catholics (p.209-214). Casson (2013) also found the students' attitudes towards RE were variable (p.93) and that when mass was celebrated in school the students' 'participation in…the mass was taking place on a variety of levels' (p.39). O'Keefe and Zipfel's (2007) findings for regular church attendance was higher than Casson's or mine with some fifty-five per cent saying religion was relevant in their lives (p.115). Grace (2002) found in his research there were mixed responses from the students in their discussions on Catholicity, but 'In general [they] spoke positively of their experience of Catholic religious teaching and liturgy in the schools' (p.233).

Almost all students were committed to the values of honesty, anti-bullying, compassion, fairness, equality, anti-discrimination, keeping promises, and healthy living. Commitment to the truth was absolute among a substantial group of students, but others would lie depending on the circumstances, including whether the lie was to a teacher or to a parent, with fewer

---

[7] Though their research was in the Catholic sector they do not claim their findings are specific or peculiar to students attending such institutions.

willing to lie to a teacher. My findings in this area or theme of student morality echo those from other research. O'Keefe and Zipfel (2007) found that only a total of nine students in their quite large sample would steal or cheat if they could get away with it (p.95), and Grace (2002) found that there was an absence of bullying in four out of five of his research schools (p.233). In discussions with students, Casson (2013) found that they trusted each other not to steal from their bags (p.74).

It seems clear that, within the concept of citizenship, a majority of the students have a commitment to the values of national pride, community and belonging, and fairness and equality. They are also committed to respect for others and learning from other cultures. A minority of students actually mentioned the value of participating in sport and being inspired by the Olympic and Paralympic Games, but that might be because a number already do take part in sport both within and outside of school. A number of students mentioned the international atmosphere produced by the Games, but only two students spoke of being part of an international community.

In addition to the values outlined above, all the students valued anti-racism, anti-discrimination, anti-prejudice, respect, a general openness to immigrants, to inclusion, democracy, and respect and obedience for laws and lawful authority. As such, my findings under the heading of citizenship tend to confirm other relevant research. O'Keefe and Zipfel (2007) record similar findings in their study. Ninety per cent of students stated that racism should not be tolerated and claimed that their school encouraged respect for other races and faiths (p.106). Surprisingly to me, only thirty-one percent thought asylum seekers should be supported (p.100) - in my sample support was unanimous. On the other hand, two-thirds valued diversity and eighty-seven per cent valued the opportunity to mix with different cultures and faiths (p.101). Grace (2002) also found that the majority of his sample reported 'a multi-ethnic and multi-cultural harmony in their schools' (p. 233) while Casson (2013) found a number of links to the local, global and other faith communities (pp.137-149).

In my final theme, that of service to others, the students showed that they are committed to the values of caring for others and openness to all people in the world regardless of ethnicity or creed. They accept that they have a responsibility towards those in need locally, regionally, nationally and internationally and, in doing so, provide evidence that they consider themselves as being part, at least in some sense, of these four communities. Again, these are consistent with other research. Casson (2013) also found that giving to charities was an important aspect of Catholic schools' ethos (pp.119-120) as did O'Keefe and Zipfel (2007, pp.124-125). These charities are further evidence of links between these schools and the wider community and are inextricably related to citizenship values.

Conclusion
I examined three specific criticisms with reference to Catholic secondary state-funded schools. The research was conducted in one archetypal Catholic school in the North of England, which happened to be located in an area which had little ethnic diversity. The research could not substantiate the criticisms as far as the non-probability sample of forty

students was concerned. In fact, far from having the negative effects stated, the opposite was true: the students were tolerant and open to others and able to mix well with people and had a sense of belonging to a number of different communities. They contribute to promoting community cohesion in a number of ways, not least by their commitment to the values of equality, respect, fairness, anti-discrimination, anti-prejudice, anti-racism and other spiritual, moral and religious values. In addition to exhibiting a strong bonding social capital, the students had links with local, national and international communities, demonstrating a bridging capital. In addition many of the students possessed strong spiritual and moral capital and a smaller number demonstrated religious capital.

If I have interpreted the data accurately, and even if these findings can only strictly be said to apply to the sample group, the research results do not support the view that being educated in a Catholic secondary state funded school will necessarily result in fragmentation in society. Neither is it true that the students make no contribution to community cohesion. Therefore it is not justified to oppose these schools on the basis of these specific criticisms and I concluded that the best educational arrangement in a pluralistic, multicultural, multi-faith and inclusive society is to ensure parents have a choice of schools to which they can send their children

References

Alexander, H. (2007) What is common about common schooling? Rational autonomy and moral agency in liberal democratic education, Journal of Philosophy of Education, 41. 4. 609-624.

Allen, R. & West, A. (2009) Religious schools in London: school admissions, religious composition and selectivity, Oxford Review of Education, 35. 4. 471-494.

Casson, A. (2011) The right to 'bricolage': Catholic pupils' perception of their religious identity and the implications for Catholic schools in England, Journal of Beliefs & Values, 32. 2. 207-218.

Casson, A. (2013) Fragmented Catholicity and Social Cohesion, Oxford, Bern, Berlin, Bruxelles, Frankfurt am Main, New York, Wien, Peter Lang.

de Souza, M. (2006) Rediscovering the spiritual dimension in education: promoting a sense of self and place, meaning and purpose in learning, in: K. Engebretson, G. Durka, R. Jackson, A. McGrady & M. de Souza, (eds) International Handbook of Religious, Moral and Spiritual Education (Part 2), Amsterdam, Springer, 1127-39.

Flynn, M. (1993) The Culture of Catholic Schools, Homebush, St Pauls.

Grace, G. (2002) Catholic Schools: mission, markets and morality, London, New York, Routledge Falmer.

Grace, G. (2003) Educational studies and faith-based schooling: moving from prejudice to evidence-based argument, British Journal of Educational Studies, 51. 2. 149-167.

Haidt, J. (2006) The Happiness Hypothesis, London, Arrow Books.

Haidt, J. (2013) The Righteous Mind, London, Penguin.

Hand, M. (2003) A philosophical objection to faith schools, Theory and Research in Education, 1. 1. 89-99.

Hansard (1991) http://www.hansard.millbanksystems.com/lords/1991/mar/04/education-amendment-bill-hl, 526, cols. 1275-1276, [Accessed 30 January 2012].

Hirst, P. H. (1985) Education and Diversity of Belief, in: M. C. Felderhof, (ed) Religious Education in a Pluralistic Society, London, Hodder & Stoughton, 5-17.

Hunter, A.M. (1965) Design For Life, London, SCM Press Ltd.

Judge, H. (2001) Faith-based schools and state funding: a partial argument, Oxford Review of Education, 27. 4. 463-474.

Levinson, M. (2007) Common schools and multicultural education, Journal of Philosophy of Education, 41. 4. 625-642.

Macdonald, I., Bhavani,T., Khan, L. & John, G. (1989) Murder in the Playground: Report of the MacDonald Inquiry into Racism and Racial Violence in Manchester Schools, London, Longsight Press.

Marples, R. (2005) Against faith schools: a philosophical argument for children's rights, International Journal of Children's Spirituality, 10. 2. 133-147.

Morris, A. B. (2008) Fifty Years On: The case for Catholic schools, Chelmsford, Matthew James Publishing Ltd.

O'Keefe, B. & Zipfel, R. (2007) Formation for Citizenship in Catholic Schools, Chelmsford, Matthew James Publishing Ltd.

Osler, A. & Starkey, H. (2005) Changing Citizenship, Democracy and Inclusion in Education, Maidenhead, Open University Press.

Osler, A. (2007) Faith Schools and Community Cohesion, www.runnymedetrust.org/publications, [Accessed 14 June 2012].

Osler, A. (2010) Students' Perspectives on Schooling, Maidenhead, Open University Press.

Pring, R. (2007) The common school, Journal of Philosophy of Education, 41. 4. 503-522.

Reich, R. (2007) How and why to support common schooling and educational choice at the same time, Journal of Philosophy of Education, 41. 4. 709-725.

Sheldrake, P. (2007) A Brief History of Spirituality, Oxford, Blackwell.

Short, G. (2002) Faith-based schools: a threat to social cohesion?, Journal of Philosophy of Education, 36. 4. 559-572.

Thiessen, E. J. (2001) In Defence of Religious Schools and Colleges, Montreal, McGill-Queen's University Press.

Troyna, B. & Hatcher, R. (1992) Racism in Children's Lives: A study of 'mainly white' primary schools, London, Routledge (in association with the National Children's Bureau).

Van Ness, P. H. (1996) Spirituality and the Secular Quest, London, SCM Press.

Aspects of Parental Involvement in a Catholic Secondary School

Jonathan Lawford

Editor's Note:
This extract is taken from a small study which forms the background to, and one element of, an, as yet, uncompleted EdD thesis having a wider focus on parental involvement. It is to be submitted for examination before the end of the academic year 2016-17.

Background and Research Methods

This study focuses on the nature of parental involvement at a single Catholic Secondary School in the North of England and sought to establish whether a hypothesised 'joint religious enterprise' was evident in the interaction of school and parents in the education of their children.

It uses an interpretive research paradigm with a small group of parents (n=24) so the collected data are non-statistical and subjective, particularly so because of my status as 'insider researcher'[1] having a personal relationship with those parents who agreed to take part. For these reasons it is recognised that the findings from such a small sample taken from a single school preclude extrapolation of any firm conclusions to a wider context.

The term parental involvement covers both ways in which parents are practically engaged with their children in their academic and social activities in school – 'spontaneous involvement' - and in strategies designed to enhance the positive impact of those activities – 'interventionist involvement' (Desforges & Abouchaar, 2003 p.84). Desforges & Abouchaar have argued:

> *'The very clear and consistent finding [from their extensive review of literature is] that when all other factors bearing on pupil attainment are taken out of the equation, parental involvement ..... has a large and positive effect on the outcomes of schooling.'*
>
> (Desforges & Abouchaar, 2003 p.87)

'Spontaneous involvement' might be parent/child conversations about school work, parents being proactive in contacting school, accessing the school web site, parents initiating school visits and parents engaging in their child's homework. Interventionist involvement could include parents' evenings, responding to school reports, opportunities for one to one meetings with a member of staff, school newsletters, educational activities for parents, parent groups and using parents in the classroom. From the school's perspective, the aim of these forms of interventionist strategies is to establish a partnership between a pupil's family and the school, one of whose main functions is that of assisting parents - as the prime educators - in their task

---

[1] For a discussion of 'insider research' see, among others, Jones, (2001); Ganga & Scott, (2006); Mercer (2007); Hopkins, (2007); Crossley et al (2015).

of bringing children up in the Catholic faith (Stock, 2005, pp.3-4). This implies that education as a religious enterprise will be a prominent feature of home/school interaction. This study asked the question, 'Is this the case at St. .... Catholic Secondary School?'

In seeking at least a preliminary answer, theoretical constructs derived from American research were used as a framework for the interpretation of parental comments made during the interviews. This research identified six themes that should be evident in schooling in which a joint religious enterprise is a reality; namely, 'the primacy of parental role in education', 'parents as witnesses in the world', 'continuing parental catechesis', 'parent/school/church collaboration', 'parents as witnesses in the world', 'parental involvement' and 'school choice' (Frabutt et al., 2010).

The main instrument for data collection was interviews with parents supplemented by school records of pupil progress and their academic attainment in public examinations. The sample comprised a group of twenty-four families having children in Year 11 in the academic year 2012-13. Each was given a reference number to preserve their anonymity which is used when quoting comments they made in the sections below. The study used semi-structured interviews with those family members who agreed to take part in the investigation. They had been given a list of indicative questions prior to the interviews taking place. These focused on ways in which they felt involved in the life of the school; whether it was important for them that their children attended a Catholic school and, if so, whether it was possible to quantify that importance and the value they placed on their own religious faith (if any); and their active involvement, or otherwise, in helping with homework? Specific activities which formed a focus of the interviews with parents are based on descriptions developed by the National Foundation for Educational Research (see table 1 below).

Table 1

Types of Parental Involvement

Spontaneous Involvement	Interventionist Involvement
Parent/pupil conversations	School contacting home.
Parents contacting school	Parents attendance at parents evenings
Parents initiating school visits	Parents responding to written reports
Parents engaging in their child's homework	Parents responding to invitations to school events.
Parents accessing the school website	Parents attending one to one meetings with a member of staff.
-	Parents reading the school newsletter
-	Parents attending educational activities
-	Parents involved in parent groups
-	Parents supporting in the classroom

(SOURCE: NFER 2007, p.1)

Findings: Evidence of a Joint Religious Enterprise

I have used categories of religious self-identification derived from research into children's religiosity (Casson, 2011) and from work in America (Frabutt et al., 2010) as a way of evaluating parental understanding of, and attitude towards, education provided by a successful secondary school with a Catholic religious character. That amalgam of attitudinal understanding I have named a 'family faith factor'. Its characteristics include a strong religiosity according to the self-identification categories from the work of Casson (2011) - see table 2 below - an understanding and acceptance of the primacy of parents in the education of their children (Sacred Congregation for Catholic Education, 1965; Frabutt et al., 2010; Stock, 2005, 2012) and acting as witnesses to the Catholic faith (Frabutt et al, 2010).

Table 2

Catholic Self Identification Categories

Category	Identifier
Hardcore	Regular Mass Attendance.
Baptised	Baptised but not practising. Notion that it is Baptism that makes you Catholic.
Halfway	Baptised and received Holy Communion once. Takes issue with some church teaching.
Pilgrim	An emotional dimension to religion. Has had a one off religious experience.
Golden Rule	A right way of living rather than a right way of belief.
School Catholic	School acts as church.
Catholic Atheist	Baptised but doesn't believe in God
Family Heritage	Has a Catholic family history and wants to perpetuate this.

(SOURCE: CASSON, 2011)

Because the prime concern of this study was the interaction between parents' faith, or religiosity, and the impact it may have on decisions and actions regarding their children's education, the interviews centred around four main questions, namely, is the Catholic faith important to you; what were the reasons you decided to send your child to a Catholic school; do you teach your child about faith or do you ever talk about faith at home; and, do you think Religious Education is an important subject for your child to study? As one might expect there were variations in their statements and convictions

The Importance of Catholic Faith

The great majority of parents of children stated that their Catholic faith was important to them and their families, though the ways in which it was expressed varied from those claimed a high level of personal and familial religious practice, for example:

> *'It's important to my wife and I'd like to think it's important to my daughter as well.'* (24)
> *'I think we are a religious family. We do go to Church quite a lot.'* (4)
> *'I've been brought up as a Catholic and all my family are Catholic and I always think they have better morals being a Catholic. When you go to Church you know you've always got that place to go to as well.'* (9)
> *'My mother brought us up Catholic, we always went to Church and maybe when I was younger I wasn't always happy about that and I can understand and I can see why children aren't but I brought my children up that way. I*

38

was determined my children were going to be brought up Catholic and I always take them to Church and when they're old enough they can make their own mind up and hopefully they'll do what I did.' (16)

In contrast, there were parents whose comments suggested their level of adherence was more a case of intellectual assent to the idea of belonging, or a matter of personal identity, rather than a commitment and/or involvement in religiously motivated activity. For example:

'Yes, because I think it teaches you right from wrong. I think it gives you morals and principles to stick by.' (12)
'Yes it is very much so because I'm a practising Catholic. Both children have been christened Catholic, gone through Catholic schools and I just think it's important just to have those values.' (15)
'Yes, very much so because I think it's the guidelines for your life. Just to know that there should be no bullying, treat other people as you'd treat yourself. That's how I was brought up through the Catholic faith. I think it's just to be a better person.' (11)
'Very important, I and my brothers were brought up in a very Catholic environment, we went to Church every Sunday with my parents. I'm not still a practising Catholic but now my children have grown up they've not really followed it through but which is their decision at the end of the day, they don't practise the faith each week.' (21)
'It's not important to me but it's important to me for my children.' (5)
'I don't believe, I wouldn't class myself as a religious person but I do believe in the Ten Commandments and I think the Ten Commandments give morals. Morals are a massive thing in my life I just think it's about being a good person.' (6)
'I don't go to Church. In that respect it's more of the way you live your life, is more in line with the ethos and principles of it all.' (22)

One parent, who identified themselves as a non-Catholic, argued:

'It is important as part of history and you have to believe in something.' (10)

Preference for a Catholic School

One of the consistent purposes for providing Catholic schools in England since 1850 has been to assist parents in fulfilling that responsibility (see, for example, Bourne, 1906, 1929; Stock, 2005, 2012). This stance has subsequently been affirmed in a variety of official church documents, all of which emphasise the primary role that parents have in developing the faith of their children and argue, therefore, that parents should have the right to choose a Catholic education for their children (Sacred Congregation for Catholic Education, 1965, 1977; Sacred Congregation for the Clergy, 1997; Pope Paul V1, 1975; Pope John Paul II, 1979, 1981).

Many parents, particularly those of children who achieved high levels of academic attainment standards in national examinations, consistently identified the school's Catholic character as the major reason why they had chosen it; a reason cited by all those parents who were themselves baptised Catholics. Typical statements included:

'Faith is very important and one of the reasons that I had never even considered another other school but a Catholic school for my children.' (2)

'It is because I am a practicing Catholic and I felt it was important. I wouldn't send my children to a non-Catholic school. If the local Catholic school had a bad reputation then I would look at another Catholic school and I would travel. I think it helps build the way in which a child grows, loving, kindness, etc.' (16)

'It is because my wife's a Catholic and she goes to Church every week ... all of her sisters come round and they all go to Church together.' (24)

'I got to spend time in a Catholic school on a secondment and loved the way that it was very family orientated, the values that were driven in that school, the principles, the Catholic Church. I loved it, so it was my personal experiences as a professional.' (3)

I wanted him to go to a school that was going to encourage and support the Catholic faith.' (8)

A larger number indicated that their Catholic family/cultural heritage was an important element in their decision making;

'I went to Catholic schools so it [sending our children] is just following a family tradition in Catholic schools. I wouldn't have wanted anything else because I think our beliefs are very important.' (18)

'Well because it is something that I was brought up in. I went to a Catholic primary school as well as St. ... as did all my family so I feel completely happy sending mine to Catholic schools, so it was never not an option.' (4)

'Mainly because the family is Catholic and I wanted him to have that same level of religion and education.' (1)

'I was brought up Catholic went to a Catholic school and it's just something I really do believe in. I just think it's the best education, I just think besides education its morals, its ethics and it's just a whole round thing.' (11)

'It was because my upbringing was Catholic and I do think there is a different ethos at a Catholic school than there is at other education settings. I think the behaviour is completely different.' (7)

'Well, it's through my experiences of coming through a Catholic school and my wife coming through a Catholic school.' (20)

'It was important to me. My husband's not a Catholic but that was the one thing that I did insist on was the fact that if we had any children the they would be brought up in the Catholic faith and he didn't really have much of an opinion in the matter so that was just something we did.' (21)

'All my family are Catholics and we wouldn't dream of sending our children to a non-Catholic school.' (17)

'I sent my children to Catholic school because their dad is a Catholic and I wanted to agree with him.' (14)

'I think it was because of the bonding, it's difficult to explain, I like the family unit and I like how you meet other families and people in the same situation, not just that school, I find it at Church as well.' (2)

A few argued that the reputation of the school as a provider of high quality education/good examination results was one, or the, major factor.

'Other parents looking from the outside in say Catholic schools are better, you know they seem to have better grades and all that and I always say to them well they have religion and it's amazing the way they say that's ok as if certain people would like to be Catholics. Another reason why we chose it is because it is important to our family.' (9)

'It just wouldn't have been anything that I hadn't considered because obviously I go to my local church. It is for lots of reasons really not just because it's Catholic but for their academic history as well. I just think it's massively important that they have Catholic values and I think Catholic schools traditionally tend to be better and stricter and you know I'm certainly all for that.' (15)

'I just think the discipline's better. I think they get a better education in a Catholic school.' (12)

'It was mainly the primary school that we sent them to had a very good reputation and that's what we wanted at the time so I have to be honest the faith came secondary.' (13)

'We wanted the best school, especially when he had worked really hard in primary school so that's why.' (10)

'I think it is far better than the state school system. I think the teaching is better. The management of the pupils is better.' (22)

Religion in the Home

The majority of parents stated that, in various ways and at different times in their child's lives, different facets of religion and the Catholic faith were topics of conversation at home; those having high, rather than low attaining children academically, being more likely to make such statements

'Oh, yes, some of the books we bought for him were like 'My First Bible' and we always explained Palm Sunday and Easter. Then when he brought work home for his RE I used to have a read with him, I used to say "oh, we did this and we did that" and I think that was quite a good bond.' (9)

'Oh, yes, we were quite an open family, we have talked about faith and who believes this and who believes that. I think your faith gets challenged as well and I think that can have an impact about how you feel sometimes.' (18)

'Yes absolutely, every day. I mean my son sometimes comes running down the stairs because he's very interested in what's topical.' (4)

'Yes. It could be a debate, we do discuss it and even as my daughter has become older, they'll be discussions in the house about religion and the faith.' (16)

'Yes we do, but my son and I definitely have opposite opinions.' (2)

'My daughter and my sister in law have done so all the time.' (24)

'My younger son is coming up to his Communion. He will say we've done this in RE, what does this mean? Anything to do with the Church or Faith then we would go to my older son.' (3)

Yes, certainly when they were little. They had the children's Bibles with the very early Bible stories and certainly supporting the RE aspect from school we had more discussions really. So I think lots and lots of discussions and I think he can't get how it used to be. I've never forced them when I go to Church every Sunday.' (15)

'It's just general conversations. It's like when you sit down and watch certain programmes and then you have a discussion on how that affects you as a family and how it affects you as a person.' (19)

'Yes, when my daughter took her holy communion we had homework and I'd sit with her and go to meetings and really embed it into her.' (11)

'My son has a lot of arguments with his Dad about the Catholic Church because his dad is definitely not Catholic so he used to be really good at arguing for the Church.' (8)

'Yes, we've discussed things like that but he's getting to that stage now you can see that he's thinking about it ... I've given him the foundations and if he wants to take that further he can.' (20)

'With one of my children; he talks about it a lot because he likes to look at different views, so yes.' (23)

An additional minority of parents were more hesitant in claiming religion, Church attendance or matters of faith as being regular topics within the household, while at the same time indicating that the subject was not completely ignored:

'Yes, little bits but not as much as I did when they were younger because obviously they'd been to Church, they know what it's all about.' (12)

'We have talked about religion at home. I'm sure I am probably, deep down, a believer but it doesn't focus highly in my life but I have tried to make it focus in my children's lives.' (5)

'Well sometimes she does when she has Religious Education.' (14)

'We must have done at some point.' (1)

'No. Sometimes I asked him questions. I always say you don't need to go to the Church to be a good person, so we are always talking about being a good person and we teach our children to respect each other.' (10)

On the other hand, a quarter of the sample indicated that such subjects were never part of family discourse.

'No, not really.' (7)
'No, not as a rule.' (13)
'No, not overly, I wouldn't say so. We don't go to Church.' (22)
'No, it [the topic] doesn't [arise].' (6)
'I didn't really feel it necessary because she was getting that in school and we were going to Church so I didn't really feel the need for that.' (21)

The last quotation above is indicative of a wider view among the population at large that, while many people are not committed to any religious faith, learning about religions and religious practices is an important element of a 'good education'.

Religious Education at School

There are media reports of claims that Religious Education can be of general benefit to pupils and communities by both parliamentarians and educationalists (Howse, 2014). There was near unanimity in my sample that they valued the inclusion of Religious Education within the curriculum and that the school gave it a high priority. Within that general agreement, however, various reasons were provided though, when the question was raised, some parents stated that it was important to them but did not specifying why that was the case:

'Yes. I think it is important through primary and secondary.' (16)
'Absolutely, that's why he'll be going to a Catholic 6th Form college.' (4)
'Yes, she's done quite well in it I think.' (21)

Relatively few parents gave reasons that were rooted in their concern for the development of their children's Catholic faith[2], though those that did seemed convinced about the efficacy of the school's religious education courses in that regard.[3] They stated:

'I just think it helps them as practising Catholics. It just strengthens their faith, reinforces everything and keeps us in touch with religion.' (17)

---

[2] While faith development may be one of the reasons why the Catholic Church provides schools and, consequently can be regarded as a legitimate pupil outcome of an education in a Catholic school, it is a difficult variable to quantify or evaluate. Nevertheless, these parents were clear that it is important for them.

[3] This could be the focus of future study but Religious Education (RE) may also provide support for them to develop their own child's faith development. The nature of RE means that through the academic study of religion some catechesis can also take place. For example, Year 10 pupils study Mark's Gospel in depth which may lead to a more spiritual appreciation of the Gospel and homework could be set to encourage this appreciation through dialogue with parents.

'Yes I do. Sounds like contradictory as I don't believe in my own Faith but I want the children to be embraced in it. I work in quite a multi-cultural office and we have Muslims and some Jewish people and they really embrace their Faith and I love watching that and that's why I think it's important for our children to have Religious Education so they have got that feeling. I want them to have that sense of belonging and I think that for me they get that through coming to a Catholic School and studying RE.' (3)

'Yes, I think it's really important for Catholic schools to know about religion. I think it's very interesting for children to pick up on things like that. I envy Religious Education, when I was younger I never had that experience myself." (14)

A larger number of parents indicated that developing their child's moral values, and therefore helping in their child's future life, was the main reason why Religious Education was important. What they seemed to suggest is similar to the 'golden rule' self-identification category (see Casson, 2011, p.127 and in table 2 above). These parents referred to the morals and values that they wanted their children to have when they were older and looked to the school to inculcate them.

'Yes they need to have that little bit of faith instilled in them so that they can then make decisions in life and decide which way they want to go.' (19)

'Definitely, I think it guides them. I think it gives them their views as well. I think it teaches them morals and principles and the wrongs and rights; it guides them.' (12)

'Yes because I think it gives them something to think about and I just think it gives them values and I think somebody who's got those values will hopefully stay on the right path in life.' (15)

'Yes because I think there's much more to religion than just 'is there a God? Or isn't there a God?' I just think that it's all about morals really; it's all about being a good person, looking after each other. I just feel that religion is more than just should you or do you need to go to church.' (6)

'Oh yes, RE was one of the subjects that she did enjoy and from her feedback, she really engaged in it and liked it for the debating side. I think just recently she did attend some classes and said 'I'm going to be a better person now', so it did have an impact somewhere along the way on her.' (22)

Some argued that they believed the school's Religious Education lessons helps children fit into a multi-cultural society and develop some empathy with others holding different views to their own.

'I think it gives her an understanding of the world and her faith, whilst obviously she is brought up Catholic and I might not reinforce that at home, but I do think it's important that she understands that, but they do all sorts of different religions as well which I think is important.' (7)

44

'Yes I do. It's hard to explain. I think it is how horrible society can be and it helps you deal with the horrible things that come along.' (2)

'Yes because RE's not like it used to be when I was a child, it's more about tolerating other people's religions and beliefs and ways of life. So I think it helps for people to find out other people's beliefs.' (5)

'Yes I do because it's just different views and different ideas.' (23)

'Yes I think RE is important so he can make up his own mind when he's had all the information.' (13)

Others referred to the academic or educative value of the subject:

'In life probably the religion would help you more but on the table when you go for a job what helps you more is having your Maths and English.' (20)

'It's good for your education for understanding the world. ... what you learn in early days you will carry for the rest of your life.' (10)

'Yes I do because it was a subject I quite enjoyed myself when I was at school.' (1)

That all but one of my sample stated (in their various ways) they valued the inclusion of Religious Education in the curriculum may be a contributory factor for their decision to send their child to a Catholic school. This may be because they see the school as an important assistant in the task of bringing their children up in the Catholic faith and that they recognise their joint religious enterprise with St ... Secondary School. It may also be indicative of a perception that, generally, Catholic schools provide more than the potential for good academic attainment, and other outcomes, such as faith development or the development of moral virtue, are also an important.

Summary and Conclusion

The Catholic Church argues that its schools, in addition to serving the common good, act to further the mission of the Church and assist parents in their task of developing their children's understanding of, and responding to, God as revealed through scripture and the life of Christ. This implies that effective Catholic schools and committed Catholic parents will place a high priority on their joint religious educational enterprise. The findings of this small scale study suggest that may be the case in St. ..... Secondary School.

Research elsewhere strongly suggests that, all things being equal, Catholic schools are more academically effective than similar secular institutions (Willms, 1985; Convey 1992; Morris, 1994, 1998, 2009; Benton et al., 2003; Arthur & Godfrey, 2005; Prais, 2005; Yeshanew et al., 2008; Godfrey & Morris, 2008.). Possible causal factors that may explain this apparent phenomenon include the advantages that Catholic schools, provided for baptised Catholic pupils and with staff who are themselves predominately baptised Catholics, may have in developing within the institution a sense of Gemeinschaft-like community (Tönnies, 1988) having a shared comprehensive doctrine of good education and conception of the 'good life' (Strike, 2000; Morris, 2005).

National and Diocesan inspections deem St. ..... Secondary School to be 'outstanding'. Given the nature of parental involvement in the school highlighted in this study, it may be the case that a 'family faith factor', including their support for and appreciation of the quality of Religious Education, is positively associated with educational outcomes that have led to this judgement. If that proves to be the case, finding ways of enhancing their joint religious enterprise can be of benefit to all involved. Further investigation, perhaps on a larger scale, seems warranted.

References

Arthur, J. & Godfrey, R. (2005) Statistical Survey of the Attainment of Pupils in Church of England Schools, National Institute for Christian Education Research, Canterbury, Canterbury Christ Church University.

Benton, T., Hutchinson, D., Schagen, I. & Scott, E. (2003) Study of the Performance of Maintained Secondary Schools in England – Report for the National Audit Office, Slough, National Foundation for Educational Research.

Bourne, F. (1906) The Catholic Attitude on the Education Question (transcript of an address delivered at Blackburn, 25th September 1905), London, Catholic Truth Society.

Bourne, F. (1929) Declaration by the Archbishops and Bishops of England & Wales on the Subject of Education, Essex, Catholic Parents Association.

Casson, A. (2011) The Right to 'bricolage': Catholic pupils' perception of their religious identity and the implications for Catholic schools in England, Journal of Religious Beliefs & Values, 32. 2. 207-218.

Convey, J. J. (ed) (1992) Catholic Schools Make a Difference, Washington, National Catholic Educational Association.

Crossley, M., Arthur, L. & McNess, E. (eds) (2015) Revisiting Insider–Outsider Research in Comparative and International Education, Oxford, Symposium Books.

Desforges, C. & Abouchaar, A. (2003) The Impact of Parental Support and Family Education on Pupil Achievement and Adjustment: A Literature Review, RR433, Nottingham, Department for Education & Skills.

Frabutt, J. M., Holter, A. C., Nuzzi R. J., Rocha, H. & Cassel, L. (2010) Pastors' views of parents and the parental role in Catholic schools, Catholic Education, 24-46.

Ganga, D. & Scott, S. (2006) Cultural insiders and the issue of position in qualitative migration research, Forum Qualitative Social Research, 7. 3. 1-8. Art. 7, http://nbn-resolving.de/urn:nbn:de:0114-fqs060379, [Accessed 18 March 2014]

Godfrey, R. & Morris, A. B. (2008) Explaining high attainment in faith schools: the impact of Religious Education and other examinations on pupils' GCSE points scores, British Journal of Religious Education, 30. 3. 211-222.

Hopkins, P. E. (2007) Positionalities and knowledge: negotiating ethics in practice, ACME International E-Journal for Critical Geographies, 6. 3. 386-394.

Howse, P. (2014) Religious education 'helps communities get along' [online, 18th March], www.bbc.co.uk/news/education-26617395, [Accessed 18 March 2014].

Jones, M. (2001) The issue of bias and positionality in cross cultural, educational studies, enhancing the validity of data through reflective-reflexive approach, paper presented at the Higher Education Close Up Conference 2, Lancaster, Lancaster University, 16-18 July.

Mercer, J. (2007) The challenges of insider research in educational institutions: wielding a double-edged sword and resolving delicate dilemmas, Oxford Reveiw of Education, 33. 1. 1-17.

Morris, A. B. (1994) The academic performance of Catholic schools, School Organisation, 14. 1. 81-89.

Morris, A. B. (1998) Catholic and other secondary schools: an analysis of OFSTED inspection reports, 1993-95, Educational Research, 40. 2. 181-190.

Morris, A. B. (2005) Academic standards in Catholic schools in England: indications of causality, London Reveiw of Education, 3. 1. 81-99.

Morris, A. B. (2009) Contextualising Catholic school performance in England, Oxford Review of Education, 35. 6. 725-741.

National Foundation for Educational Research (2007) How are Schools Involving Parents in School Life, London, NFER.

Pope John Paul II (1979) Catechesi Tradendae (Catechesis in our Time), Vatican, The Catholic Church.

Pope John Paul II (1981) Familiaris Consortio (The Role of the Christian Family in the Modern World), Vatican, The Catholic Church.

Pope Paul VI (1975) Evangelii Nuntiandi (Evangelization in the Modern World), Vatican, The Catholic Church.

Prais, S. J. (2005) The Superior educational attainments of pupils in religious foundation schools in England, National Institute Economic Review, 193. 70-73.

Sacred Congregation for Catholic Education (1965) Gravissimum Educationis (Declaration on Christian Education), Vatican, The Catholic Church.

Sacred Congregation for Catholic Education (1977) The Catholic School, Vatican, Catholic Church.

Sacred Congregation for the Clergy (1997) The Catholic School on the Threshold of the Third Millennium, Vatican, The Catholic Church.

Stock, M. (2005) Christ at the Centre, Coleshill, Birmingham Diocesan Schools Commission.

Stock, M. (2012) Christ at the Centre (Revised Edition), London, Catholic Education Service.

Strike, K. A. (2000) Schools as communities: four metaphors, three models and a dilemma or two, Journal of Philosophy of Education, 34. 4. 617-642.

Tönnies, F. (1988) Community and Society, New Brunswick, Transaction Books.

Willms, J. D. (1985) Catholic school effects on academic acheivement: new evidence from the High School and Beyond Follow-Up Study, Sociology of Education, 58. 2. 98-114.

Yeshanew, T., Schagen, I. & Evans, S. (2008) Faith schools and pupils' progress through primary education, Educational Studies, 34. 5. 511-526.

Teacher Voices: Values in a Catholic Secondary School

Alison Clark

Editor's Note:
Alison, a member of staff in the Education Faculty of Liverpool Hope University during her doctoral studies, received a PhD award for her thesis Voices on Values: Perceptions, Reactions and Effects in a Catholic School *in 2015. It comprised three main sections and twelve chapters (together with five appendices). The majority of this extract is taken from chapters 8, 9 and 10.*

Background

This case study was undertaken during the academic year, 2012-2013. The school concerned had gained a Leading Aspect Award for its values-led approach in 2010, which was deemed innovative and deserving national recognition as best practice. Following this, an Ofsted Inspection in 2011 referred to the school as 'characterised by a palpable ethos' and an 'inclusive, harmonious community', where 'students have a well-developed moral sense' (Ofsted, 2011).

The headteacher commented that when he took up the post in 2006, "... teamwork, and culture and ethos ... needed renewing", and he saw his role as giving 'confidence' to the school community (HT, 2012b, 8). His understanding that essential and formative values were central to school renewal meant he worked hard to ensure that 'values' became an embedded, prominent and explicit feature of its expressed ethos. Following wide discussion and negotiation, five core values (Respect, Co-operation, Stewardship, Compassion and Honourable Purpose) were identified for this purpose and finalised by the senior team.

Although the values terminology had been in place for several years at the time of the research, it was clear that the headteacher did not see them, simply, as static, unchanging aspirational statements, so while arguing 'values are at the core of what I think is the main motivational driver in terms of leading a good church school' (HT, 2012a, 6), he regarded their implementation as subject to on-going change and development.

Research Methods

I spent thirty-eight days at the site so that I became a familiar figure in a variety of setting within the school and had three main data collection mechanisms: semi-structured interviews, observation and school documentation.

I held formal interviews, staged over the year, with self-selected teachers and volunteer students from year seven, year ten and years twelve and thirteen.[1] Interviews were paralleled with observations in lessons and of school life in general; for example, the canteen at lunch,

---

[1] Although the thesis included data derived from pupil discussions and interviews, none have been included in this extract [Ed].

the social areas, and days spent shadowing pupils. I also attended staff meetings, special events such as school performances and award evenings, assemblies, and some after-school club events. I participated in the liturgical life of the school, in order to experience it from a student and teacher point-of-view: this involved attending a Year Seven Retreat, Remembrance Day liturgies, Christmas liturgy, Lenten reflection, Easter liturgy, and weekly Mass. I also made use of official school documentation, including the school magazine, weekly newsletters, various leaflets about aspects of school life, policy statements and other information from the school website, including letters to parents and the virtual 'Guest Book'. My aim was to experience, as far as possible, school life during a full academic year in order to generate a multi-layered 'painting' rather than a 'snapshot' of its operational ethos.

At the beginning of the academic year, twenty-one members of the teaching staff volunteered to take part in individual interviews. Twelve teachers in this self-selecting sample were female, and nine were male. Five of the teachers were new to teaching, and another two were experienced teachers but new to the school. The latter were able to explain how their first impressions of the school contrasted with their previous experience. Seven of the sample had been in the school for ten years or more, so were able to speak about the changes brought about since the headteacher was appointed six years before the start of my research. Three teachers held senior management posts. A further three had recent or current experience of pastoral middle management roles, and six were, or had recently been, academic department leads in the school. All subject areas were represented in the sample. Five of the teachers had training or mentoring roles outside the school, with other institutions.

Personal details were not sought although most volunteered some information, particularly about their religious affiliation. There was a range of faith positions in the sample: eleven self-identified as baptised practising Catholics; others were practising in different Christian traditions; two gave no direct or indirect indication of their religious or philosophical convictions. In addition to those teachers who took part in formal interviews, many others took part in informal discussions. All contributions shaped my understanding of the school and it purposes. Informed consent was obtained from all participants, and all the data were anonymised in accordance with the University and British Education Research Association ethics guidelines (BERA, 2011).

The full dataset was analysed using a MaxQDA computer programme which created detailed coding which, together with my comments, memos and other contemporaneous notes, helped generate common themes, key words, and identify important differences (Silverman, 2005, p.105; Robson, 2002, p.459, quoting Miles & Huberman, 1994, p.9). The code system was developed both by *a priori* themes (the template approach), and also by the concepts used by the teachers in the interview setting (editing approach, linked to open-coding of a grounded theory style). I also used word counts (quasi-statistical approach) and aimed to find common and outlier themes (quasi-statistical and template approaches), and the connections (or not) between themes (axial coding of grounded theory style) and ultimately draw conclusions through refining the codes (selective coding of grounded theory style and template approaches). Overall, the methods of analysis chosen linked most closely to the 'template' approach suggested by Robson (2002, p.458).

Research Findings – Values, Teachers and Pupil Formation

This section focuses on how teachers brought the expressed values of the school into their professional life and the ways in which they influence/affect the pupils in their charge. In official Vatican documents about education, 'formation' is understood as shaping of the students in all aspects (see, for example, CfCE, 1988,§100). In a similar way, it can be argued that ethos shapes 'human perceptions, attitudes and beliefs' (McLaughlin, 2005, p.311) and that the shaping of habits goes beyond the intellectual, and arises in distinct 'environments of practice' (Smith, 2013, p.9) where habits are formed through what is seen and experienced.

My findings suggest that, in this particular school, the creation of individual priorities and meaning by teachers through the way they interpreted the Five Core Values, for example as a role model, brings together a set of beliefs, intentions, activities and reflection through which they engaged in the formation of their students' values. In other words, the values terminology and activities of teachers bringing that language and meaning into their environment contribute to the activity of *shaping* within the Formation Process.

Teachers in the study believed they had an important role in values formation and it was linked with providing values that would be a legacy for life, '... we're here ultimately for the children and we're here to pass on something to them, and I think, "Well values and all those things are so, so important" ...' (TZ.137). It was also felt that school was the right place to support development of values, '... it's our job as well to draw out that, sort of, goodness, if you like, in them all' (TW.116).

Formation also went beyond simple acknowledgement of values, and involved action, 'It's making the values so that the children not only understand them but grasp them and take ownership of them and put them into action' (TU.46), and actions were encouraged in a purposeful way in the school, 'I think the fact that they're continually being, kind of, harassed to do good and to contribute' (TE.96). Some teachers wanted to explore how the values could be communicated in a meaningful way, which went beyond merely cognitive understanding, as argued by Smith (2013, p.9) through giving opportunity to explore and express values, as summarised here:

> *'I think it's digging down and what the basis is, what's the foundation of that value and how can you practically make that an understandable experience, you know? What does it look like in practice? What does this teaching look like in practice, and it's about giving experience of that in a practical way.'* (TD.93)

The Formation Process: Premise and Strategies

I would argue that teachers start from, what I call a 'Formation Premise' and implement a 'Formation Strategy'. Such processes of formation may be the clue to how teachers encourage dispositions where values may be inwardly attached (Hadaway, 2006; Donnelly, 2000). The final comment above – illustrating a commonly held perspective within the school

- indicated that the formation of student values involved both *knowing* and *doing*. Part of *knowing* was both understanding the basis of the school's values, and what they might mean, and also what the values 'look like in practice'. Part of *doing* involved purposefully created opportunities through 'giving experience'. I observed a number and variety of instances of these principles in action in the school as teachers worked through the inevitable tensions inherent in developing both in themselves and their students, first outward attachment and, subsequently, inward attachment to the school's values (for a discussion of these two forms of attachment, see Donnelly, 2000). The following detailed study of an individual teacher, Ms Dean [*not her real name – Ed*], working with her students illustrates her being both a role model and also seeking, actively, to shape the thinking of her students. Though it shows a single teacher in action in the school, I would also argue that she provides clues to how teachers generally within the institution think about the process of shaping students in values. She has pre-existent ideas about formation, which I call Formation Premises, and has Formation Strategies to make these premises evident to students.

Pupil Formation – A Case Study
This event happened within the first month of Ms Dean starting at the school. In the earlier part of the interview, she had indicated that being 'approachable' was important to her, a key part of her self-identification as a teacher and an idea she held in contrast to other teachers: 'I think I'm a bit more approachable. So, I think [students] tell me a lot. I like that with them' (Ms Dean.79). Therefore, a premise from which she worked was that she should be approachable, and students needed to know this. She then used a strategy that she believed would make it possible for the 'approaching' to happen. She stated, 'They come to me at break times and lunch times and they're always there actually. Yes, so I try and co-operate with them as much as possible, really' (Ms Dean.79) showing that she made a choice to stay in her classroom at breaks and lunch time, rather than go to the staffroom, a strategy she hoped would communicate her approachability to students. She indicated that the strategy worked, and students took up what was offered, 'I never have a whole 45 minute lunch, never' (Ms Dean.19).

A further insight into her teacher world-view was seen in an event which she explained at length in interview, and which I will discuss in detail below. Ms Dean explained how she managed a school uniform infringement concerning excessive makeup. She had a particular perspective on persons, that is, her students deserved to be valued for who they were rather than for their superficial appearance. For this she drew on the aspirational ethos of the school, 'Aspire not to have more, but to be more', which she explained was meaningful to her, '... our kind of motto of 'Don't aspire to have more, but be more', I think that, I love that, I love saying that to the children.' (Ms Dean.23)

The students in question did not share her view of beauty. Ms Dean explained:

> *'We all went round the room and said one thing, of where we would wear makeup and where we would go without makeup. Who we would wear makeup in front of who we wouldn't; and quite a lot of mine were similar to theirs, like I said, I wouldn't come to school without makeup on and they*

went, like well Why?" and I said, "Because I feel quite comfortable with makeup on. But I said, "I do feel comfortable without it as well. I'd happily nip to ASDA in the evening or the morning with no makeup on. [They said] We don't believe you! I said, Honestly, I'll prove it, I'll take mine off. I said, We'll do it together, you take yours off, I'll take mine off. They were like, You won't, you won't, and I said, Honestly, I will, so I did mine first, and they said, I can't believe that you've just done that! and I said, I know, I have to go to a meeting now! So I just wanted to make them feel like they didn't need it, you can be confident without it ... but the more you do it, the easier it gets, you don't need it. So I just wanted to show them it is OK, we don't need it.... but I thought well, why am I preaching to them saying they don't have to have it, if I can't do it myself, so I thought, No, do it, so I took it off!' (Ms Dean.57-59)

When she said, 'So I just wanted to show them it is OK, we don't need it', her intention was to change students' perception of self. This indicated that she was involved intentionally in formation of students' attitudes and behaviour. There were other ways she could have handled the situation, for example, she could have quoted school rules without allowing discussion, and excluded the students from the classroom until their makeup was removed.

She could have simply ignored the whole issue. However, she acted on her beliefs, her Formation Premises: a sense of obligation to support school rules, beliefs about the value of persons, and a personal interpretation of *teacher*. She explained that it was important to her to live out values, '... why am I preaching to them saying they don't have to have it, if I can't do it myself?' At times, the premises may be expressed as explicit statements, for example, through choices and consequences language.

I call the method of putting formation into action Formation Strategy. The teacher believes, consciously or unconsciously, that this method will enact the Formation Premise. Other teachers may have taken the alternative action listed above, the choice of which would be based on their particular (and different) Formation Premises. The first Formation Strategy Ms Dean used to deliver the Formation Premise 'we don't need it [make-up]' was to hold a discussion with the students about self-image: this fitted with the norm of the environment of the school. She used another Formation Strategy when she removed her makeup, hoping the students would follow her example. She made a connection between the behaviour she showed and her intentions for student behaviour, indicating she believed that in this way, students would be formed in values.

It also showed that she had assimilated a key aspect of the school's aspirational ethos, 'Aspire not to have more, but be more'. It is possible that this message was already a personally meaningful concept to her, but working in this particular school had given her a language, and a right, to express it. I would argue that the school's aspirational motto had become part of her *way of being a teacher*; that is, incorporated into her teacher-worldview and teacher-actions and is illustrated in the way she sought to use her own values and beliefs, supported by the school's aspirational ethos, with the intention to bring about the transition from ethos of outward attachment to inward attachment (Donnelly, 2000). This episode also indicated other aspects of the Formation Process. Ms Dean made a decision to suspend the teaching activity momentarily in order to prioritise this personal issue and in doing so attempted to manage the situation in this way was likely to be consistent with policies and practices in the whole school.

Values and Relationships

For Ms Dean, and many of her colleagues, relationships were very important elements of their self-view of 'teacher': 'I would have to say it's at the core of everything I do here, before anything else' (TZ.11). Another teacher commented that having appropriate relationships was a hallmark of the entire staff:

> *'I know I have a professional working relationship with my students, I've never considered I was too friendly, I've never considered I was too cold. I think it's a really good balance and I think there's a lot of staff that have a similar working relationship with the students that I do.'* (TM.10)

Some spoke of relationships in more personal terms about caring for students, which involved helping both their learning and management of any personal issues:

> *'I think when the students come and talk to me, when they have got a problem, whether it be with the content [of a lesson], or something else, shows that you've got a good relationship with them. I think you have to have that relationship in order to educate them, I think, anyway.'* (TN.122)

The juxtaposition of these two themes, enabling learning and care for the students' personal issues appear to be linked here with the concept of educating; in her view, education itself was dependent upon the quality of the relationship. Such a view might indicate why teachers worked hard to create a relationship with their students, so they really knew them, as shown in the following comments:

> *'[Central to the role of the teacher] is emotional intelligence, but it's more than that. A real understanding of where that student is and an understanding of what an important role we have.'* (TK.154)
> *'In terms of everyday dealings and what I think kind of fires the, you know, the classroom relationship, I would say Respect is really important.'* (TE.65)
> *'I think she [the student] is just in a perfect position now ... because of those relationships and because she's understood the Respect and Co-operation is important, it's transformed everything.'* (TI.117)

Relationships were also linked to a wider moral purpose, as seen in the following comment where it was linked to a discussion on Stewardship, from a senior teacher concerning the goals of the school:

> *'I think it's about relationships. The root of it is about relationships and how we work together and how we've got a moral responsibility to care for those*

outside of our community and see our role in the global picture as well.'
(TD.29)

Values and Choice: Negotiation, Challenge and Ownership of Learning

Teachers indicated they had strategies for values formation of students, beyond being a role model, one of which was the emphasis on dialogic relationship. This was described as involving negotiation of choices and reflection on possible consequences. However, negotiation had limits. While formation, or values acquisition, ideally involved voluntary commitment by the students (Silcock & Duncan, 2001, p.245), many teachers also indicated that they were the final arbiter of school rules. Therefore, the power base ultimately lay with them, and negotiation had limits although they perceived that they went the 'extra mile' for students, particularly to help them understand the reasons for the school's expectations.

Concepts of responsibility and ownership on the part of the students were prominent, indicating that the students needed to take responsibility for outcomes, 'So it's that ownership of their own progress, but, obviously, teacher led, but there is a huge ownership' (TY.7). As one teacher put it, 'the aim is holistic formation' [and] 'they are treated more like young adults where the emphasis is put on them ... You are not so much teaching them just to pass an exam, you are teaching them to be young people at the same time as advancing their academic knowledge' (TY.3).

Such comments indicated that teachers did not necessarily distinguish between their academic and moral responsibilities; often merging the two. For example, another teacher begins talking about education and learning, but his reflections quickly take on a wider perspective of his role.

> *'I do think that education isn't imposed on them, really. It's about motivating and making them take, or helping them to take, responsibility for themselves rather than taking responsibility for them and telling them what they need to achieve, really. 'It's not always easy, you know, because a lot of them would far rather you did all the work for them. Making them responsible members of society, I do think is, is key. Responsible for themselves and their own success and their own achievements in life.' (TS.20-21)*

A key part of developing a sense of ownership of their lives and learning was through the role of dialogue. Here again the place of reasoning is emphasised, along with a relationship that is based in one of the school's values. Part of the reason for having dialogue with the students about personal, academic and moral issues lay in the perception that it was deemed important to formation:

> *'I just think that saying to a kid, "You have to do it because we say so", and not giving them a reason, is just going to make them start to resent all of this instead of buying into it. Because I think if you can buy into it, then you're going to be a better person.' (TX.83)*

Values - Respect and Co-operation

Other core values were also linked with relationships, in particular, Respect and Co-operation. This indicated the way that the values language had permeated how teachers thought about their relationships, and found these terms meaningful in conceptualising and explaining them. There was not just a sense that students' needs should be met, and their emotions and circumstances understood, highlighted by the term, Compassion, but also that a good relationship required a level of autonomy and independence for the students. This was understood as having been achieved through compassion leading to trust, and trust bringing confidence that enabled the student to be autonomous and to co-operate. An example is given here in relation to the choice of subjects for GCSEs, showing how values operated in the relationship and so established trust:

> *'And the relationships, and the quality of the relationships that have developed, mean that those kind of conversations can take place ... It's done in, you know, a very honourable purpose sort of way that then brings about co-operation ... so there's a trust, there's a trust there. So those relationships, the quality of the relationships is absolutely vital, I think, and that enables those kind of curriculum decisions to take place for individual students, you know, the individualised curriculum for them.'* (TK.13)

This was further explained in a profound way by the following teacher, linking the development of trust directly to experiencing compassion. He explained that as compassion towards the students focused on meeting their needs, so the students were able to trust the teachers they were working with, which led to co-operation:

> *'Where I think I've seen is perhaps a fruit of compassion is co-operation, and that, you know, particularly for some of our children who have not had good, you know, not had the same opportunities perhaps as others and therefore can be more inclined to be looking inwards to their own needs. As we give those, as we show compassion for each other, we see greater co-operation.'* (TU.46-47)

The cycle of values generating trust and encouraging development and expression of other values was indicated in this teacher's thinking, and were part of the Formation Process. In this instance, the Formation Process could be seen as cyclical, a positive spiral of the values generating attitudes and behaviours, generating a response. The relationships that existed were fundamental to formation as suggested by another teacher, 'I think they [values] develop almost entirely by the interaction of the people they work with' (TS.58).

A similar link between respect from the teacher, experienced as trust, appeared to encourage students to be co-operative; in fact, it was seen as essential if the students were to be able to show co-operation, 'I think one of the main reasons it works really well is this great deal of respect of the students. That means I can give them the trust. So without that trust, they wouldn't be able to do the co-operation' (TI.61). In an interview several months later, the teacher repeated the importance of trust in developing a different kind of teacher-pupil relationship:

> *'If you've got that trust with them, you've got that strong relationship, you know. I don't like the idea that they just think it's a one-way street, kind of this spectrum of me at the top and they've all got to listen to me, and they've got to do everything I ask. Sometimes you learn more from asking them than you could learn from anywhere else.'* (TI.141)

The following quotations, illustrate the importance teachers' attached to the need to establish mutual **Respect** as a central role in productive teacher–student relationships. It was experienced by students primarily through their teacher's willingness to enter into dialogue and discussion. In turn, teachers believed it helped students take ownership of their own learning and develop positive behavioural attitudes.

> *'You've got to take people with you and I think there has to be ownership ... if I'm going to give like my students, for example, ownership of something, we have to enter into some sort of dialogue. That has to be a meaningful, fruitful dialogue that's based on, kind of, mutual respect ... it's about then having a joint common view on moving forward.'* (TK.76)
>
> *'I think that the students who walk in my room and behave the way they behave, because I've built up a respectful relationship with them, which I know has come from me initially, but they kind of follow through with that. On that vehicle, we can address things like "Is that really the right answer; is that really the way we should be doing this?" ... and I'm comfortable to bring that up.'* (TM.30)

These comments may indicate that there was a belief in the role of discussion as forming the mind and so contributing to the process of formation. In a question about how a direct challenge of the school values would be managed – for example, if a student took a materialist attitude to the prospect of winning on the lottery, this teacher responded, 'Nobody would ever say, "You know, that's wrong." I think we all encourage open dialogue into why you think like that - "Justify that statement".' (TF.94). This enquiry style changed their way of being a teacher, and indeed their view of *teacher*:

> *'You know, to question the values that we have I think it's probably quite a healthy thing ... I guess my outlook would be to support an exploration of that idea, the positive and the negative and not see myself as an enforcer of a view.'* (TB.53)

Not all teachers found this easy to do, as shown in a moment of self-reflection:

> *'I think it's quite frightening the first time you do it, because the one thing as a teacher, you like the ownership of the lesson, but it's more a case of guiding it rather than dictating the pace, sometimes.'* (TY.25)

In a similar vein, adopting such a style could change how students responded quite radically, 'We can go much, much deeper and they even challenge me, and I think a good teacher will challenge and a good student will challenge their teacher' (TZ.106). There was a strong perception that being involved in a school's values approach may lead to changes not just in the students, but also in their teachers. Here we see that the Formation Process was an iterative experience: the interaction between teacher and student, and reflection of the teacher leading to new ways of working in the environment, and reshaping of those involved, as they journeyed through the school year.

Through these illustrations, the complex picture of how teachers interpreted the school's values within their interactions and relationships with students is shown. At times it appears linear, and at others there is a cycle or feedback loop. In both models, the activity of formation, or Formation Process, was rooted in beliefs about the purpose of education for which the language of values provided a platform.

Teachers used the language of values to shape relationships, and their environment. They were aware of the responsibility they had not just to be a role model in values, but also advisor and often carer, the latter particularly shown when teachers spoke about what **Compassion** meant (see below). The environment and ethos of the school, functioning in a systematic way, in particular the negotiations of classroom interaction and the sharing of personal encounter were also central to this process.

Meeting the Needs of Students: Compassion
One particular aspect of the desired student-teacher relationship was expressed as 'having care for the students', which was frequently linked to the core value, **Compassion** which manifested itself in the wish to understand the personal background and concerns of students. When asked about the relative importance of the different core values one teacher argued, 'I think Compassion [is the most important] because, at the end of the day, a lot of these students have issues' (TZ.75).

Similar views were expressed by others who regarded Compassion as an important aspect of being a teacher and which provided a vocabulary that helped encompass what student-teacher relationships meant:

> 'They know they're going home to, not a great scenario. There's a lot of other facets to the interaction between you and the student, but definitely, the Compassion element ... [is most important].' (TQ.79)
> 'I think Compassion has got to be in there. There's got to be that understanding, that sort of caring side as a teacher ... My understanding of it is it's all to do with empathy and care, actually, because for some of these students we are the most constant adult that they see.' (TJ.64)
> 'And the Compassion bit, I think that's the bit where you see past some of the, you know, you remember that they are children and there's the, kind of, emotional thing going on there with them. Despite that I said Respect is really, really important, equally, I do believe in everyday giving them a

second chance to show that; and that comes from Compassion, isn't it, in a sense? That's why I want to encourage it amongst them with each other.' (TE.66)

Though generally accepted as important by all teachers, the term appeared particularly important to those who had had a pastoral role, either as a tutor or through the head of year responsibility:

'... compassion for each other, I mean, being a form tutor, and sometimes some of the students that I teach will come to you with things that are maybe happening. When I was head of year Compassion would play a big part in the role we had.' (TZ.71)

However, the importance of Compassion was not regarded to be of value just for teacher effectiveness, but also as one element in the strategy for student formation. Students were encouraged to have compassion for each other. One teacher indicated her belief in this proposition by drawing on a personally meaningful quotation as she sought to link the way in which she conducted herself and the relationships inherent in her role as 'teacher' to the school's core values.

'There's a really good quote from [an author], which is something like, "Hate is a failure of the imagination". I think that's the bottom line. If you can imagine what someone is going through, everything else will follow, I think, you know, and that's Compassion, isn't it, on some deep level?' (TE.68)

A link between Compassion and empathy, particularly for considering the feelings of others in the classroom, was also made by other teachers, '... they [the students] show some compassion, particularly in [my subject] when it goes wrong' (TR.29), and occasions when students were encouraged to be compassionate, 'You can show compassion for other people if they are different from you, or if they're experiencing something that's tough' (TJ.37). The link of Compassion with understanding others was a dominant theme, which had implications for the pedagogy used in lessons, to provide opportunities for discussion and listening, so students developed those skills effectively:

'Compassion is linked, in a way, in that they've got to, ... they've got to be able to understand other people's point of view and show empathy and show respect to one another in terms of their opinions or values, as much as mine is. Understand that we have to understand, you know, other people's opinions and other people's backgrounds for making those decisions.' (TI.61)

This was explained as a key part of sport, and compassion was central to how the students related to each other, particularly in how they gave feedback in peer assessments,

'... we do a lot of pupils assessing each other and saying "look, if you did this, this and this, you would improve," so that shows Compassion through trying to almost peer teach them.' (TY.64)

Although Compassion was talked of mostly in terms of empathy and kindness, it was also linked to high expectations, both of behaviour and of outcomes for the students, as the concept of 'tough love'. The teacher below indicated that compassion was not just a feeling but also significant in guiding how he behaved when he had to have difficult conversations with students:

> *'It's about, it's about, at times, what I'd describe as 'tough love'. It's about actually picking somebody up, pulling somebody up when they need to be, but in a very measured way, and in a very compassionate way.'* (TK.15)
> *'I used to use the core values, and flip it back so they knew where they were, and there was that consistent approach with it, you know, for some of them, the 9 to 3 was the safest place and the most consistent thing in their lives. It was just always that consistent approach of, "I'm not going to waiver my expectations of you," within that, and I think that really helps across the board.'* (TY.31)

It seemed, therefore, that the school's emphasis on values helped to set standards and enabled consistency in teachers' expectations of the students.

Values Expression: Values and Christian Faith

It may be assumed that the teachers in the study, given that they had chosen to work in a Catholic school, would think that values-based education might operate best in a faith-rich environment. However, in this case, many were able to draw on experiences in different types of schools both with a different religious character and with a secular base (Stock, 2005) and the perceived contrasts informed many comments. There were also teachers who had no religious affiliation.

Their collective perspectives were important factors in understanding their views about student formation in this particular religious school context. Using data from observations as well as interviews I examined three different views of the relationship between Values and Faith: the link between values and the Catholic faith; values separated from any religious faith; and the challenges arising from any possible causal links between values and religious faith.

Explicit Expression of the Catholic Faith

The headteacher reintroduced the word 'Catholic' into the title of the school on taking up the post in 2006, and teachers commented how he had given a renewed importance to the explicit Catholic basis of the school, for example, '... going back six or seven years, our renewal and refocus, in terms of putting religious practice and spiritual experiences back at the heart of the college' (TD.48).

Teachers described the school as a mix of diverse forms of Catholicism ranging from 'traditional' (TD, TH, TW) to 'modern'. Most illustrated the 'traditional' element by pointing to the Victorian-style statuary and formal types of worship, including weekly Masses led by a local priest, the presence of a Tabernacle in the Chapel with the reservation of the Blessed Sacrament. During the year of this study, there was also a whole school mission in the Spring

Term in which the sacrament of Reconciliation was made available. Having chosen to be part of a Catholic school, their presence in religious events was compulsory, but there were choices the students and staff could make about their level of participation.

I first heard the term 'modern Catholic' at an Open Evening talk by the headteacher (Fieldnotes02, pp.101,109) Teachers were familiar with it and directed my attention to modern-style religious artefacts, the use of choruses in Mass and clapping and uplifted arms during worship as examples of it. There was also use of Taizé Community worship including quiet reflection and choruses with actions:

> *'The Head is brilliant at making them sing, because all the staff sing, which, I'm not comfortable singing and I certainly wouldn't have done it in my last school, but here, it seems to be alright! I'll even clap in Mass and if necessary, I'll do the movements to the song whilst we're in front of the kids.'* (TH.21)

There were various examples of both modern and traditional icons displayed in the school, for example, an image of the Mother and Child at the bay window of a corridor, and the Risen Christ in the entrance foyer (Figures 1 and 2 below). This mix was, for the headteacher, an expression of the school's Catholic character.

> *'... in terms of the iconography of the college you will see some modern expressions of traditional faith concepts. That might be through a new set of words, like, "Aspire not to have more but to be more". That might be through a statue of Our Lady that is designed as a mother and child that isn't necessarily the gaudy plaster-cast statue you might see in churches. It might be through the statue of Christ at the front with open arms symbolising welcome and inclusion.'* (HT, 2012a, 16)

He argued that a focus on Jesus' life, death and resurrection, supplied the narrative that informed the institutional worldview and the meaning underpinning its values.

Fig. 1: Our Lady, corridor

Fig 2: Risen Christ, foyer

The term 'modern Catholic', as used by the headteacher, involved more than contemporary artefacts and the use of guitars in worship. His intention was to acknowledge and accommodate two contrasting perspectives within orthodox Catholicism; the exclusive and the inclusive.

> *'It's in that sense I use the word "modern" Catholic, which I suppose means inclusive, open, modelled on what I think the person Christ was all about where, you know, everyone was welcome. He didn't compromise his values in the process. So some things are right and some things are wrong. So I, kind of, believe in moral absolutes and the need for values and teaching people about that; but Jesus was radically accepting of people.'* (HT, 2012a, 18)

His position was based on a theological understanding of the person of Jesus, and Jesus' actions towards both supporters and opponents. The intended model for the relationships in the school was to show that inclusivity whether those in the school believed the same things or not.

However, he also drew from Jesus, within the framework of acceptance of the person, a belief in challenging the rightness and wrongness of actions and formation of values. This emphasis on formation in values, moving from outward to inward attachment (Donnelly, 2000), was not limited to those who held a particular faith position, it was for all. The teachers in the study accepted this role, but experienced it in individual ways.

His inclusive approach to both the pedagogical and nurturing tasks of the school was also discussed in relation to faith and liturgical activity. Although some teacher used the phrase 'modern Catholic' most did not, but tended to use 'Catholic' or aligned religious practices to a generic 'Christian' approach, distinguishing it from anything specifically 'Catholic' along the lines of:

> *'It's [religious] faith in general. I think they teach that having a "faith" as a good idea, rather than, "This is our faith".'* (TN.91)

There was a commonly held view that the concept of community required everyone to take part in all aspects of school life, including participating in the faith dimension, 'We are a religious community within the bigger community' (TD.73). This belief in the importance of being both a Catholic *and* an inclusive community raised discussion about the expectation of participation for those who did not fully subscribe to the Catholic worldview. The grounds that all should be involved had several justifications. One was, as stated earlier by the headteacher, that Christianity was interpreted as inclusive, not exclusive, with a focus that all were welcome to Jesus; a belief echoed by several teachers, for example:

> *'The entire ethos is based on the Christian faith and the Catholic faith, it's based on caring and I suppose, you know, the "suffer the little children" idea.'* (TH.14)

Another teacher appealed to universality of creation:

> '... we're all equal and, you know, we're all made in the image of Christ. Therefore, you know, if we share that then we should share the same values.' (TB.47)

Another was the belief that it was important to develop children spiritually within a holistic education:

> 'So, academically, I think that's obviously really important, but to be able to leave having a better understanding of who they are; you know, that we've offered time for that personal growth and personal reflection, and really just in terms of recognising where they are on a faith journey and the idea that if they're not on that journey, it's never a "no-start", and if they fall off the path, then there's always opportunity to come on again.' (TD.84)

The inclusion of all through their presence in the faith activity of the school also fulfilled the mission of the church school to support personal faith, as seen above, in all members of the school community, 'I think it's just part of our ongoing work with young people really, and with the staff, in terms of spiritual experiences and, you know, giving different opportunities to experience that' (TD.46). Spiritual development included an understanding of what church was about for some students who did not know, even if they were Catholic:

> '[I] really believe that you have to make that Catholicism inclusive. That's what we're supposed to be as a church and for most of the children that come through us, you know, we are the experience of church.' (TD.119)

For some teachers, the mission included healing, a purpose in life and experience of love:

> 'I would hope that a lot of children will come here and just have a sense of God's love through what we do, and a sense of understanding of his will for them. And also I think particularly those children whose, you know, lives have been broken for whatever reason, that they may have experienced something of God's love, you know, through what we all do, through what I do and from those around them.' (TU.69)
>
> 'An expression that I remember from my previous school that I worked in, which was also a Catholic school, there was this notion that "Christ was in every classroom" and is in all relationships. And I think I felt that there, but not as profoundly as I do here. So something is a bit different.' (TK.29)

The focus on Love as shown in Jesus' life, expressed within an inclusive community, was a key theme that the school wished to embrace. However, in a diverse school population, there was a challenge to how inclusive worship, especially as the ideal for the 'modern Catholic' community for which the school strove was that everyone could be involved in religious practice at some level.

A starting point was a refusal to make assumptions that everyone would know and/or understand Catholic religious practices. Consequently, students (and staff) who were not Catholic were shown the purposes and mechanisms of, for example, making the sign of the cross, and genuflecting before the blessed sacrament, so that they could, as one teacher said, 'blend in' (TS.11). Although this might be superficial forms of inclusive behaviour, it was seen as a minimal way that non-Catholics (students, their parents and teachers) could appreciate and more easily take part in elements of Catholic culture. Such symbolic actions were seen as steps in the process of integration necessary for access to the meaning of the actions, which might come later; reflecting outward attachment (or compliance) rather than inward attachment.

There were assemblies that utilised the forms of a religious service, but not necessarily using traditional religious symbols. For example, on Remembrance Day (November 2012), students and staff placed fallen autumn leaves on the table at the front of the hall during an assembly in memory of those who had suffered in war. The act of carrying a leaf to the front represented their participation in a reflection on war. It was explained that part of the planning for the inclusive nature of the event was the choice of a non-religious symbol. The act of all present quietly processing forward was intended to create a worshipful act where all could take part.

> *'Again, it's trying to use language and symbols that the students would commonly be able to relate to like fallen leaves as opposed to red poppies and a symbolism of light. So it's kind of, again just trying to make sure that the language and the symbols we use would have a normal, common theme to them, a common understanding to them.'* (TD.11)

Another example of the inclusive approach related to the weekly Mass, attended by all in a tutor-group in turn. It was explained to students outside the chapel, that at the right time they would all line up and process to the priest in front of the altar, but would indicate if they were not receiving the wafer, by placing their right hand across to the left shoulder. This would indicate that they were to receive a blessing instead. The explanation was that all students should attend Mass as part of this school community, and all should show respect for others; but personal choice would guide the nature of their involvement. In a similar way, on Ash Wednesday, in 2013, all students received ashes on their forehead, but could choose to keep or remove the mark, before they left the chapel. This was explained:

> *'They are expected to join in, but I like the fact that the pressure's then removed by saying, you're allowed to do that in your own way as long as it's respectful, and what we want is you to respect each other and respect others' right to do whatever it is that's comfortable for you.'* (TR.52)

63

The juxtaposition of Respect - one of the Five Core Values - within the context of religious worship was used above to justify attendance of all. Compulsory attendance was a way of preventing marginalisation of both those who wanted to express faith through attendance, and for those who did not have a faith but who would be identified by non-attendance. Given the possibility that those with a faith might be unwilling in front of their peers to show it if the Mass was optional, one teacher stated, 'It gives everybody the chance to be there without going, "Oh, I want to go to Mass".' (TG.93)

Through this approach to worship, several things were achieved. The important opportunities for formation provided in the assemblies and reflective religious activity of the school were both through cognitive means and seeing the habits of others as role models, as well as having opportunity to acquire habits. It has been argued that time for reflection is an important element in values development (Hadaway, 2006; Hawkes, 2010). These times were seen as an expression of the worldview of the school, stating what was of worth, and the systems in place to support time and place for this also expressed that worldview. It reminded staff of the holistic education and was an example of the inclusive, loving community. The particular religious character of the school was a prominent element of its ethos and a way of putting that ethos into action. It provided a fundamental purpose along with academic purposes and outcomes for students. Therefore, as the values of the school and the Christian faith of the school were two aspects of the ethos, my attention now turns to the relationship between the Five Core Values and the faith of the school and how teachers understood the relationship.

The Relationship between Values and Religious Faith

There were two distinct perspectives held by teachers. One view promoted the idea that faith was the leading aspect of the ethos in the school, with the five Core Values as its expression.

> 'Faith was the "fire" behind the values,' '... it's one way of firing up and holding together a kind of value system. It's one with creating community.' (TE.76, also TF.34)

The other saw the Core Values as central to how the school was involved in the formation of students, and indeed, central to the perceived strengths of the school. In this view, faith had an important part to play as an opportunity to express the values, especially Respect, but faith was also seen by some, potentially, as a problem. There appeared no clear link between the personal faith position of the teacher and the views they expressed, and although the central position of the Faith of the school was expressed more strongly from those with an active Christian faith, it was not necessarily the case.

Values with Religious Faith

A linkage between religious faith and values was taken for granted by many teachers. They were felt to be a natural component though not necessarily the exclusive property of people of faith.

'Because it's a faith school, so our values are based on faith.' (TN.91)

'I think the values have probably come from the fact that we're a faith school.' (TX.70)

'I think, for me, from my perspective, the values are the kind of-, in a way they're the visible manifestation of aspects of the faith.' (TK.121)

'I think our values come from faith and I think this [Faith] is where all these [Values] have come from. I think these [Values] are a translation of this [Faith], so our core values are a translation of our faith beliefs.' (TM.73)

'It's the whole understanding, the whole, you've got the faith dimension supports the values and the values support the faith dimensions.' (TY.79)

'... [Values] naturally fit with faith, you don't have to be a Christian to be someone who lives by these values, of course, you know? But again, I think they naturally flow from someone of faith ... .' (TU.50)

Some teachers felt that the religious character of the school helped develop their understanding of values because they felt they had 'permission' (TR.20) to talk about topics that would not feel comfortable discussing in a secular institution.

> *'I think "love" is something that is an important word and I like the idea, because it's quite a controversial word as well, isn't it? ... If you use the word "love" in, say, an assembly or classroom in a secular school, it could be misinterpreted ... but it makes it much more clear and acceptable to do it through faith ... .'* (TI.67)

This seemingly mutually supportive association was expressed in various metaphors. For example, faith was an 'anchor'; a focal point for interpreting values (TY); a 'hanger' for values, allowing deeper 'exploration' (TD.75 and 58).

It was felt by some that values could be taught better through faith (TI), and a personal faith commitment helped guard against the danger of paying 'lip service' to values (TU.54, TF.35). Religious faith was also referred to as a 'framework' for the students, so they had a structure to react to, or reflect upon (TE.76) because, it was argued, students needed to know what was important before they could decide whether they agreed/accepted it for themselves. It was also felt that the faith of the school would help the school create a 'strong identity', which would then strengthen the values approach in the whole school. The view of the teacher below - not a practising Catholic - was that the 'success' and acceptance of the schools values strategy was inextricably linked to its religious character:

> *'... Whereas in a non-faith school ... you've got to find a way of creating that culture without the faith ... how do you develop children who buy into it in the same way, without the, the sort of ... structure of the faith? And can it be done? Can it <u>really</u> be done? Not just lightly, but can you have it as an all -, I think you can create a very nice school which is highly successful and children are on board, and you can do that, but can you underneath all that*

have a very strong identity behind the morals and that side of the teaching?' (TR.58-59)

On the other hand, in linking values and faith some teachers tried to overcome possible misinterpretation of values terms:

> *'Now, values, you see, that doesn't say "good values", does it? It just says values. Now, to some, the values might be entirely opposite to the ones we live by, and I think it's important children understand that the values we live by through our faith are the ones like these ones here.'* (TU.50)

That the school's values were a subset of religious faith (rather than the reverse) was held by most teachers, Catholic and non-Catholic. Most spoke of how the school's religious character helped to clarify and explain the values, since it provided a 'fundamental background' (TS.39). Another teacher explained:

> *'There needs to be some worldview, you know, that holds them [values and community] together, as it were, and I think that's what faith does here.'* (TE.76)

This 'fundamental background' of faith provided the basis for enabling teachers to talk about values and manage the Formation Process. The connection between faith and values seemed to empower teachers to embrace strategies for student formation, especially as the combination of faith and values was closely linked with practical expressions of good.

> *'I think, what we've got now, you know, with things like the "Pay it Forward"[2], the merit-plus, and they are going to India. We have bought in, if you like, all the, sort of, interesting aspects of our faith and what we are about as people. We have, sort of, sewn into that the more, traditional things that we, as Catholics, as Christians, believe in.'* (TW.28)
> *'Because the young people see the two together, they almost, now, can see, more the value [of them]. Some still might value the "Pay it Forwards" and all of that, far more than the other, but it's almost like we are giving them both. It's a bit like pick and mix, at the moment, we are giving you both and you can choose and select.'* (TW.28)

Providing students with choice within a clear structure was an important element of the school's 'inclusive community' policy. There was sensitivity to the various religious backgrounds of students enabling a degree of diversity in understanding of the school's

---

[2] The phrase 'Pay It Forward' was derived from a book of the same name (Hyde, 1999) which the headteacher adopted. He used it to promote the idea that, in response to any received kindness, individuals should undertake three good deeds towards others. Showing kindness to three different people unrelated to the initial actions created a programme of self-sustaining consideration for others within the school – a mechanism for sustaining an harmonious and benevolent community.

values which promoted community solidarity wherever students were on their 'faith journey'. Teachers saw the values as the pre-eminent cohesive force and having universal appeal:

> *'I would say because we have children here from different faiths that we all ... know the values and we're working towards those values ... .'* (TG.73)
>
> *'I think, in terms of the values that we look at, our values that are common to ... all faith dimensions, really. In Buddhism, you'd find the same, in Islam, you find the same, and what it's giving us is a very practical way of putting our faith into practice. We can have the values without having the faith, these are equally generic values, they don't have to have a religious purpose, we happen to identify them with the Gospel. You could identify them with any scripture, but you can identify them in humanism, or atheism.'* (TD.71)
>
> *'We specifically identify Stewardship with the notion that we're given the planet as a gift, and we've got to respect that and pass it on, it's, kind of, moral obligation with that, but equally, somebody of no specific faith, I think, can find meaning and understanding in terms of their role in society and the contribution that they can make through the values. They don't have to directly link to a faith practice or a specific faith, but I do think that, you know, we spend a lot of time showing that these are, kind of, values that are generic to faith and non-faith.'* (TD.71)

The Core Values framework was important for teachers' understanding of the school as an inclusive Christian community and, although it could be understood without recourse to any form of religious faith (see Figure 3 below), they were strongly linked to, and informed by, Catholic faith and social teaching.

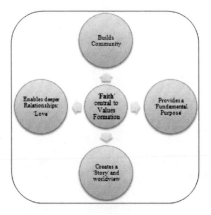

Fig 3: Centrality of Christian Faith to Values Formation

Within my self-selecting sample, the idea that values and faith were a positive combination was an accepted reality. However, while the linkage was strongly presented by teachers, there were aspects that caused some concern. One example was that the focus on values might diminish the centrality of the Catholic faith and the school lose sight of its core mission:

> 'So I think as much as the values support the faith to make it more approachable to children, I think there's a time, as well, we become adults and we say, Well, this is what we're about, and this [Faith] is our core purpose and what we believe in, and therefore you're part of the community.' (TR.47)

Another commented that the emphasis on both fixing on particular values, and on less overtly religious values terms might lead to loss of understanding of a distinctly Christian (and Catholic) message. The teacher struggled to find how self-sacrifice might be explored as a value, a concept that was integral to the Christian tradition, (The Bible, John. 15:13), when it was hard to link to the established terms:

> 'I was thinking something like, well, I suppose elements of self-sacrifice. Quite literal self-sacrifice, which hopefully, they're never going to have to do. Maybe if they joined the army and what have you, they may find it difficult to see, for instance, laying down your life, being as an Honourable Purpose.' (TQ.90)

In the end they link it to Honourable Purpose, but with a sense that this connection might – or might not - be fully understood by students. So, while the faith and values were seen to have created a framework (religious faith) and also an expression (values), some teachers questioned the way this link was articulated.

Values without Religious Faith

In contrast to the majority of voices described above, the Five Core Values were seen by some as universal moral expectations without having any necessary association with religion. The values were entire in themselves, with the telos of becoming a 'decent human being', not needing faith to give meaning to them. They questioned whether religious faith was an essential ingredient for student formation, and prioritised values over their faith framework on the basis that the Core Values provided the inclusive element of the school, while affiliation to religious faith was not.

> 'I think ultimately the emphasis on talking about being a good person is regardless of faith. So try and promote, try and talk to their, sort of, inner self about, well, "We're asking you to be a decent person, we're asking you to treat people nicely and be treated nicely. You can't really argue with that, you know? That's not a big ask of you".' (TR.47)
>
> 'I don't think they're [Values] communicated around religion, I think they're communicated more about being a good person' (TF.20)

'... So when I'm speaking to the children about, "Have respect for your teacher," I'm not quoting any passages from the Bible and relating it back to the Catholic faith. I'm speaking to them as, like, there are values; we're not relating them all the time to religion.' (TF.22)

Others, while accepting that committed religious affiliation was useful, being formed in values did not depend entirely on faith. For example, it was argued that the values underpinning the activity 'Pay it Forward' 'speaks to the hearts and minds of young people' (TW.27), while faith might not necessarily do so. Another teacher commented:

'Values, it's kind of universal to all of the students; whereas faith is exclusive to some.' (TI.67)

'I like about how [the headteacher] approaches faith in our school is that he's very good at showing children why it doesn't matter what your faith is, these [values] are good things to be doing.' (TR.16)

'... all those core values, none actually have anything religious about them, doing nice things for each other, there's nothing religious about it' (TR.61)

Therefore, seeing the values without faith and presenting them independently of faith, was a course of action open to teachers (see figure 4 below).

'I don't really talk about religion, about faith, about Catholicism, about any of those things in lessons. I just talk about the Values. So if someone's not respecting the prayer, I don't talk about, "This is a faith school, this is a Catholic school, you have to do it." I try and talk about you not being respectful to those in the room that do want to observe the prayer ... it means that I feel I have the tools to really buy into what the school's about without having to address the faith side of things, which doesn't really fit with me personally.' (TX.70)

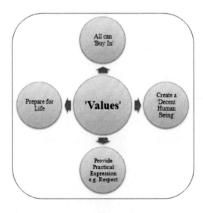

Fig. 4: Values' role in the school, without reference to faith

69

An important point to draw out here is that the values message of the school enabled this teacher to feel that he was supporting the school's ethos, in a way that had integrity for him. The implication derived from such views was that the school's values could have one *telos* of moral formation, disassociated from religious faith. The adopted values approach to educational formation operating independently of any religious interpretation can be seen as a solely humanistic and practical rationale.

When teachers spoke about the detachment of values from faith, my questions to them were designed to understand the degree of importance they placed on the school's Values approach to education. A common response was a fairly straight-forward statement along the lines '... [teachers are] fully aware of how important the ethos and values are, and how it underpins everything.' (TF.96) The vision of the headteacher, purpose of education and the values of the teacher were also cited as the justification:

> *'It's how strongly leadership says, "This is what's important in school," that values and means - the thing is about [headteacher], you see, he does mean it, you know, in terms of wanting it integrated into the [school] ... there is a consistent message coming from the top about, "This is what we stand for. These are our values".' (TE.104)*

Another teacher commented:

> *'If the community is trying to genuinely create, I suppose, adults moving out of school with a good set of values and caring and compassion and so on, then I don't think that needs a faith. It needs people with values, and people with values, I think, can generate people with values.' (TS.39)*

A values ethos in these views needed something to justify it, a 'back story', and if not faith, the 'story' became the personality and vision of the headteacher, or the unified example of the teachers. Here, the story behind the values was one of personal authority: the values were justified because of the persons who were presenting them. I concluded that none of the teachers felt that values could simply just exist, without a justification. Fundamentally, the issue of values came back to the question, 'Why should I expect others to do this?' Catholic/Christian faith provided answers, but there were also a range of answers that that satisfied teachers, without reference to faith.

A further comment on the link between faith and values raised the issue of whether schools with a religious character were automatically schools with positive values. This was rejected by several teachers who had previously worked in such a context, where values had not been as evident, despite the religious character of the school (TI, TE, TF, TG, TW). The difference lay in the persistence of teachers to make the values prominent, according to one teacher:

> *'... we could be a faith school and not produce students with any decent set of values because the faith isn't as embedded within the school. And yes, it*

could go wrong if there isn't a buy in to that faith and to that... you know, real significant desire to give students values, because it's not easy, you know, it's not easy, when you see kids all being horrible to each other to actually pull them back and get them to see that that's not the way to live your life, I suppose.' (TS.39)

The way that teachers were to use values suggested above was that they formed a dialogue for reflection on how to live life, rather than a command, and this approach was due to a view of life as a whole, not just the moment at hand. It may be that this is how the values became 'embedded' and habitual: not telling, but suggesting a different way to live a life. All teachers felt there needed to be values in the school, but to be more than simply the expressed values.

The work of the teachers was central in being consistent in the activity of reminding, challenging students to consider how to live their lives. This could all, arguably, be achieved without faith, with the systematic delivery of ethos, inspiring headship, and committed teachers.

Faith in the school: a challenge to inclusive community
The concept, and reality, of an inclusive community was, for some teachers, in jeopardy because of the school's religious character, so a common term applied to 'community' was that people should feel 'comfortable'. This necessity was linked to that faith dimension.

'So it's not just a Catholic school for Catholic practising families, and what we make sure is that students are very comfortable joining in with all religious liturgies.' (TD.3)

One teacher wondered whether it was hypocritical to involve people in any overtly religious activity, particularly acts of worship, unless they were 'believers'; another whether students should be excused if they did not believe in God.

'A lot of children are going through the motions. A lot of children don't have faith, and there is a bit of me that, but there's half of me that doesn't like this at all, you know, that finds it a bit of hypocrisy, making children say prayers that they don't believe in - the prayers I mean.' (TE.76)

One form of resolution of this issue, for most teachers, was to argue that by opting to seek a place at a Catholic school parents (and the students) knew in advance what would be involved.

'... it's taken as implicit that that's what you do, because you're in a faith school, you've chosen to come here, and this is part of our daily routine, if you like.' (TJ.86)

The school's approach took reasoning seriously in relation to this aspect of school life, and there were descriptions of how teachers would engage in dialogue with students on this more than any other area discussed. Some saw students questioning as a natural expression of teenagers reacting to the requirements of school; and learning to cope with what you might not want to do was a life-skill.

> *'You know, it's hard, because some of the kids do say, you know, "We don't want to go." But, actually, when they're there I think they quite enjoy it ... I think it's at an age where they don't know what they want, really.'* (TG.90)

For others the conversation was almost redundant since, they argued, the school achieved both the integrity of a faith position, while also being inclusive for non-practising Catholics and those with no religious affiliation, because of the centrality of its Five Core Values which supported the expectations of involvement by all who wanted to be part of the community.

> *'So, it isn't about being a subscriber or not a subscriber kind of thing, you know. I'm not in the club and therefore I'm not part of that, because there's a whole continuum of views and that actually-, I think I would say that there will be aspects which are about values and that whether you have faith or have no faith, or undecided, those values have got value and, you know, to think about that.'* (TK.125)
>
> *'... [Children who say] "I'm not a Catholic, I don't want to be here, you know? I didn't choose to be in a Catholic school." But actually, those Five Core Values, remove that conversation, because they aren't directly about our faith even though they promote what our faith stands for ... And I think that's true in a lot of the ways thing are approached [here] that it's open to your interpretation as a child and it promotes what the school believes in and the faith that the school has, but it doesn't necessarily force them to have the same beliefs.'* (TR.28)

There were, however, some teachers for whom the school religious activities were, clearly, a challenge. For example, during a school Mission it was decided to provide the Sacrament of Reconciliation and have Exposition of the Blessed Sacrament. This decision was explained and justified by reference to the purpose of the school as 'witness to the Catholic faith' and argued that, as such, the right time to venture into a new experience (for the school) of Catholic worship. This was not a decision undertaken lightly, and reflecting after the event, one teacher remarked:

> *'Were the students ready for it? - which I think they were; but more, really, not the students, but the staff, their experience of the mission. Because I think staff do feel included in religious life, and comfortable with it, but we're taking everybody out of their comfort zone with that one ...'* (TD.45)

My Fieldnotes record some negative reactions to the Exposition of the Blessed Sacrament (Fieldnotes09, pp.3,5) suggesting there was both confusion about the place of religious activity in a Catholic school, and also the education priorities behind the decision to promote it.

Another aspect of the school's Catholic culture and practice which prompted discussion by all the teachers was the requirement to hold a tutor-group Mass. Many teachers were perfectly happy with the 'compulsion', given the basic expectation of the school's values to listen, be respectful towards and tolerant of others (even if not personally committed to any religious practice) to which all members of the community could subscribe. One teacher recalled a discussion with a student:

> *'You can't force participation in the actual worship, but a presence that shows a respect for everybody else, and it is part of us as a community ... I just said, It might not be an act of worship for you, but there's reflection in there which you can take on your own level ...'* (TD.77-78)

On a few occasions, concern was expressed that the intellectual demands inherent in some religious activities in the school may have inhibited the engagement of students with (various) special educational needs, for example, occasions that demanded a lengthy period of reflection and quiet, such the Advent or Lenten Services.

> *'I think of kids now who aren't prepared to buy in, a lot of them have some sort of special need, that focuses their brain very clearly on what they want and find it very difficult to be flexible; and I think they are worked with... with compassion, really, and with understanding ...'* (TS.41)

Efforts were made in this respect and, in many instances, special arrangements were made. This was not seen as contradicting the inclusive community ethos, rather, as it was seen as an expression of Compassion. Teachers did not feel this was an issue for other students, who, they felt, recognised that the excusal arose from a student's particular need. Teachers also experienced understanding of particular needs in relation to faith matters, and the dialogic approach that they used when discussing values as part of the school's pedagogy equally when there was a clash between personal values and requirements of the Catholic faith; one example was the topic of abortion. The use of the dialogic approach at all levels of relationships in the school enabled diverse perspectives to be discussed without compromising either personal or the Catholic perspectives. This would be an example of 'adaptive management', (Seddon, 2005, p.179), which could support teachers attaching to the values of the school through the experience of dialogue; the structures of the school were not just for students, but equally, from the headteacher, also for them.

Tensions between Values and the Catholic and Christian Faith
My discussions with teachers allowed them to explore questions about identity and purpose: what kind of school was this, and what was the purpose of the education in the school? The concepts that were most frequently used to describe the school were 'Catholic' and 'Business/ Enterprise', perhaps unsurprisingly, given the name and nature of the foundation.

In extended answers, 'Christian' and 'Values', were also used. The commonest answer from the research group was 'Catholic': 'Oh, there's no hesitation. It's Catholic first' (TK.27), but often this was configured in a complex way. Their use of phrases about faith and of values in the responses suggests that some teachers saw the two concepts as complementary, side by side; others saw them partially overlapping as in a Venn diagram, but the most common description was of layers, with Faith under Values. That is, values were the outward expression of faith, with religious faith as the narrative underpinning the values. Consequently, the school's values approach to its educational enterprise was seen by many as a way of making the faith dimension practical and, as such, values and faith were interconnected,

> *'I do think that whilst fundamentally we are a Catholic school and Catholic-, it's hard to separate Catholic values from Christian values... so basically it's the same thing.'* (TS.11)

In this view, to understand the values fully, faith was needed as an explanatory background, and for the faith to be understood, the values were needed as a tangible expression of it.

> *'... link the values to concrete ideas, like stewardship and the environment. Then on top of that, the layer underneath that is the Christian value of having linked that to the Bible. I think that's what it's better than, "Here is the religious view. You will take this religious view." That wouldn't work, I think.'* (TH.59)

However, there were voices that expressed difficulty with the link between faith and values. One teacher commented that the twinning of the concepts may alienate some students and, if so, prevent them from engaging with values:

> *'I don't like to link them completely to faith, because we have a lot of students who have struggled with their faith and have no faith at all, and I don't want them to feel excluded by linking them up like that.'* (TZ.89)

The way that some teachers dealt with this tension was to link the values only to Christian themes, ignoring any potential denominational differences.

> *'... when I see faith, it's more "Catholic" faith, whereas, values are more "Christian".'* (TC.82)
> *'I think the faith is - the values are what is our day-to-day bread and butter. I do think, you know, we link everything to the values, but that comes back to our Christian faith ... we have linked it, very much, to a Christian ethos here. So therefore, that's where our values stem from.'* (TH.58)

There was also concern expressed about how teachers might be perceived by their students and some felt they trod a fine line in being faithful to the Catholic tradition, but not being seen as overly religious or, worse, a 'religious zealot'.

'Because, what I don't think we can allow ourselves to be is seen to be - what's the word I'm looking for? Almost like, just like a gospel squad, almost.' (TQ. 97)

'I don't think day in, day out -, we don't bang on about Catholicism so much, but we do talk about Christian faith and a Christian life. Therefore, I think we're linking it to the values, therefore, brings the faith out without being the, I suppose, the religious zealots, that I think the kids would shy away from having linked it to values.' (TH.59)

Figure 5 (below) serves to illustrate both the differing ideas about values and how the majority of teachers in the study saw the values operating in the school. The Five Core Values take centre stage as the universally acceptable, uniting aspect of the ethos; layered beneath them are the opportunities and spaces to engage with values both iteratively and cyclically.

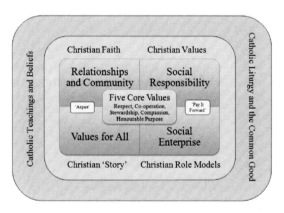

Figure 5: Values and Christian Faith

Underpinning the activities was a Christian story of values and faith, and the basis for that was the explicit Catholic message and activity expressed in the narrative and liturgy of the school.

Summary and Conclusions

Two questions were central to this research: how the Five Core Values influenced the school's day-to-day activities, and how they affected the role and work of individual teachers in this particular Catholic school.

Values, linked to moral and character education, were a live issue in the school where teachers spoke of the school's espoused ethos as having a profound influence on them in their general educative role and specific responsibilities towards their students. All the participants believed that, in this Catholic context, they were strongly linked to religious faith, although some teachers felt that they could exist without faith. The majority believed that faith was naturally expressed in lived-out values. However, some regarded Catholic faith, primarily, as a useful background rather than central to the school's educative purpose, while others believed that, while the faith had an important educational role, it was easier for them to connect with their students through values than through religion.

Although the Five Core Values were recognisably linked to the Catholic faith, and supported by the systems and structures of the school - both visible (the artwork) and semi-transparent (the policy decisions about use of time and space) - they were assimilated to a lesser or greater degree into the teacher's pre-existing worldview, and their understanding/acceptance of student formation [*as described in official Catholic documents – Ed*] as a legitimate role for an educational system.

While the school context challenged teachers to reflect in this way, many also drew on their experiences in very different schools. Nevertheless, I found there was a connection with, and application of, the Five Core Values to the relationships they forged with students which went beyond simply using values language to being a formative element of being a role model. This involved conducting dialogic relationships and enabling a degree of autonomy and choice for students, as a sign of values being lived out in the life of the school community.

There was also evidence of the Five Core Values being interpreted diversely, with some terms acquiring more meaning in particular contexts for some teachers. For some, the values were rooted in the Catholic tradition, for others, in their practice as a teacher. The priorities given to some values over others indicated an individual interpretation and ownership of the concepts. Some teachers felt that being able to utilise the language in this varied way was an advantage. To others, it evidenced confusion about meaning and application. Such diversity of interpretation may only be a problem if there was the expectation from school management that all teachers should assent to the school ethos in the same way. Beneath what might be seen as outward attachment, or possibly compliance, the individual interpretations of the Five Core Values could be argued as a strength, in that, such ownership could enable movement towards inward attachment, as seen in their explanations of the values in practice both in the school as a whole and in their own sphere of the classroom.

While there was diversity of views on the nature of the link between faith and values in the perspectives of teachers, all agreed that the values were a common meeting ground in the diverse school community. Furthermore, the focus on values was seen to enable all to participate in religious events, supporting in teachers' view the idea of inclusive community. In this respect, the values were seen by many as universally relevant and cohesive, and empowered teachers in the role of formation.

The school's aspirational language created a way of talking with and nurturing young people. It also helped them reflect on their varied roles and experiences, as a teacher of a particular subject, a year group leader, a senior manager, or a form tutor. Some teachers spoke of the school's espoused ethos as having a profound influence on them in their general educative role and specific responsibilities towards their students' formation. The values also generated and confirmed the idea that education should be a holistic activity, personal, social, moral as well as academic, which aimed for more than academic qualifications.

While the teachers did engage with the aspirational ethos of a school, they also brought prior beliefs about education and being a teacher to this process; their own aspirational ethos. This included their beliefs, intentions and hopes for students, drawn from a personal view of educational purpose. This became a base for negotiation with, and assimilation of, the values language and aspirations of the school. The diversity of views indicates that teachers in the study actively engaged with all aspects of the school's aspirational ethos, but in an individual way; choosing aspects of the faith and values ethos that were most meaningful to them. The occasional mismatch, however, between aspirational values and particular decisions created problems for some teachers in their alignment to the school's aims and aspirational messages which, they felt, hindered them in their day to day work.

There was conviction and emphasis in the way that the teachers in the study spoke about the school's values. They confirmed that the headteacher had merged the Catholic worldview with values in such a way that enhanced both aspects; the values benefiting from the Christian narrative, and the Catholic faith being exemplified in values-driven activity for the common good. All teachers were very aware of the values-based nature of their role, evidenced in their reflections on the purposes of being a teacher, and the way they created narratives of stories and examples that express that purpose. Several teachers mentioned the values approach as one that they would miss if they moved to another school. The values terminology prompted deep reflection, in some instances in relation to how the values might be understood in relation to particular roles and responsibilities.

The school's Core Values enabled the teachers to have more than a simple perception of the agency of their role. They contributed to an understanding of the school as an inclusive community and, for many, were seen as the glue that held it together. Teachers felt an obligation to incorporate values language into their daily interactions, at times as a tool to redirect behaviour or guide relationships. They thought of the ethos as educative not just through what may be learned about values, but also through the way that values supported learning.

There was clear evidence from the ways in which the teachers used the language of values, and in their everyday work, that they had assimilated, or were in the process of assimilating, the school's values and aspirational ethos into their personal worldview, explicitly accepting their professional position as moral role models.

In respect of my two research questions, therefore, I concluded that the Five Core Values did influence the day-to-day activities of the school, and did have an impact on how the teachers in the case study understood their role in the school. There is a danger, however, that the strong emphasis placed by the school on its Core Values may result in a secularising effect with a consequent lessening emphasis its Catholic character and purposes.

References

CfCE - The Sacred Congregation for Catholic Education - (1988) The Religious Dimension of Education in a Catholic School: Guidelines for Reflection and Renewal, in: Libreria Editrice Vaticana (2004) Church Documents on Catholic Education 1965-2002 (Vatican Translation), Strathfield, NSW, St Pauls, 143-188.

Donnelly, C. (2000) In pursuit of school ethos, British Journal of Educational Studies, 48. 2. 134-154.

Hadaway, B. S. (2006) Preparing the way for justice: strategic dispositional formation through the spiritual disciplines, in: D. Smith, J. Shortt & J. Sullivan (eds), Spirituality, Justice and Pedagogy, Nottingham, UK, Stapleford Centre, 143-165.

Hawkes, N. (2010) Does Teaching Values Improve the Quality of Education in Primary Schools? A study about the impact of values in a primary school, Saarbrucken: VDM.

Hyde, C. R. (1999) Pay it Forward, New York, NY, Simon & Schuster.

McLaughlin, T. (2005) The educative importance of ethos, British Journal of Educational Studies, 53. 3. 306-325.

Miles, M. B. & Huberman, A. M. (1994) Qualitative Data Analysis: An Expanded Sourcebook (2nd edition), Thousand Oaks, CA, Sage.

Office for Standards in Education (2011) Inspection Report, Manchester, Ofsted [reference anonymised].

Robson, C. (2002) Real World Research, (2nd edition), Oxford, Blackwell.

Seddon, J. (2005) Freedom from Command and Control: a better way to make the work 'work' - the Toyota system for service organisations (2nd edition), Buckingham, UK, Vanguard Education.

Silcock, P. & Duncan, D. (2001) Values acquisition and values education: some proposals, British Journal of Educational Studies, 49. 3. 242-259.

Silverman, D. (2005) Doing Qualitative Research, London, Sage.

Smith, J. K. A. (2013) Imagining the Kingdom, Grand Rapids, MI, Baker Academic.

Stock, M. (2005) Catholic Schools and the Definition of 'Practising Catholic', Coleshill, Archdiocese of Birmingham, Diocesan Schools Commission.

Pupil Voices on Religious Faith and Practice

Mark Dumican

Editor's Note:
Two separate, but connected, sections have been taken from Mark's M.Ed thesis investigating the respective and cumulative roles played by school, home and parish in the pupils' understanding and commitment to Catholicism. The first considers the pupils' explanations and discussions about their own Catholic backgrounds. The second is concerned with their actual religious practice.

Part 1 - Sources of Catholic Culture

Introduction

Understanding how the pupils perceive their own Catholicity can provide valuable insights into the development of the religious character of Catholic secondary schools that exist, in part, as an arm of the Church trying to place Christ and the Church's teaching at the centre of its educative role (Stock, 2005, p.3). The absence of empirical data from pupils means that the conclusions drawn from other research into this area are almost exclusively from an adult perspective (Grace, 2002).

It is my intention to give pupils an opportunity to voice their perceptions and understanding of what it means to them to be a Catholic and to practise their Catholic faith. This first section provides an overview of the extent to which major cultural influences in the pupils' Catholic formation comes from the institutional Church and other sources, including those of family and friends. The second is concerned with their religious practice within the parish and at school.

Sources of Culture: Family, Friends and Material Needs

In the event, pupils' views of the influence of family and friends highlighted two distinct patterns. One, perhaps unsurprisingly, identified family as the predominant factor. The second linked friends and school to the family as important formative influences.

Pre-eminence of Family

Some pupils stated clearly and firmly that their family was the most important influence on their lives. It had the greatest impact of their attitudes, values and behaviour and was the source of their determination to do well at school and in life generally. They had no doubt that all other influences came a very distant second. Simply being with family and 'spending time together' was very important and if something 'went wrong' it would 'override' everything else. They saw the family as a unit, providing mutual help and support through the good and bad times. The closeness of the relationship meant, for them, that everything would be fine, no matter what happened; family provided a constant source of security. As a consequence, they felt strongly motivated to work hard at school so that their parents would be proud of them. It was one way of returning the parental love and support they so clearly enjoyed, expressed as 'a need to return that support' (PG3.1) when, perhaps, the relationship would be reversed.

> *'My family have always been there to support me, they've fed me, clothed me and I owe them everything. If things changed and went wrong then it would be my turn to support them and help them through it because they have always helped me.'* (PG5.2)

Their close relationship with parents, with whom they 'could discuss anything' emphasised that their own happiness depended upon the happiness of the family unit; 'if their family was OK, then they would be also and vice versa.' (PB2.2)

While there were common views about the family *per se*, there was greater variation when they talked about whether Mass attendance was important to their family. For some, a natural part of family activity included attending their parish church each week. This both generated and supported close familial ties, but it was recognised that their Catholic beliefs, practice attitudes and values were primarily sustained by and through the family.[1]

> *'My parents have brought me up following the rules (of Catholicism) so that I follow a good life and become a good person, it is just the way we believe we should live our lives.'* (SG2.1)

Others thought living a 'Catholic life' far more important than attending Mass every week although for these pupils, attending Mass at Christmas and at weddings and christenings was a very important expression of family solidarity.[2] Though there were these attitudinal variations, they appeared to have the same source. The vast majority of pupils aligned themselves with their parents' view about the importance of religious practice, contrary to findings suggesting the current generation of young people had very strong filters that restricted the impact of external influences (including those of parents) than might have been the case in earlier times (Smith & Denton, 2005). Rather than filtering parental messages before making their own decisions, they were very open about how much their views echoed those of their parents, especially on the issue of attendance at Mass and their own religiosity. This seemed to be both natural and obvious since, 'family simply should always come first' (PB4.1). For this group, the overall consensus view is illustrated, perhaps, by the following:

> *'Because you live with your family all the time, they influence you in everything. I know you go to school every day and it does affect you, but nowhere near as much as your family. It all really depends on what type of family you have, I'm lucky to have a good one.'* (LB5.1)

---

[1] Such statements are in marked contrast to the view that, within the general population, belief in God is becoming less of an institutional collective consciousness and more of a personal choice - see Davie, (1999).

[2] Indicating a belief that to be a Catholic one must practise, albeit sporadically, a view consistent with findings reported by Davie (1999).

Family, Friends and School

A second group of pupils, while still recognising the importance of their family, did not afford it the same prominence. Their lives were influenced variously, they argued, by a combination of family, friends and school, each of which had different impact upon them and their own attitudes and values.

They recognised that at some point they would have to live their own lives and live away from their parents, but knowing they would always be there for them was a great source of comfort and very reassuring to them. They suggested, however, that at age 16 and in their final year at school although family had been most important up to this point, now friends and school had a greater influence. Since their friends were undergoing experiences, for example, the pressures of taking public examinations, which their families were not, pupils felt they should 'expect to take a back seat' (LG4.2).

When asked to differentiate between the sources of influence, they indicated that their families were very loving and supportive and had taught them how to be 'good' people, but friends had helped to develop them socially and the school had encouraged and pushed them to be the best kind of people they could possibly be, mainly through the ways in which they interacted with, and showed their respect for, others. They readily acknowledged the impact of peer group pressure and felt that it was important for them to have 'the right type of friends' (SB1.2). They recognised that their judgement in this area of their lives was of particular importance and decisions could result in positive, constructive support or, alternatively, it could be a negative, and destructive. They felt the combined influence from the three sources had helped them become independent, 'make the correct decisions in life' (LB1.2), and would ultimately define them. For some pupils, part of their independence involved them choosing to attend Mass, though actively living by Catholic values was seen as the more important factor. This would seem to support findings that young people have a very strong emphasis on their own culture which affected the way they made ethical and moral decisions (Greeley, 1998).

At the time of this research, GCSE examinations were just six months away for the pupils involved. Perhaps, reflecting the pressures they were under, they indicated that their families and, to a lesser extent, their friends had to accept that their school work and preparation for the looming examinations had to take priority over everything else. Their families seemed to accept their preoccupations and assume that they would 'return to normal' at the end of the academic year (PB1.1). Some pupils felt this was quite a selfish approach, but as it affected their entire future they felt they had no choice but to take this approach, it just had to be that way. In doing so, however, only two pupils added themselves to the list of influences and pressures that contributed to their 'selfishness'.

> 'My family and friends do mean everything to me, but I have to focus on my schoolwork and do my best for myself because you have to be selfish sometimes to do the best for yourself instead of helping everyone else.' (NB4.2)

Material Needs/Desires

The term which pupils applied to clothes, computer games, games consoles, mobile 'phones, music and eating out was 'stuff'. I will also use this term to describe these items in this section. For the most part there was a great deal of agreement amongst the pupils, but a minority of alternative views expressed were very diverse. Contrary to research suggesting young people were profoundly individualistic,[3] claiming their moral perspectives as being independent of any religious influences, most pupils in this sample acknowledged that their views came from, and were very much in tune with, the Catholic Church's social teaching., though some cited their family's [religiously based] views on material possessions which they had absorbed.[4] On the other hand, while agreeing the influence of their parents' attitudes and practices influences on their own moral and ethical decision making, a minority were adamant that religion had no part to play in the way they conducted themselves.[5]

That there was an existing perception of teenagers as being selfish and materialistic was freely acknowledged by most pupils but, many argued, it was erroneous. They felt that while it might be true of a minority, it was a media inspired exaggeration. On the contrary, most felt they were not very materialistic and always endeavoured to put others before themselves, traits evident in their generally selfless and non-materialistic friends. These observations highlight the problem with generalisations of adult perceptions of young people; they will be correct for a certain number of pupils and totally incorrect for others.

Pupils explained they had changed their views over their five years in school. When they were younger they would 'base their happiness on getting stuff' (PB2.2). Gradually, they became more concerned with what they could achieve in life and the type of person they could become. The pupils thought they 'had matured and grown up a lot' (PG4.3) and as they were in Year 11 and this more mature attitude to material possessions was rooted in their developing religious faith. While they recognised how fortunate they were to have new 'stuff' (and they did enjoy receiving/obtaining it), they did not regard acquisition or accumulation of stuff as overly important or the means to happiness: there were far more important things.

> *'Being able to buy things and being materialistic just doesn't matter to me, I use my faith to guide me, to think about what I can achieve and the type of person I can become.'* (PG1.1)

When they talked about examples of extreme poverty and reflected upon their own material wealth, which in their own estimation was not very great, pupils expressed some level of shame at their own materialistic outlook. A number thanked God for being in such a (relatively) privileged situation and identified Gospel teaching as having helped them form a view on this subject. While they felt very grateful to have the latest 'stuff', it made them think about people who were less fortunate then themselves. Recognising 'that situation was

---

[3] See, for example, Smith & Denton (2005); Schweitzer (2007) and Rossiter (2010).

[4] See, for example, Fuller (2001) and Crawford & Rossiter (2006).

[5] Such views are consistent with some American research - see, for example, Greeley (1998).

not right' (LG5.4) seemed to motivate them to help others as much as possible. They recognised that, unlike many others in the world, they did not have to worry about whether they were going to eat every day and such reflections gave them 'the proper perspective' (LB3.3).

They also pointed to the pressures to conform to peer-group standards in term of their material possessions (PB1.3; LB5.1) while claiming that it applied to a minority. For example, one pupil expressed occasional envy when thinking about 'how others had better stuff' and how much more expensive it was (PB4.1) but claimed such feelings did not last very long when set against the [material] support of parents. Another was 'quite materialistic [but] not as grateful' as they should be to my parents since it was important not to be selfish and to show appreciation for what they had (LB1.2). On the other hand, most acknowledged those who did not have the possibility of similar choices about what they bought or consumed and, in making the comparison, felt very privileged, grateful and happy with their own circumstances.

Most pupils professed they would prefer to have all the 'stuff', but recognised it was not necessary, simply nice at the time, but far from the most important thing in life. They felt lucky to be able to afford 'stuff', as there were so many people in the world who could not even hope of having anything like the possessions they had and felt very privileged to be in a position where they could purchase 'stuff' without thinking about it too much. They acknowledged they would feel a loss if it was taken away. These pupils argued that materialistic ambitions could be good. They intended to go into careers that pay well so they could afford to help others and in that sense money was important, but the only reason it was important.

> *'Money is really a means to an end; you need it to look after your own family first, then it should be used to help others less fortunate.'* (SB3.3)

They did however, think it was 'important to be able to handle money properly' (SB2.2). The problem with money, they argued, came when people dedicated their lives in pursuit of it, when they were obsessed with always having more and became consumed by their own greed. They recognised that it was easy to succumb to such temptation but such a lifestyle would be very superficial. Consequently, they felt their own focus should be on 'being happy with what you have and being close to family, friends and those you love' (LB2.1) and keeping their material in perspective.

The pupils also recognised how much (in terms of material possessions) they received from their parents and thought it was important to earn enough money when they were older to be able to help them in return.

> *'You think your phone and clothes and stuff are important, but when you really think about things you realise they aren't important at all, you realise your family and friends are all that matter.'* (LG3.1)

One pupil described how he was often 'told off' (PB3.3) by his parents for being too selfless, as he really did not care about having the 'stuff' and only focussed on what he could do for others and how he could help them. He did not like other people who got obsessed with it because 'it distracts them from becoming better people.' (PB3.3) Another pupil spoke about how buying 'stuff' is about 'fitting in sometimes, it is just the modern world, it is how things are' (PB5.2) even though such conformity might not help them to 'develop or grow'. Conversely, as they matured 'it became less important' (PB5.2).

One girl identified pressure particular to her sex. There is 'enormous pressure on girls when going out, especially to parties', not to wear the same thing twice and therefore the need to 'buy fashionable clothes was huge'. It was, therefore 'vital to have the clothes' and this social imperative outweighed all other considerations (SG2.1). Another agreed the need to purchase stuff was often overwhelming so obtaining the latest 'iphone or new clothes' was a very high priority. This was just the way things were and that 'everyone was really like that, even if they didn't admit to it' (SG5.2). Two boys also acknowledged their need for material possessions. One pupil felt that his parents should give him 'lots of money to spend' as of right (LB4.4) when he was out with friends. The other thought it was very important to be able to buy 'stuff', because shopping is 'just very enjoyable' and you have to 'fit in and not feel left out'. By having all the latest 'stuff', this 'made you feel good about yourself' (LB3.3). Such expressions were, however, were very much in a minority.

Section Summary
This section explored the basis of pupils' Catholic cultural formation, in particular, the extent to which the contributing influences and pressures came from their formal association with the Catholic Church. Whilst some stated there was no direct formative influence on them from Church teaching, the majority recognised it had an impact on their own values and also their attitudes towards their families, friends and material possessions.

All pupils acknowledged that their behaviour was influenced by their social environment and that for the majority of pupils this involved some influence derived from Catholic social teaching, albeit primarily mediated through parental attitudes and teaching rather than their own formal religious practice and Mass attendance.

Part 2 – Religious Practice in Parish and School

Introduction
Researching religious identification of practise within a faith tradition is a complex issue because of the many variables which combine to influence the data (Ammerman, 2003), not least those that are associated with teenagers in their transition from children into adulthood. It is important to note, therefore, that the construction of pupils' views will be in a state of transition (Smith & Denton, 2005; Smith & Snell, 2009) not a final result but more of a point in the progression of understanding; a record of how they felt at a particular time.

Research into the Catholic identity of children attending Catholic secondary schools has identified four different typologies to describe their practice; (1) **practising** Catholics who attend church every Sunday; (2) **sliding** Catholics who attend church some Sundays, but less than weekly; (3) **lapsed** Catholics who never attended church on Sunday, and (4) **non-Catholics** who may have been baptised in the Catholic Church and who may or may not be practising members of other denominations (Francis, 2002). While using these categories as a starting point I found several distinct sub-groups emerged based on the pupils' responses during their interviews (see table 1 below).

Table 1

Catholic Typology – Year 11 Pupils (n = 242)		
Self-Identified	**'Francis' Categories**	**Research Sample Sub-Groups**
Catholic – 95%	Practising - 9%	1.1 – The Family Catholic
		1.2 – The Committed Catholic
		1.3 – The Transformational Catholic
	Sliding - 41%	2.1 – The Halfway Catholic
		2.2 – The School Catholic
	Lapsed - 45%	3.1 – The Faith-into-Action Catholic
		3.2 – The Prayerful Catholic
		3.3 – The Golden-Rule Catholic
		3.4 – The Catholic Atheist
Non-Catholic – 5%	Non-Catholic - 5%	4.1 – The Former Catholic
		4.2 – The Resentful Christian
		4.3 – The Personal Christian

The previous section explored the sources of pupils' Catholic formation. Families are the primary influence since their attitudes and practices, including choosing to educate their children in a Catholic school, provide the cultural norms within which they live and grow. This section explores how pupils viewed attending Mass in their school and parish communities and the impact, if any, those experiences had upon on their own religious identification. It is important to set the particular context for what constitutes 'practising' the Catholic faith at school. Primarily this comprises attendance at religious services, whether in school assemblies of various types or formal liturgical events, such as Advent and Lenten Masses. Such events are compulsory in the sense that they form part of the normal life of the school. In addition there are voluntary religious activities, including 'House Masses', organised during the pupils' lunch time.

Religious Practice by Category (1): Practising Catholics – A Brief Overview

Three sub-groups, having varying levels of religious commitment, emerged within a category which can be defined as 'practising Catholics' (Francis, 2002) where the pupils' religious culture is rooted in, and sustained by, links between the home, parish and school.[6] There were pupils who happily and unquestioningly attend Mass every week with their family; it is

---

[6] School based research suggests that 'practising Catholic pupils are likely to have more a positive view of their Catholic school than those with different socio-religious backgrounds – see Egan (1988).

part of their 'normal routine' (PB2.1, PG3.1, PB4.1). These I have labelled Family Catholics (**1.1**). Others, who attend Mass every week wanted to get more involved in practical ways[7] but only in their parish setting were labelled 'Committed Catholics (**1.2**) (PG5.2, PB2.2, PB5.2).There were also pupils who are particularly active both in their parish and in school. This latter group, labelled Transformational Catholics (**1.3**), are involved in IMPACT (Involving More People At Church Today) and seek to encourage other pupils both to attend Mass and try be agents for the development of more 'youth friendly' parishes (PG1.3, PG4.3, PB1.3, PB3.3).

When the 'Practising Catholic' pupils talked about their religious practise during the interviews they had a clear sense that the celebration of the Eucharist at Mass was central to any religious practice. Religious faith and practice had 'an important part to play for the common good' of society (PB3.3) so that in practising their faith they aimed to become 'better people' (PG2.1) - evidenced in their efforts to help others, both familiar to them and unknown.[8] Acceptance of and adherence to Catholic social teaching meant that they felt that it was important 'to be the best person they could be' (PB4.1) and 'help as many people as they could' (PB5.2). They held a very clear view of 'right and wrong' (PG4.3) and that they should be aware of the consequences of their actions. If they 'had done something wrong' they 'felt bad about it' and regarded making use of the sacrament of reconciliation as a natural way of putting things right and ensuring that such actions were not repeated (PG3.1). They talked about 'wanting to pray' (PB2.2), to have a relationship with God, 'trusting God to guide them' (PG4.3) and that He was 'constantly with them' [which] they never forgot about' (PB3.3).

They saw an on-going synergy between church and school teaching, providing key messages about the type of person they should/could become through practising and living their Catholic faith. They agreed that the complementary aims of parish Church and school to involve pupils in the practise of their faith were worthwhile; aims which they were happy to endorse.

Some pupils went further. Those in the IMPACT group argued that they could help others find and/or develop their faith through the religious activities of parish and school. In addition they felt that, if their peers did so, they would derive personal satisfaction from the encouragement they had provided. All regularly attended Mass in their parishes and in school.

In contrast, many in the other three categories (sliding, lapsed, non-Catholic) only attended Mass in school. For these latter groups, school was the only place they associated with any religious practice, though they viewed school in a positive light, describing it as the place

---

[7] They act as altar servers, readers and Eucharistic ministers (or are on the waiting list to be one).
[8] The language used when expressing the idea of unknown others being their brothers and sisters echoed that found in research by the Catholic Youth Ministry Federation (2010).

where they should and could explore what religious faith meant both liturgically and their daily lives.

1.1 The 'Practising Family' Catholic

These pupils attended Mass every week, but did so, in part, from a sense of familial duty. They recognise the strength of their family's commitment, attend mass out of love for their parents and wish to avoid any adverse impact on familial relationships, but acknowledged that without strong family bonds they would simply stop going. A general view that Mass attendance was a matter of duty rather than a personal commitment was articulated by one pupil as:

> *'Going to Church I feel is like a parental duty, I mean it is just something I do because of them.'* (PG3.1)[9]

Some dutifully professed to 'believe in God' (PG2.1) but were less sure whether they had to practise their faith to be faithful to God. These pupils liked attending the major celebrations of the year, such as Easter and Christmas because 'it is like everyone is celebrating' (PB4.1), but much less so at other times of the year where they felt attending Mass was a chore. On many occasions, however, once they were actually in Church they 'didn't mind' it because 'it is a good time to be quiet and reflect upon what is going on' (PG3.1) in their lives. These pupils actively seek 'a good relationship with God' (PG3.1), where they can 'trust in him' (PG2.1) and that He is always with them but pondered whether they could have these things without attending weekly Mass.

It seemed that school staff provided the motivation for them 'to be the best they could possibly be' both academically and in their religious practice. Following the tenets inherent within what are known as 'Gospel values' was expected in school and these pupils reported it had a major positive impact on their commitment to their faith. Religious Education lessons and Mass attendance had strengthened family inspired Catholic identity and practice.

They enjoyed attending both the compulsory and voluntary school Masses and were keen to talk about the additional wider opportunities the school had afforded them for the exploration of their faith. For example, they cited assemblies, pilgrimages, the St. Vincent de Paul Society,[10] the twin/partner school in South Africa, special curriculum days devoted understanding world hunger, poverty and ways in which they might be alleviated. As one pupil said 'there is always something going on to get involved in' (PG3.1). Perhaps more importantly, they thought school provided a vehicle for pupils who felt detached from their faith to re-establish contact and involvement.

---

[9] Such attitudes are consistent with, for example: 'practising' (Francis, 2002); 'core' (Fulton, 2000); 'patrimonial' (Hervieu-léger, 2000); 'hard-core' (Casson, 2012); and the archetype 'Daniel' (Catholic Youth Ministry Federation, 2010).

[10] The St Vincent de Paul Society (SVP) is a lay Catholic organisation providing practical assistance to those in need – irrespective of ideology, faith, ethnicity, age or gender. It was formed in Paris in 1833 and has been active in England & Wales since 1844. For more details see www.svp.org.uk

They also commended the school's balanced approach; providing many opportunities for religious participation but allowing pupils to make decisions as to whether they took advantage of them. They argued that where such involvement was entirely voluntary, those active pupils received the respect of their peers (perhaps providing a source of psychological reinforcement as to the benefits of 'being religious').

1.2 The 'Committed' Practising Catholic

Pupils in this sub-group felt that while attending their primary school they had given little thought to their Mass attendance but following transfer to the secondary school began to understand why they went to Church and slowly moved from a passive form of Catholicism to a more active role, for their own benefit and that of others. They felt the school was a positive influence on their faith, citing the large numbers of teachers who prayed with them in lessons and during all the school's liturgical events.

Committed Practising Catholics were regular mass attenders though their religious practise was parish orientated and, for the most part, derived from parental attitudes (PG2.1, PG3.1, PB4.1). They had little enthusiasm for religious practice outside their own particular parish (including faith based activities at school). Even though they recognised and valued the contribution and opportunities the school had afforded them, they very much felt the major influence on their faith had come from their own families and when their families and school were 'saying the same thing' (PB2.2) it had a major influence in what they believed and the way they behaved. The family remained, however, the major influence on how they would think and behave. As one pupil stated;

> 'If school are saying the same things as your parents it really makes you think because it's not just your parents, they are backing each other up and it makes the message more valid and more likely to stick with you, so you do it.'
> (PB4.1)

1.3 The 'Transformational Practising' Catholic

Pupils in this sub-group had started the IMPACT group (see above). They attended Mass each week in their parishes and also in school. They identified how important their families were in developing their own religious practice in the same forthright manner as the previous two sub-groups in this category, but also recognised the school as being similarly influential.

Two pupils attended Mass every week though their parents did not.[11] Both stated that school had provided the motivation to them to practise their faith and, as a consequence, they gained a tremendous sense of well-being. They appreciated the opportunities they had in school and recognised that without its influence they would not have chosen to practise their faith. They both 'had that feeling inside' (PG1.3) they wanted to practise their faith and the distinction between school and parish, and indeed any other place of worship, simply was not there.

---

[11] Although in both cases the parents had taken them to Church when they were younger.

Because of the transformational effect it had on their lives, it was the practice of their faith *per se* that was important, not the location where it took place.

All members of this group of pupils talked openly, and proudly, about their faith. They actively encouraged other pupils to do the same and, to some extent, 'felt different to the other pupils' (PB3.3). Consequently, statements that they did not enjoy attending [*compulsory- Ed*] school Masses came as a surprise. They explained that as everyone had to attend them within each year group, and they knew fellow pupils who really did not want to be there because they were not baptised Catholics or were self-proclaimed atheists, they saw their attendance under compulsion as detrimental to the individuals and their own practice. In a similar way within school generally, but especially their Religious Education lessons, they expressed some resentment towards those pupils who professed to being atheists on the basis that they were taking advantage of perceived benefits of education in a Catholic school, both academically, spiritually and morally, yet they did not subscribe to Catholic religious and social teaching. They voiced strong disagreement with the school's decision to make Advent and Lenten Masses compulsory, since it led to a form of dishonesty for non-practising pupils. As one put it:

> '*In a way it's sort of mocking, because if Jesus wants you to choose to get into the kingdom of heaven, it must be your choice to go to Mass and I know people do not want to be there and they shouldn't be.* ' (PB2.2)

In contrast, they felt 'much more comfortable in their own faith community' (PG1.3) when attending Mass in their own parish because those attending did so out of a sense of commitment similar to their own.

All these pupils argued that IMPACT would have a greater influence on their peers than the teaching staff, or indeed anyone else would/could possibly have, precisely because, as fellow pupils they shared a common youth cultural outlook on life and, perhaps more importantly because of that, they were not in any sense authority figures 'telling teenagers what to do'.

Religious Practice by Category (2): Sliding Catholics – A Brief Overview
Pupils who could be identified as 'Sliding Catholics' had many of the same characteristics as the 'practising' group, apart from their approach to Mass attendance. They claimed to believe in God, to pray and adhere to the values and teachings of the Catholic Church but had little motivation or desire to attend Church, even when their families did so.[12]

As with the first category, it quickly became evident that this category did not have a totally homogenous view and two distinct sub-groups emerged. The first sub-group (**2.1**), which I call 'Sliding Halfway Catholics', are those who attend Church occasionally, both in school at

---

[12] This characterisation is consistent with typologies derived from other research, for example, 'sliding' (Francis, 2002); 'intermediate' (Fulton, 2000); 'patrimonial' (Hervieu-Léger, 2000); 'halfway' (Casson, 2012); 'routine' and 'family' (Catholic Youth Ministry, 2010).

the voluntary Masses and their own parish. The second sub-group (**2.2**), 'Sliding School Catholics', go to Church occasionally in their own parish, but actively sought to go to Mass regularly when they were in school.

Unlike the three Practising Catholic groups, who afforded minimal attention to the influence of their teachers, 'Sliding Catholics' highlighted teacher-pupil interaction as a potential source that could affect their Mass attendance in school and religious practise generally. It seemed that these pupils actively looked for exemplars of individuals 'living their faith' within the school community. They commented on teaching staff noting the lived reality of some and its lack in others. They gave example of teachers saying prayers at the end of lessons, being prepared and able to discuss issues raised by pupils in various subjects from a religious perspective. They stated they would 'connect with the genuine staff who lived their faith' (SG2.1) and actively seek to do so, whereas, they were much more likely to 'not even make an effort towards the staff who were not genuine'. (SG2.1)

2.1 – The Sliding 'Halfway Catholic'
This sub-group were pupils who attended [*non-compulsory - Ed*] Mass occasionally both in their parish and in school. In a similar way to those in the IMPACT group in the 'practising' category (**1.3**), these pupils separated their experience of attending Mass in school and their parish. They did not particularly enjoy the Masses where all pupils from the year group must attend in school, because they felt uncomfortable (SG4.1), although this was on aesthetic rather than religious grounds.

> *'It is hot and cramped and this detracts from the experience.'* (SB4.1)
> *'[It is] really boring sometimes and then could be more interesting depending upon what is going on, certain parts of the Mass are more important than others, for example at communion you feel more in the presence of God, but the other parts you can just zone out and think about something else.'* (SB3.1)

For this group, the physical location for liturgical celebrations was important. Where the Mass took place in the local Church, and especially when the school Jubilee celebrations took place in the diocesan cathedral, pupils reported that they enjoyed the experience. The physical environment enhanced the experience and they 'enjoyed Mass much more'. Because religious matters were commonly discussed in school, reflecting its religious character, it was the only place in which they felt they could talk about faith and issues arising from it. Since their attendance in their parish church was spasmodic[13] they felt school together with parents were potentially major sources of external influence on their faith commitment and practice, though they acknowledged that the actual impact was marginal.

On the other hand, where parents held the view that 'living the faith was more important than attending Church' children strongly endorsed such sentiments. Their school experiences

---

[13] Other things were afforded a higher priority, for example, playing sport, attending clubs and general peer-group socialising.

appeared to have had some positive influence on their lives. They viewed the religious aspects as an integral part of the education it provided. As one pupil stated 'the key messages of the school are to love God, love yourself and each other' (SG4.1), and, as a way of life, it was something they wished to pass on to their own future children.

2.2 – The Sliding 'School Catholic'

Unlike the sub-group above who were half-heartedly involved both in school and their respective parishes, these pupils liked attending Mass in school and actively sought to do so, but did so in their parishes only very occasionally (SB1.2) regarding it as irrelevant for living good lives (SG3.2). They were happy and very comfortable in attending Mass in school, they liked getting involved in the Mass preparation and organisation and they would 'listen more' (SB1.2) and 'pay more attention' (SG3.2) because of this involvement.

> '[Attending Mass in school] is good because everybody is together and you can see everybody is there, if you go to your own church, you don't really know many people, so it is really nice to be with all your friends and celebrate Mass together.' (SG5.2)

They involved themselves in the work of the school St. Vincent de Paul Society, other school based charity work and the IMPACT group. They enjoyed the number and variety of religious experiences provided by the school, for example, through the curriculum, extra-curricular activities and access to confession, but the main plus-point about such school based events was the choice the school afforded to pupils whether or not they become involved.

They felt the school had a 'massive effect' on the way they thought about their faith (SB1.2) but outside that environment 'would not bother' (SB2.2) and 'definitely would not believe in it'. (SG5.2) The ability they had developed, and the opportunities provided by the school, to translate religious faith into practical actions was very important to this group. For them 'practising' went far beyond just attending Mass. What they called 'living the faith' was a crucial component of their belief. When exploring this notion, they argued that they loved and cared for each other because doing so was the most important part of their Catholic belief and, further, several stated that school had a huge influence in encouraging them to live their lives in this way. They felt the school had made them think about issues in the world during their Religious Education lessons and these, together with the many other opportunities for Christian action provided by the school, had encouraged them to evaluate themselves, their lives and think about what having faith actually meant. As one pupil expressed it;

> 'The way I used to live my life was probably pretending, without even being aware I was pretending. I would say that the way I live my life now is more genuine.' (SG3.2)

Pupils in this group were able to reconcile their actions with the Church's social teaching reinforcing their strongly held view that to be a Catholic meant you had to make a difference in the world.

Religious Practice by Category (3): Lapsed Catholics – A Brief Overview

There was the greatest diversity of opinion about Mass attendance, generally, within this group. On the other hand, their views about religious observance in school were all remarkably similar. Many of the pupils wanted to point out that when they were younger, particularly during primary school years, on the occasions they attended their parish Church, and they 'got something out of it' (LB5.1). It seems that the strength of the link between their primary school and Church also helped them to 'feel comfortable' (LG4.2) on those occasions.

In a similar way to those in the 'Sliding Catholic' category, pupils who defined themselves as 'lapsed' recognised the major influence their parents had in shaping the way they thought about Church and their faith. Most reported that their parents regarded 'living the faith' as more important than attending Church; statements repeated by them during their interviews. They also readily identified the extent to which teachers illustrated their religiosity in the ways they carried out their responsibilities. It was abundantly clear to them which members of staff actively tried to teach and act in a Christian way, not just by including prayers and religious themes in their lessons, but in the way they cared about and spoke to pupils.

> 'The teachers do mention God and Christian things and then others don't mention it at all, I can tell you, it is clear to us (the pupils) whether they (the teachers) believe in it or not.' (LB2.1)

They felt very strongly that their actions that defined them as being a 'good' or 'bad' person; it had nothing to do with attending Church. It was, for them, much more important to develop a set of 'good' values and attitudes which, in turn, they argued, should be the measure of 'being Catholic'.[14]

Apart from the 'Catholic Atheist' sub-group (3.4), the pupils felt Catholicism had influenced the way they conducted themselves; they viewed it in a generally positive light and wanted to pass it onto their own children. People who attended Church but did not lead a 'good life' were 'just kidding themselves' that they were doing what God wanted (LB2.1).

3.1 The 'Faith into Action' Lapsed Catholic

These pupils, baptised Catholics, attended Mass in school but not at their own parish. They felt that their words and actions defined them as Catholics. They believed in God and could remember attending church when they were younger and were still encouraged to attend Mass by their parents. When they did, very occasionally, attend a parish Mass it was a case of following a family tradition to which they attached little importance. On the other hand, when they attended Mass in school (or in the local Church as part of a school organised activity) they stated they felt quite at ease though sometimes unsure about the thought of

---

[14] Though the ten pupils in this group indicated that they had 'lapsed', they all strongly identified themselves as 'being Catholic' but had divergent views about the nature of their own Catholicity.

attending Mass. However, once they were involved they stated that they enjoyed it and thought whether it was something they should do more often – though such thoughts did not, it appears, translate into a change in their normal practice.

It might be expected, for a group of pupils who had decided that outside the school environment they would not to attend Mass, the compulsory school Masses would be resented. This was not the case. Pupils said they appreciated the fact the school made them attend the Advent and Lenten masses and, in a few cases, it had led them to occasionally attend the voluntary 'House Masses'. However, they felt it was hypocritical to 'just go to Church and then tell people you go to Church' (LB5.1), it was much more important to actually follow their faith with 'what you say and do' (LB2.1). The pupils were involved with the IMPACT and St Vincent de Paul groups in school and viewed their 'faith in action' (LB2.1) as far more important than 'just attending Mass' because 'that is how you really make a difference' (LB5.1).

> *'It's wider than just going to Church and just being there, what's really important is actually just doing it [following the teachings of the faith].'* (LG2.1)

They reported that their involvement in Religious Education lessons at Key Stage 3 and Key Stage 4 (GCSE Religious Education courses) enabled them to acquire a greater understanding of Catholicism and acknowledged how other curriculum activities had a part to play in talking about faith which, in turn, had had some positive effect on their views. They liked the way the school gave them information and explanations about matters of faith, whilst at the same time emphasising it was up to them, as individuals, to make up their own minds and then draw their own conclusions as to what was really important.

Being able to talk about faith issues in school, while not necessarily being in agreement with Church teaching, was seen as very positive; they had no worries about expressing their opinions. They liked the debates that took place in their Religious Education lessons, especially now they were in Year 11 because it gave an opportunity for everyone to express a view, the merits of which they could judge for themselves. Such discussions were highly appreciated.

3.2 – The 'Prayerful' Lapsed Catholic

These pupils did not attend Mass in their own parish and expressed their religiosity through prayer; they did not feel the need for Church. They felt it perfectly acceptable to separate the Catholic Church from a Catholic school, seeing the school as providing all the religious input about their faith that they needed – or wanted. Religious practice was, for them, a very personal matter and argued that the best way to have a relationship with God was directly through prayer.

Most pupils in this group believed in God and could remember attending Church when they were younger as their family attended. They no longer attended because they had no-one to go with (their family had stopped attending), but felt they had retained a relationship with God because they continued to pray.[15] They liked 'being Catholic', but not being subject to any Church teaching. The following statement encompasses the feeling of many of the 'Prayerful Catholic' pupils.

> *'You must look at the evidence [whether organised religion is a source of good] and then decide for yourself and then interpret that in your own way so you can decide for yourself how you want to lead your life.'* (LG4.2)

They found Mass 'boring', needing to be brought up to speed (LG1.2), that it could become 'more lively, instead of somebody just stood at the front talking to us.' (LG4.2) and was 'weird-ish' (LG4.2). Church 'isn't relevant anymore' (LB1.2), and, consequently, 'needed modernising' because it 'is totally out of date with the real world' so that 'nobody listens to what it has to say' (LG4.2). Interestingly, they did not apply this view uniformly. They argued that Church traditions were important because 'if you change everything, you would have a completely different religion to the one you started with' (LG1.2), but the 'essential parts keep you anchored' (LB1.2).

Although the thought of attending compulsory Mass in school was unwelcome they claimed to enjoy the occasions when they did so and were grateful they had had no choice in the matter. If they had, they would choose not to attend and 'would miss out on being all together as a year group.' (LG4.2). Some of them argued, paradoxically, that the school could do more to encourage pupils' involvement in voluntary Masses, rather than it being the 'same ones all the time' (LB1.2).

Some pupils in this sub-group were members of the school's St. Vincent de Paul society and emphasised that their involvement came from wanting to make a difference in other peoples' lives. While they valued any prayer that was accompanied by thoughtful contemplation of the meaning of the chosen words, they argued that anyone who just said 'the words' but did not put 'faith into action' were just 'going through the motions' so it did not matter whether such individuals went to Church or not. Contemplative prayer, even if sporadic in nature, was 'better than saying the words but not leading a life of faith' (LG4.2).

Praying was clearly important to them, but only the type of praying that meant something because it was really thought about. This sporadic approach was considered much better than praying every day but just saying words and not leading a life of faith. It was no surprise, therefore, that these Prayerful Lapsed Catholic pupils linked their ideas about faith leading to positive actions to the example provided to them by the teaching staff, noting a high degree of variability in the conduct they observed. They also viewed the aims and activities of the

---

[15] Their separation of spirituality and religiosity, feeling connected to the Catholic Church but rejecting compliance with Church's teaching in favour of a highly personalised view of what being 'Catholic' means, is consistent with other research. See, for example, Berger (1973); Baumer (1977); Moberg (1979); Fuller, (2001); Alexander & McLaughlin (2003); Eckersley (2005).

IMPACT group favourably, supporting the way they were trying to influence liturgical celebrations.

> *'Talking about that stuff makes you think what you would like to do to change the Church and what is wrong with it and what you think would make it better, so makes you think more and understand the issues and what you actually think about it.'* (LB1.2)

3.3 – The 'Golden Rule'[16] Lapsed Catholic

These pupils were not sure whether they believed in God. As the school was the only place these pupils experience Mass, they thought about their feelings towards it a lot. Simply by putting the Advent and Lenten Masses on the calendar and making them important was initially seen as just something the pupils had to put up with, but as with the previous two sub-groups, they too expressed being thankful they had been involved. Having been born into a Catholic family and, subsequently, baptised into the faith, these pupils saw having a Catholic education – which was regarded in a positive light - as an integral part of Catholic life. The pupils identified the Catholic character of the school by pointing to religious artefacts, such as a crucifix in each classroom, as well as religious activities such as the compulsory and voluntary Masses. Such things 'really meant something' but, when required to attend school Masses they;

> *'... just put up with religion like that [because it was] in school ... it was boring and there 'isn't the time because of other priorities' ... we live in a generation where you are not bothered if it is not interesting, it must grab your interest.'* (LB3.3)

Even those pupils who expressed their doubts about the existence of God readily acknowledged the positive influence of the school's Catholic character on what they thought and how they behaved. They felt that subscribing to religious faith was very much a personal issue. It had great personal benefits, helping them make informed decisions about big issues in their lives, but having faith and attending Mass, to them, were entirely separate issues. Faith was something that was in constant flux, something 'you could never be sure of.' (LG3.3) However, they also cited the positive influence of those staff whom they identified as 'acting in the right (Christian) way' while at the same time identifying some individuals as having a contrary impact. Despite the variation in role models that the teaching body provided, these pupils felt that the school had 'kept their faith going' (LB3.3) and without it their religiosity 'would have just slipped away' (LB3.3), though, when pressed, they were unsure what that religious faith might comprise.

---

[16] I have adopted this title from Casson (2012) describing young people had a real thirst for understanding their role in the world, of self-understanding, of the ability to develop relationships and enquiry into how they could develop a perspective on life, whilst at the same time having a great deal of uncertainty about whether religion plays any part in this understanding. See also, Priestly (1985) and Wintersgill (2008).

3.4 – The 'Atheist' Lapsed Catholic

A small number of baptised Catholic pupils professed to not believing in God. Knowing what was right and wrong and living a good life, they argued, did not require having any recourse to religion. They really did not want to attend the compulsory Masses and felt they just had to put up with the religious aspects of school. They recognised the school tried to encourage and inspire them to live a Catholic way of life, but felt the efforts to be irrelevant to their lives (LB4.4); that Mass was 'actually quite strange' (LG5.4) and, at times, boring. Although they 'got nothing' from Mass attendance, they felt perfectly comfortable but they would rather spend their time 'doing something else '(LG5.4).

However, they recognised the school's emphasis on academic achievement and 'making the most of themselves' was, at least in the eyes of the school hierarchy, part of its religious message, though the 'pressure do well academically was sometimes overpowering' (LG5.4), especially in Year 11. They also saw benefits in attending a Catholic school, 'because they do better than the non-Catholic schools' and that 'everyone seems happier and nicer' (LG5.4) and, consequently, they would not want to be in a non-Catholic school.[17]

Religious Practice by Category (4): Non-Catholic   Brief Overview

Five per cent of pupils (n=10) in the sample identified themselves as non-Catholic. Three pupils had been baptised as Catholics (whom I have designated as 'Former Catholics' 4.1). The other seven had been baptised in the Church of England. Five of these professed to being 'anti-religious' (designated as Resentful Christians 4.2) and two stated they had a personal relationship with God (designated as Personal Christians 4.3).

All ten do not attend Mass outside school and, even when they remember attending in the past, they have not been to a church 'for a long time' (NB2.1). One of the ten had been an altar server for a time in primary school but stopped before he transferred to the secondary phase because his 'belief stopped' and, as he phrased it:

'I don't think I will ever reconnect because I just don't want to.' (NB5.2)

They felt they had to excuse the religious aspects of the school when in conversation with their peers outside school. They were embarrassed and explained it [*religious practice – Ed*] away as something they 'had to do' (NG1.1). Even though they disliked attending Mass the pupils acknowledged that the religious character and associated activities of the school were instrumental in 'making it a good school' (NB5.2) and, as such, and they would 'put up with it to get a good education' (NG3.2).

Although school was only forum in which they ever received religious messages they found them to be very positive, especially those relating to fulfilling their human potential.

---

[17] These attitudes closely match with 'The Catholic Atheist' identified by Casson (2012) who were happy to be in a Catholic school solely for the apparent superior quality of education they provide rather than for any holistic influence gained from Catholic values and beliefs.

Understandably, achieving the best possible GCSE grades was their most important goal especially during their last year in school. They felt the school put a lot of pressure on them to achieve the best grades possible which they found was quite oppressive at times,[18] though understandable as enabled access to higher education and the potential to 'a good salary'.

4.1 – The Former Catholic

The three pupils in this sub-group had been baptised as Catholics but no longer considered themselves to be part of the Church (NB3.1). They acknowledged that the school had tried to encourage them not only to attend Mass, but to believe in living a Catholic life but they felt those efforts to have been ineffective. As one stated;

> *'The school has tried to make me believe in God and Jesus and His teachings. Some of it is important I suppose, but I don't really believe in religion, school is the only place I've heard about it.'* (NB5.2)

These pupils felt that they 'should not really be there' (NG1.1) when there were Masses provided in school, but did not mind 'being part of it' (NB3.1) because it was part of school life; but if they had the choice they would not choose to attend. They felt that practising faith was for old people because 'they are worried about getting into heaven' (NB3.1).

When they were in Mass they felt like they should be doing something else and were generally bored, sometimes they really disagreed with 'what the priest is saying' (NB2.1), if it was to do with God's omnipotence, they felt like standing up and disagreeing, but would not do that out of respect for the Priest and would not anything which would 'offend the school' (NG1.1). They stated that, given the option, they would not want to have attended any other school. They also acknowledged and applauded the school's contribution to their academic progress but had no belief in God.

> *'If I am being really honest I know it sounds really stupid, but I don't care if I go to Hell or something if I don't pray, I don't believe in it, you're just going to die anyway.'* (NB2.1)

4.2 – The Resentful Christian

Some pupils regarded themselves as Christians but had not been baptised into the Catholic Church They very strongly disagreed with having to attend the twice yearly compulsory whole school Masses, feeling both hypocritical in doing so and resentful for missing the lessons that would normally take place at these times. They felt quite strongly that they should not be there and believed they should be in the lessons they were missing instead. They identified their non-religious parents as being the main influence in their lives and, consequently, attributed their own current religious antipathy to the expressed opinions of

---

[18] They also felt there was 'no hiding place' from the school's emphasis on high academic attainment since it effectively involved parents in promoting and encouraging academic success. Some pupils felt such all-round pressure was not necessarily good for them.

their parents when they were younger. They claimed never to think about God, religion or religious practice apart from when they were in school and did not want to have anything to do with religion. As one pupil said:

> 'My Mum and Dad are not very religious, so I have not been religious, it just follows, we're just not interested in religion and that's it.' (NB4.2)

Some pupils in this sub-group went further, professing to be 'anti-religious' and argued that it was a direct cause of many of the ills in the world (NB5.2).

In stark contrast to the generally anti-religious attitudes described above, and most surprisingly given the vehemence with which they were expressed, all the pupils in this sub-group stated that they enjoyed their Religious Education lessons, appreciated learning about the Catholic and other faiths and valued their consequent increased understanding of a variety of beliefs and value systems.

4.3 – The Personal Christian

The two pupils who comprised this subgroup, though not baptised, claimed a form of personal Christian relationship with God through prayer. Praying and thinking about 'what it all means' had helped them to become 'better people' (NG4.3):

> 'It [praying] helps me because it is like thinking about being kind to each other, treating others with respect, loving one another and just trying to be closer together.' (NG4.3)

Although they did not particularly enjoy attending Masses in school, they appreciated why the liturgies were held and expressed no strong concern about their compulsory nature: it was 'part of the package' of attending a Catholic school and part of the wider messages the school tried to give about living as God would want. (NG4.3)

They recognised, and seemed to value, the positive effects of the link between the school's activities, in the widest sense, with the tenets of the Catholic faith and its social teaching. The school had been a major influence, both in terms of showing them a religious outlook of life, manifested in the requirement to know the difference between the right and wrong informing a positive way of life – which included high academic achievement and 'being the best person they could possibly be'.

They attributed to the school their understanding of appropriate behaviour towards others, an emphasis on being polite and courteous. They also noted the encouragement the school gave them to think about their actions and their consequences, to be independent in their thinking and doing what they knew to be right. As one stated;

> 'School has changed me a lot, obviously I am more mature as I have grown up, but I am 'more' because of this school.' (NB1.3)

Section Summary

Based on four main pupil categories (Practising Catholic, Sliding Catholic, Lapsed Catholic and Non-Catholic) this section explored the pupils' views on religious identification, the sources of their religious practice, if any, and, where they did practice, whether they perceived differences between that which took place in church and in the school. There were nuanced differences within each of those main categories, leading to the delineation of a number of sub-groups.

All 'Practising Catholic' pupils attended Mass, linked its celebration to their understanding of what it meant to be Catholic, and helped form their social attitudes and practice. They were aware that for some, both pupils and staff, that there was a mismatch between the ideals expressed in the school's expectations and their behaviour.

Those pupils who adopted a religiously 'transactional' approach in their lives, and who were the most visible proponents of Catholic action, were, surprisingly, censorious of their fellow pupils who attended Mass but professed no belief in God. They were equally censorious of the school in requiring such pupils to take part/attend.

Sliding Catholics accepted and generally welcomed the religious influence of school. It supported their sense of well-being which they felt was derived from their religious backgrounds, helped sustain their strong affinity towards the Catholic faith and encouraged their sense that they were 'good Catholics'

These general attitudes were shared by the majority within the 'lapsed Catholic' category and in three of its four subgroups who regarded Mass attendance and other religious elements of school life in a positive light.

The exceptions to this were Catholic Atheists (Lapsed Catholic, sub-group 3.4) and pupils who identified themselves as non-Catholics. Though small in number, these pupils simply 'put up with' the religious character and practices of the school, whilst at the same time, recognising the part they played in generating and sustaining its ethos, including its academic and social effectiveness.

Overall Conclusions

The purpose of this research, presented in two main sections, was to give a group of secondary school pupils an opportunity to voice their perceptions and understanding of what it means to them to 'be a Catholic' and to 'practise' their Catholic faith. These two separate, but connected, themes sought to investigate the degree to which, in a particular Catholic school community, the Catholic faith tradition is being preserved within the religious cultural triumvirate of parish, school and home. As with much research, a relatively simple question gives rise to a very diverse and nuanced answer.

Four main factors, however, were identified. This research showed, albeit in one particular school only, that parents have by far the greatest influence on their children when it comes to

99

the transmission of religion, belief and practice and therefore influences within the triumvirate are not equally weighted. For the majority of pupils the school is the place where they encounter the explicit values, attitudes and beliefs of the Catholic faith. It showed that, whether pupils self-identify as 'practising', 'sliding' or 'lapsed' Catholics, they all strongly identify **with being** Catholic, and in retrospect it showed, I suggest, that the use of pre-defined categories for identifying different 'types' of Catholic may inhibit understanding of what 'being Catholic' means to young people.

There is a paucity of research in this particular area and I hope my findings will add to that body of literature that others might find it useful in some way. My argument is that such research should consider the pupils' own understanding of *what it means to be Catholic at their age* since, for many pupils in my sample, the practice of their Catholic faith through parish church attendance seems alien, but living by Catholic values, attitudes and beliefs, as exemplified in the school, seems a perfectly natural thing to do, as does attending occasional school Masses and other acts of collective worship.

References

Alexander, H. A. & McLaughlin, T. II. (2003) Education in religion and spirituality, in: N. Blake, P. Smeyers, R. D. Smith & Paul Standish (eds) The Blackwell Guide to the Philosophy of Education, Oxford, Blackwell Publishers Limited, 356-73.

Ammerman, N. T. (2003) Religious identities and religious institutions, in: M. Dillon (ed) Handbook of Sociology of Religion, Cambridge, Cambridge University Press, 207-224.

Baumer, F. L. (1977) Modern European Thought: continuity and change in ideas, 1600–1950, New York, Macmillan Publishing.

Berger, P. (1973) The Social Reality of Religion, London, Penguin.

Casson, A. (2012) Fragmented Catholicity and Social Cohesion: faith schools in a plural society, London, Peter Lang International Academic Publishers.

Catholic Youth Ministry Federation (2010) Detailed Typology: mapping the terrain, London, CYMF.

Crawford, M. L. & Rossiter, G. M. (2006) Reasons for Living: education and young people's search for meaning, identity and spirituality, Melbourne, Australian Council for Educational Research.

Davie, G. (1999) Religion and Modernity: the work of Danièle Hervieu-Léger, in: K. Flanaghan & P. C. Jupp (eds) Postmodernity, Sociology and Religion, Basingstoke, St Martins Press.

Eckersley, R. (2005) Well and Good: morality, meaning and happiness, Melbourne, Text Publishing.

Egan, J. (1988) Opting Out: Catholic schools today, Leominster, Gracewing Publications.

Francis, L. J. (2002) Catholic schools and Catholic values? A study of moral and religious values among 13-15 year old pupils attending non-demoninational and Catholic schools in England and Wales, International Journal of Education and Religion, 3. 1. 69-84.

Fuller, R. (2001) Spiritual but Not Religious: understanding unchurched America, New York, Oxford University Press.

Fulton, J. D. (2000) Young Catholics at the New Millennium : the religion and morality of young adults in western countries, Dublin, University College.

Grace, G. (2002) Catholic Schools: mission, markets and morality, London, Routledge Falmer.

Greeley, A. (1998) Catholic Schools at the Crossroads: an American perspective, Dublin, Veritas.

Hervieu-Léger, D. (2000) Religion as a Chain of Memory, New Brunswick, N.J., Rutgers University Press.

Moberg, D. (1979) The development of social indicators of spiritual well-being for quality of life research, Sociology of Religion, 40. 1. 11-26.

Rossiter, G. (2010) Perspective on contemporary spirituality: implications for religious education in Catholic schools, International Studies in Catholic Education, 2. 2. 129-147.

Schweitzer, F. (2007) Religious individualization: new challenges to education for tolerance, British Journal of Religious Education, 29. 1. 89-100.

Smith, C. & Snell, P. (2009) Souls in Transition: the religious and spiritual lives of emerging adults, Oxford, Oxford University Press.

Smith, C. & Denton, M. L. (2005) Soul Searching: the religious and spiritual lives of American teenagers, Oxford, Oxford University Press.

Stock, M. (2005) Christ at the Centre: a summary of why the Church provides Catholic Schools, Coleshill, Archdiocese of Birmingham, Diocesan Schools Commission.

Wintersgill, B. (2008) Teenagers' perceptions of spirituality: a research report, International Journal of Children's Spirituality, 13. 4. 371-378.

Part 3: Aspects of Engagement and Performance

Five research papers are included in this section. Two are taken from doctoral theses; the other three are edited versions of reports commissioned either by the National Centre for Christian Education (NCfCE) itself or by outside bodies. These three reports are concerned, in different ways, with Academies; two with those provided by the Church of England, the third with institutions established in collaborative ventures between the Catholic Church and the Church of England.

A three year research programme was commissioned by the 'Church of England Academy Services Limited' (CASL) from the NCfCE in 2009. At that time CASL, established in 2007, was the in-house project management and service company for Church of England Academies. One of its functions was to assist the Church's development plan to establish 'one hundred new Church of England secondary schools' (Dearing, 2001). CASL's commission was in two parts. The first, a qualitative research project examined the character of the Christian ethos of a small group of Church of England Academies and the extent to which those most closely involved with the institution, staff, pupils etc., engage with its Christian educative mission. The second, complementary, quantitative research project, sought to evaluate the academic performance of a separate sample of CofE Academies.

The qualitative research team of **Alan Flintham, Elizabeth Green** and **David Moore** worked with ten Academies identified as both suitable by the commissioning body and (most importantly) the Principals of which were happy to be part of the project. The planned programme comprised four Academies to be visited during each of the calendar years 2010-11 and 2011-12 with the final two during 2012-13. Those Academies which had been established for the longest period comprised the first cohort, while the two Academies scheduled to be visited in the final year of the project opened in September 2010.

It was decided that the most effective mechanism would be based on a case-study approach, combining data from fieldwork observation, interviews, documentation and other archive material into an single 'narrative account' of our overall understanding, perceptions and inferences. That narrative would be supported by anonymised illustrative comments from some of the people we interviewed and inferences gained by the team during those interviews.

Unexpected events,[1] and individual decisions by Principals to withdraw from the research programme, necessitated changes to the original sample. In the event, by end of 2011 the

---

[1] In two instances planned visits subsequently coincided with Ofsted Inspections and had to be postponed. The Principal of a second withdrew from the programme because of difficulties in agreeing the timing of visits by the research team. The principals of two other Academies in the programme were suspended from duty - in one case just prior to the planned visits. Attempts to re-schedule following the appointment of a successor were unsuccessful.

research team had visited seven Academies – not all of which had been in the original sample.

A second, parallel research programme concerned with the Church of England Academies undertaken by **Ray Godfrey** and **Andrew B. Morris** used a quantitative approach for their project. They investigated the extent to which the Church of England educational strategy - articulated in the Dearing Report of 2001 - to provide one hundred new Church of England secondary schools met its academic objectives. That strategy envisaged the new schools would be established in areas of great social disadvantage, seek to improve educational standards and, as a result, ensure that all young people living in the locality would leave school leave with improved life chances through better and more appropriate qualifications. Central to these aims was a determination to have the widest and most inclusive admissions policies. Adherence to the Church of England or Christianity in general would not be a criterion. The schools were to be available for all who wanted them, irrespective of their religious beliefs or practice.

Their report analyses the academic performance of a small group of eight Church of England academies for which public domain data are available, including data on precursor schools. It draws exclusively upon data provided by the Department of Education school performance tables. It includes public examination and test data for the academic years 2003-04 (for the precursor schools only) to 2009-10. Following the introduction of the English Baccalaureate (EBac) qualification at the beginning of the academic year 2009-10, the performance of each academy in respect of the EBac has been included in the analysis. However, it is noted it should be interpreted with care as only a single year of data concerning this qualification are available. Seven of the eight Church of England Academies in the sample had precursor schools for which public domain data were available at the time. Only one had more than two years' public domain data on its own academic performance. Of the other seven, two had two years and the remaining four a single year's worth of data.

Constraints on the overall size of this book have necessitated some significant editing of this particular research project. After describing the general observations and conclusions that it was possible to draw from the full sample, detailed analyses of only three academies are included - those which have data for more than a single year. Analyses of all eight were featured in the original report prepared for CASL.

In addition to the effects of the editing outlined above, there are limitations in the data source of this study. The use of school performance tables ensures that there will always be some ambiguity in terms of how far each school served the interests of a less disadvantaged population and how far improved results are achieved for a more disadvantaged population. Recognising that the quantitative approach they have used can never probe beneath this ambiguity, they suggest that a more extensive longitudinal programme, including quantitative and qualitative methods, might give a more robust picture.

The more complex and challenging Joint Church Academies are the focus of **Elizabeth Green's** report.[2] She was commissioned in 2010 by NCfCE to investigate how they relate to existing academies and the maintained joint church school sector and also how they articulate their vision and ethos. At that time little empirical research had been carried out within academies and so this study sought to contribute towards our understanding of the culture and positioning of individual academies. Using a case study approach and drawing on open interviews and documentary analysis Elizabeth spent two years documenting the process of opening two such institutions and compared her findings with data from a more established Joint Church Academy.

While the vast majority (approx. 99%) of voluntary schools are Anglican or Catholic, the respective approach of each of those two Churches to the existence and purposes of their schools is somewhat different (Barber, 2012). The Church of England, as the established Church, set out to educate the nation at large. In contrast, the Catholic Church set out deliberately to create a complete and coherent system of schools for a particular community.

Consequently, Elizabeth's main research interests were focused on the ways in which jointly sponsored academies articulate their objectives and Christian ethos and the relationship between school structures and the ethos of this type of academy. Although limited in scope, it was, perhaps, no surprise that her study found joint academies to be sites of intersecting but competing fields of education, operating in relative isolation from the wider church school sector. Whilst sponsors were relatively clear about their aims and their understanding of a Christian school ethos there were crucial points at which these objectives appeared to be lost in translation which, she argued, had the potential to dilute the stated aims of the distinctively Christian based education they provide.

Gerry Bradbury's doctoral thesis explored concerns articulated, among others, by the current head of the Catholic Education Service, Paul Barber. He has argued that the Academies Act 2010, and the programme it promoted, introduced a fundamental change in the relationship between the Catholic Church and the State in respect of safeguards relating to the religious character of Catholic schools, and the rights of bishops and trustees prescribed under the provisions of the Education Act 1944. The possible impact on its existing and future educational provision, he argued, requires the Catholic Church to face the same questions and decisions about the threats and possibilities involved as it had in 1943 when the (then) Education Bill was being debated (Beales, 1950; Barber, 2012).

She looked at the parallels between the, sometimes, heated debates within the Church as to the merits of the 1944 Act and the varied response of dioceses to the academy programme introduced under the Academies Act 2010. As a Diocesan Director of Schools herself, her research was driven by her 'insider knowledge' of debates within the Church at the time and,

---

[2] Elements of the report were subsequently published in 2014 in the peer reviewed academic journal Research Papers in Education – see Green 2014.

in particular, by a comment made by a fellow Director at a conference to consider the implications of the legislation that "... we need to present a united front as we always have done or we stand to lose our schools." This perception of disunity arose, she notes, partially because of the variety of responses from dioceses which were prepared to embrace academy status for their schools, but also because of the divide between dioceses which would and those that would not allow their schools to seek academy status.

The extract included in this book concentrates on four key themes she identified which, she argues, dominate discussions in both 1943/44 and 2009/10. She uses them as a framework for her consideration of the implications of the 2010 Education Act and the dilemmas which the Catholic Church faces in reconciling its provision in a school system so radically different from the settlement of 1944.

The purpose of **Fiona Dineen's** research is to explore how primary school teachers understand their role in relation to the ethos and mission of the Catholic school in the context of contemporary Irish culture, arguing that an understanding of their lived reality is critical for planning and providing ongoing professional development for those intending to work in such institutions.

Her qualitative study is in two sections. In addition to outlining her chosen methodological framework for her research - using the concepts of habitus, field and capital (Bourdieu, P, 1971; 1977) and of spiritual capital (Grace, G. 2010) - the first section explores the historical, ecclesial and educational paradigms that influence the contemporary Catholic school, the socio-cultural context in which they operate in Ireland and the contested concept of school ethos.

The second section of the thesis describes the multiple lived realities that young primary school teachers experience of the ethos of a Catholic school. The four case studies bring into clear focus that only some of her sample have an authentic connection with the 'ideal' or 'expected' ethos of a Catholic school as defined by the Church, to the extent that they could be described as fitting the field of the Catholic school rather than mediating the mission of the Catholic school.

Her empirical findings, she argues, reflect the tensions that exist between the theory and practice of Catholic education in Church schools and, she concludes, should have particular relevance for those with responsibility for supporting the formation of educators for Catholic schools during initial teacher education and their ongoing professional formation.

References
Barber, P. (2012) Nineteen forty-four and all that: Christian schools and the political settlement, in: Morris. A. B. Re-imagining Christian Education for the 21st Century, Chelmsford, Matthew James Publishing, 9-28.

Beales A. F. C., The struggle for the schools, in: Beck, G. A. (ed) (1950) The English Catholics 1850-1950, London, Burns Oates, 365-409.

Bourdieu, P. (1967) Systems of education and systems of thought, paper presented to the Sixth World Conference of Sociology, (1966) and first published in International Social Studies Journal, 19. 3., in: E. Hopper (ed) (1971) Readings in the Theory of Educational Systems, London, Hutchinson & Co Ltd, 159-183.

Bourdieu, P. (1977) Outline of a Theory of Practice, Cambridge, Cambridge University Press.

Dearing, R. (2001) The Way Ahead: Church of England Schools in the New Millennium, London, Church House Publishing.

Grace, G. (2010) Grace, G. (2010) Renewing spiritual capital: an urgent priority for the future of catholic education internationally, International Studies in Catholic Education, 2. 2. 117-128.

Green, E. (2014) The negotiation and articulation of identity, position and ethos in joint church academies, Research Papers in Education, 29. 3. 285-299.

A Study of Ethos and Engagement in Seven Church of England Academies

Alan Flintham, Elizabeth Green & David Moore

Editor's Note

This is a report of one of two parallel research projects commissioned from Liverpool Hope's National Centre for Christian Education (NCfCE) by the Church of England Academy Services Ltd (CASL). This first project involved detailed case studies of seven Church of England Academies. The researchers' written notes/findings were collated into a first draft which was then checked for accuracy before being finalised. It comprised some 110 A4 pages and over 52,000 words in total. It was intended that CASL would receive the final report. Just a few weeks before its delivery, however, CASL ceased trading and, as a consequence, ceded all intellectual property rights to the collected data to NCfCE. In editing the report for inclusion in this book, the most important observations and overall conclusions arising from the case studies have been retained but the detailed findings relating to the individual Academies that were included in the report – comprising some 35,000 words – have been excluded.

Introduction and Context

This qualitative investigation looked for signs of Christian distinctiveness in the institutional **ethos** of seven Church of England sponsored Academies and for evidence of the extent of any **engagement** with that Christian distinctiveness by staff and pupils, and also of others connected with the various communities they served. It uses a case-study approach, combining data from fieldwork observation, interviews, documentation and other archive material into a single 'narrative account' supported by anonymised illustrative comments from interviews together with inferences gained by the research. While the small sample size requires that care should be taken before extrapolating from the findings, (for example, they should not be interpreted to as an over-arching model for effective Christian Academies), this study does provide some understanding, or 'thick description' of the quality, character and purposes of activities adopted by institutions that are all striving to implement the vision of Christian educational service of socially disadvantaged children contained in the Church Schools Review Group Report (Dearing, 2001).

Institutional Character, Ethos & Culture

Since 1998 all maintained schools with a religious character must have a description of what has been termed 'the ethos of the school' included in their Instrument of Government (School Standards & Framework Act, 1998, schedule 12. 1. G). Such schools that choose to convert to become Academies will retain both their religious and other characteristics derived from their previous designation and circumstances under the Education Act 1944 and subsequent education legislation (Hill, 2010, 2011).

The following statement was agreed by the Anglican Diocesan Directors of Education in 1999 and offered to Church of England schools as an appropriate definition of the character and purpose. It was re-stated in the report The Way Ahead, (Dearing, 2001, s. 3.24) as "...

the aspiration of all that Christian values and principles will ... run through every area of school life ... [so that] pupils will experience what it is to live in a community that celebrates the Christian Faith" (ss. 3.25; 3.28).

It is a statement of purpose that has been adopted by most Church of England schools and forms the backdrop against which the expansion of Church secondary provision – of which the Academy programme has been a major element – has been promoted. Since 1998 all schools which have a religious character must have a description of what has been termed 'the ethos of the school' included in their Instrument of Government (School Standards & Framework Act, 1998, schedule 12.1.g).

Model Ethos Statement – Church of England Schools

Recognising its historic foundation, the school will preserve and develop its religious character in accordance with the principles of the Church of England and in partnership with the Church at parish and diocesan level.

The school aims to serve its community by providing an education of the highest quality within the context of Christian belief and practice. It encourages an understanding of the meaning and significance of faith, and promotes Christian values through the experience it offers to all its pupils.

SOURCE: NATIONAL SOCIETY 1999

Notwithstanding the legislative framework, or the fact that on entering an institution a visitor will fairly quickly recognise the general feel of the place, the term 'ethos' has always been, and still remains a nebulous concept in relation to schools that defies easy definition, a problem perhaps most clearly seen in the variety of terms that have been used by those interested in studying institutional effectiveness. Other descriptive labels such as 'atmosphere', 'culture' and 'climate' are often used synonymously and indiscriminately but they all remain slippery concepts, capable of various interpretations. However, if it is a critical factor in our understanding of the effectiveness of organisations, then we need to be more precise.

Early Research
It has long been recognised that, even where schools may have very similar moral and educational purposes, some have few problems achieving their objectives, while others, drawing pupils from a similar background have many (Clegg, 1962; Shipman, 1968; Clegg & Megson, 1973). Many parents have always believed that some schools were better than others, had decided views that supported their belief, and a willingness to make sacrifices to ensure access to a particular school for their children. Nevertheless, it was not until the late 1970s and 1980s that the first significant empirical studies were published in England suggesting that the academic and social backgrounds of pupils were not the sole determining factors in a child's achievement at school in either the secondary (Reynolds, 1976; Rutter et al., 1979; Smith & Tomlinson, 1989) or primary phases (Mortimore et al., 1988).

The seminal work in England (Rutter at al., 1979) focused upon specific characteristics found to be associated with successful schools in a small sample of twelve London secondary institutions. Although the study was concerned with correlation and did not attempt to identify causality, it did suggest possible reasons that might lie in the features of schools considered as social systems. They identified an amalgam of values, attitudes and behaviours for which they used the term 'ethos' and which they used in the sense of 'what actually happens' in schools. It was something that, they suggested, might arise quite spontaneously and become habitual. Possible causal factors, they argued, included the history of the school, its expressed philosophy and chosen ways of working, shared activities between pupils and teachers toward an agreed common good which required them to work together so reducing potential conflict between them, and a variety of other variables outside the control of the school such as an academically balanced intake.

Commenting later on this research, in which she took part, Ouston indicated that the particular items associated with successful schools in their sample were merely indicators of the school's particular emphasis and were both causes and consequences of the particular school's climate. Further, it was recognised that schools in different circumstances might realise similar aims in quite different ways (Ouston, 1981).

Many other researchers at that time viewed the concept of school ethos in a similar way to Rutter et al., in as much as they linked it with a range of mechanisms or organisational characteristics in the effective schools that they have studied (Reynolds, 1982). Others have argued that it is more concerned with the way in which people deal with each other and the values which underpin the interpersonal relationships within the organisation (Bacon, 1979; Evans, 1982; Murgatroyd & Gray, 1982).

In similar work undertaken in America, Brookover, et al (1979), suggested:

> '... the cultural or social-psychological normative climate and the student status-role definitions which characterise the school social system explain much of the variance in achievement and behavioural outcomes of the school.'
>
> (Brookover, et al, 1979, pp. 135-136)

They argued further:

> '[This] clearly indicates that schools can produce whatever behaviour the school social system is designed to produce ... [and that] the school social system is no different from the family or other social organisations in that children learn to behave in the ways that the social system defines as appropriate and proper for them.'
>
> (Brookover, et al, 1979, p. 148)

Also from an American perspective, Anderson (1982) identified four recurring variables perceived, by either participants or outsiders, to be associated with positive pupil outcomes, but only one of which, the culture variable, was regarded as having a definite relationship. She describes this as "the value and belief systems of various groups within a school", but noted the lack of any understanding of how the variables interact with each other and other school factors (p. 308-404).

While it has become accepted, certainly by politicians, that there is a school effect on pupil outcomes - see for example a government review of more recent research that points to a number of institutional factors that may contribute to alleviating some of the pervasive and long-term negative effects of social deprivation (Department for Children, Schools & Families, 2009) - it has been argued elsewhere that school factors account for only 10-12% - at most - of inter-school differences, and that it is difficult to attribute those differences to any specific school factors (Goldstein & Sammons, 1997; Saunders, 1998; Gorard, 2006a). It is a complex process (Saunders, 1999; Meegan et al., 2002; Gorard 2006b).

Though the school effect may be a relatively small factor in the level of pupils' success at school, that there is some (small) institutional effect has become a focus for central and local government sponsored school improvement programmes and strategies. A number of school-based practices have been identified as being particularly supportive of pupil learning and attainment. They include, improving the quality of teaching and school leadership at all levels, the nature of teacher/pupil interaction, and developing positive school/parent involvement (DCSF, 2009). The report also notes that "the creation of a positive school culture is the key factor in the improvement of schools in socio-economically disadvantaged areas" (p. 67). It is rather vague, however, as to the composition of that 'positive culture' and the acceptable methods whereby it can be created (DCSF, 2009)

Schools as Social Systems
Examining what communities or groups value and how they interact with each other has its roots in cultural anthropology (see, for example, Mead, 1928, 1930, 1935). Discussions within this field contain common themes such as values, beliefs and rituals.

American writers adapted and popularised the concept of a group or community culture for both business and education (see, for example, Geetz, 1973; Deal, 1985, 1987, 1991; Purkey and Smith, 1983; Deal & Kennedy, 1983; Bolman & Deal 1991; Schultz, 1994; Schneider et al., 1996; Deal & Peterson, 1999; Angelides & Ainscow, 2000). However, definitions often lacked clarity as can be seen in the view expressed that the 'atmosphere', 'ethos' or 'feel of an organisation' reflects both its climate and culture [since] an organisation's values and beliefs - part of culture - influence their interpretations of policies, procedures and practices which in turn generate an organisation's climate (Schneider et al., 1996, p. 9).

From an anthropological perspective, it has been argued that a school's character reflects deep patterns of values, beliefs, and traditions that have been formed over long periods of time, influenced by social, economic and political forces (see, for example, Handy, 1976, 1988; Nias, 1989; Deal and Peterson, 1999; Furlong, 2000). Similarly, Greenfield has argued "above all, organisations are patterns of living, ways of seeing the world ... the meanings we find in our lives" (Greenfield, 1993a, p. 54) and that children "do not learn from 'environments', resources or from 'characteristics of teachers' [but] from their specific involvement with people, things and events around them" (Greenfield, 1993b, p. 21).

School Character and Effectiveness
Cunningham and Gresso (1993) argued "[A]ll schools have cultures; strong or weak, functional or dysfunctional [but] ... successful schools seem to have strong and functional cultures aligned with a vision of excellence in schooling ... strong, functional cultures [which] must be nourished, nurtured and supported through the correlates of cultural development" (p. 50). This is consistent with the long held expectation in England that schools should be communities in their own right, where children are expected to develop socially responsible attitudes, dispositions and virtues, as well as being places of formal academic teaching and learning.

Identifying what factors might generate an educational environment conducive to successful outcomes is, however, somewhat problematical. Hargreaves (1997) argues that the personal characteristics of members of successful school cultures are composed of openness, informality, care, attentiveness, lateral working relationships, reciprocal collaboration, candid and vibrant dialogue, and willingness to face uncertainty together. Others have suggested the possible importance of a shared world view, or school members having common constitutive values, as contributory factors (Beare et al, 1989; Fullan & Hargreaves, 1991; Strike, 1999; 2000).

However, the concepts developed by organisational theory portraying schools as orderly and rational systems based on shared goals may be inadequate and that they are, to some degree, more complex than many of the systems and organisation theorists suggest in comparison with other types of institution (Ball, 1987; Handy & Aitken, 1990). For example, it has been suggested that schools are essentially anarchic organisations with loosely coupled and fluid groups of individuals (Weick, 1976, 1982; Orton & Weick, 1990; Fusarelli, 2002) some of whom may not necessarily subscribe at a personal level to manifest, or stated, characteristics the organisation (Becker & Greer, 1960; Hogan, 1984; Handy, 1988; Flynn, 1993; Arthur, 1995; Morris & Marsh, 2002; Green, 2012). Consequently, the character of a particular school, it can be argued, will be combination of its official, stated, manifest or custodial objectives – the ethos statement required by legislation - and the collective responses of school members to that statement (Hogan, 1984; Donnelly, 2000, 2004).

Whether there is an optimum organisational culture for the provision of successful education is also open to question. Not all educational communities will have the same constitutive elements and, consequently, it is argued, the practical expression of their educative character will vary, producing differing educational environments yet each might be both academically and socially effective since there are complex interrelationships and influences between individuals, their families, neighbourhoods, communities and schools that act upon pupil outcomes of various kinds (Saunders, 1999). What may be important is not any particular cultural characteristics, but the degree of congruence that exists between the educative-cultural expectations and understanding of the major stake-holders in the educational enterprise. In other words, the level of agreement about the mission of the school and the degree to which the curriculum and pedagogical approach is consistent with its accepted purpose (Egan & Francis, 1986; Morris, 1996, 2005; Green, 2009; 2012).

Ethos or Culture

In a reference to the requirements of the Schools Standards and Framework Act 1998 set out at the beginning of this section, a former Minister of State for Education argued:

> *'Ethos is an incredibly important thing. And the best schools – whether faith schools or not – have understood that and have run with it.'*
>
> (Knight, J., 2009).

This somewhat simplistic statement is, to some extent, evidentially based and reflects research of institutional character that has taken place over the previous twenty-five years or so. However, within that research the multiplicity of terms that have been used – 'atmosphere', 'feel', 'climate', 'culture' and 'ethos' – have long served more to confuse than clarify (Strivens, 1985; Alldei, 1993; Solvason, 2005; Glover & Coleman, 2005). Nevertheless, two main perspectives can be discerned.

A positivist perspective views 'ethos' or 'culture' as something which prescribes social reality. In this sense, conferred by some sort of authority, it is an objective phenomenon, existing independently of the people and social events within an organisation and can, in some cases, be used to constrain behaviour (Hogan, 1984) – a school's 'ethos' statement might be just such a case.

From an interpretive perspective, an institutional 'ethos' or 'culture' emerges from individual and group interaction and is located in the realms of meaning and interpretation. In this view, it is about social interaction and social process; not independent of the institution but of necessity inherently bound up within it (Donnelly, 2000, 2004). In respect of schools, it can only be understood and researched as a process which responds both to prescription by key internal actors (both those who provide the school and those who work and study in them) and by the attendant social and political culture in which they are located.

A close reading of the literature illustrates how the terms 'ethos' and 'culture' can be used as aspiration, as an outward or inward attachment by individuals within an organisation. When we speak of organisational culture we are only concerned with the norms and values which are generally held by the members of that organisation, about the ways in which they interact with each other – in other words "how we do things here". The ethos of an institution, however, is a broader concept, combining both the objectives inherent in its defined purposes and the response of the members to those objectives. Consequently, for the purposes of this project we use the term 'ethos' as we examine the objectives of the school and the values rehearsed by those in authority, that is, the principal, governors, including church representatives and the managing authority of the school, together with the staff and pupils that, collectively, comprise the 'school community'. As such, what we hold it to be becomes a multi-dimensional concept with each dimension offering a different lens through which to research an organisation. We believe such an approach will help illuminate the essential elements of the character of Church of England Academies generally, and individually how they function effectively in their local circumstances. We take as our starting point that a Christian school ethos has a spiritual dimension (another slippery concept) and is located in the realms of social interaction. It is negotiated as well as imposed, and as a multi-faceted and multi-dimensional concept it will require multiple sources of data and different levels of inquiry.

If that is the case, to write of schools having a 'unique' character is, in many ways, overly simplistic. If it is the multi-faceted/multi-dimensional concept we claim, it will require multiple sources of data and different levels of inquiry. For the most part, therefore, we would argue that qualitative methods which focus on meaning and social construction as we explore the lived reality of engagement with that ethos as it is experienced by classroom teachers, students and support staff are arguably best placed to capture the different dimensions of institutions in our sample. One such approach has been developed by the French sociologist/philosopher/anthropologist, Pierre Bourdieu. His framework for social analysis assumes that people are always situated within a specific culture which subconsciously, rather than self-consciously, influences their ways of working and their world view (Bourdieu, 1986, 1989, 1998; see also Eacott, 2010; Green 2012).

It will provide the context for our qualitative investigation of the way that individual Church of England Academies enforce their particular (arbitrary) schools rules, norms and customs with pupils, parents and staff, that is, their particular 'ethos'.[1] While the concept of a school 'ethos' or 'culture' conducive to academic effectiveness seems to offer an appropriate paradigm for this research project, there are some drawbacks. Major problems include defining a somewhat nebulous concept, the difficulty in identifying valid independent organisational variables and also the extent to which any findings from one sample can be generalised to other institutions whose external circumstances may be very different. However, despite ambiguities in the concept and difficulties with the methodology involved in adequately measuring its precise effects on levels of academic achievement and behaviour, it seems that it is an essential element in understanding what schools are trying to do and the processes by which they attempt to achieve their aims, and this in turn is likely to shed light on what schools do and how they function. For the purposes of this study we have used the term 'ethos' as the guiding theme of our investigations.

Research Methods: Techniques and Strategies
The research brief was to identify the contribution and impact of the Christian ethos on students in Church of England sponsored academies using both qualitative and quantitative research methods as appropriate. For the purposes of the qualitative investigation it was

---

[1] This definition/approach is also used in the second study commissioned by CASL examining the academic performance of a different small sample of CofE Academies - see Morris & Godfrey.

decided that the most effective mechanism would be based on a case-study approach, combining data from fieldwork observation, interviews, documentation and other archive material into an single 'narrative account' of our overall understanding, perceptions and inferences. That narrative would be supported by anonymised illustrative comments from some of the people we interviewed and inferences gained by the team during those interviews.

Even so, our chosen approach is not straight forward. There are a number of difficulties inherent in any case study methodology that has to be addressed. These include, among others, the degree to which descriptive accounts of an institution, course or activities in one situation can be generalised outside the particular context. There are also issues concerning the way in which access to institutions and personnel is secured and the inevitably fragmentary and selective nature of the evidence that is gathered, not to mention the interactive effects between the researcher and the subject(s) being studied. In this particular case, while all members of the research team, including those involved in proving background information and preparing the initial draft report were practising and committed Christians, they were not all members of the Church of England.

Consequently, we have adopted, what some researchers regard as useful, a distinction between our methodology and methods. The former is regarded as being to do with the values, principles and assumptions underlying the researchers' approach to their subject for which we developed a conceptual map[2] that guided the ways in which we undertook the investigation and help illuminate our findings and understanding; the latter referring to the particular processes of data collection and recording.

Data collection and recording
The main methods the team have employed are interviews and observation with a (very) little documentary analysis. Restriction on the time available for the research led to the adoption of a non-participant observational approach to understand teaching and learning mechanisms within each of the seven Academies we visited. However, the subject of our study was more general; being concerned with the essential characteristics of school culture and ethos in Christian educational establishments sponsored by the Church of England. Interviews seemed to be the most appropriate and effective means for us to achieve that understanding.

We recognised that while some documentary information might be available, much of our data would come from talking with as wide a variety of individuals as possible through formal interviews or casual conversations. Given the time constraints most conversations would, necessarily, be in formal settings, making it a little harder to develop empathy with the interviewees, win their confidence and, at the same time, avoid influencing the interviewees.

---

[2] This is an adaption of ideas developed by a colleague, Dr Caitlin Donnelly of Queens University Belfast, to whom we give our grateful thanks – see figure 1.

Documents are a useful source of data in qualitative research, but they have to be treated with care. While they might give useful information for this project they do not all necessarily provide an objective truth. They have to be contextualised within the circumstances of their construction. Consequently, we have used material from the academy prospectus and/or its website as our main source of information about the proclaimed or official proclamation of each individual Academy's purpose, mission, and ethos.

Using our conceptual map as our investigatory framework our major source of data was derived from a series of semi-structured interviews with governors, staff and students who had agreed to take part in the research project.

Wherever possible interviews took place in a suitably neutral and relaxing environment chosen for us by the Academy. As is usual with this type of data collection, we worked hard to establish an appropriately relaxed rapport with the interviewees before explaining the purposes of our research. Since all had already been fully briefed about the project – at least in theory – there was little noticeable reticence shown by the interviewees in responding to any of our questions.

We recorded answers verbatim and these notes, together with other observations and conclusions were written up as soon as possible at the end of the fieldwork visits.

Sampling
Representative sampling cannot always be achieved in qualitative research because of:
- the initially largely exploratory nature of the research;
- problems of negotiating access;
- the sheer weight of work and problems of gathering and processing data using only one set of eyes and ears.

Such was the case with this project where we relied upon volunteers, both in respect of the Academies that agreed to take part and the people we were able to meet which was at the discretion of the Principal/Headteacher. Our interviewees must, therefore, be regarded as opportunistic rather than a statistically random sample, which may affect the balance of views that we obtained. Nevertheless, since we were seeking to make some generalised observations about our sample Academies, 'naturalistic' sampling as far as it was possible was desirable.

Thus, in studying teachers' or pupils' perspectives of the Christian ethos of the Academy and degrees of engagement with it by differing members of the community, we considered them in different settings, since behaviour can differ markedly in different situations - for example, the formal circumstances of a teacher's classroom or office, the staffroom, different classrooms, etcetera. We applied the same principles with the pupils and, as far as possible, tried to ensure we have sampled according to appropriate criteria, such as age, gender, ethnicity and experience.

We recognise that, although it would be advantageous to have a sample the size and nature of which would enable to make valid general statement applying across similar institutions, including those not involved in our survey, we had, in fact, an opportunity sample in those areas where access was offered and facilitated by the Academy concerned. Consequently, we recognise that that generalised claims about all Church of England Academies cannot be made by extrapolating from the findings of this small opportunity sample.

Research Validity and Reliability
The question of reliability and the internal validity of any findings arising from this evaluation is crucial if they are to have credibility. This is particularly the case with ethnographic fieldwork and case studies, which must always be subjective to some degree.

A second problem inherent in any evaluation of the sort undertaken for this Report is that the researchers are more than just active elements in the process. They cannot be totally impartial and, consequently, bring a personal bias into their research. That bias or ideology can vary and may not feature in a researcher's consciousness but, nevertheless, there cannot be, it is argued, such a thing as pure, neutral or disinterested research. Underlying such views is the concept that research is a social activity and, consequently, any findings and observations arising from it can only be understood within the context of the values, attitudes and beliefs of all the participants, including the researcher.

Consequently, we have included brief biographical details of the evaluation team so that readers "will be better able to assess the validity, reliability and generalisability of that particular research ..." (Walford, 1991, p.5). This will be the approach taken in this report. However, Walford also states "these accounts do not pretend to present the truth about the research or even about the research methods ... but they do give a further perspective on the way in which research is conducted" (Walford, 1991, p.5). Conversely, it is important for the reader to guard against assessing the validity of what we have written on the basis of our self-defined status or (assumed) integrity. However, we trust that the brief 'pen portraits' will be of some value and help illuminate our perceptions and explain any glaring errors in our understanding – of which we hope there will be few.

With this particular evaluation it can be argued that external validity is not critical. In one sense the prime purpose is not so much to generalise to other Church school providers or other Church of England dioceses, but to understand the character of these particular Academies which, depending on their development, may influence future decisions with Church of England diocese and schools. On the other hand, our investigation may show that certain ways of understanding and implementing the principles within this project have supportive or detrimental effects on the Christian character, ethos and mission.

The extent to which any such findings could be generalised might usefully be addressed in a subsequent and more extensive survey since our primary concern is to understand the findings of this particular project rather than to actively campaign in any particular direction. However, we do recognise that proponents of particular approaches to the on-going renewal and development of Church of England Academies may well use any reliable and valid findings arising from our evaluation for their own policy objectives.

Ethical Issues - Confidentiality

We used an orthodox, open and explicit approach to issues of confidentiality. Permission to undertake the research with the institutions and individuals involved was obtained initially via CASL and, subsequently, the Principals of the Academies in our sample. The purpose and nature of the evaluation was clearly explained beforehand and repeated verbally when the team visited each Academy. In addition, Principals were asked to brief potential interviewees and the school community generally. All interviewees were assured that the purpose was not to evaluate them or their performance of their roles within the Academy. All were assured, repeatedly, of the confidentiality of the evaluation process and any findings, in the sense that no individuals would be identified by name, though it was clear that it might be possible for anyone who was familiar with a particular Academy parish to make an educated guess of the source of any reported observations and inferences included in the Report.

Fieldwork

In the light of our conceptual map, and in order to understand the effectiveness of schools designated as 'Christian' in the sense of their Christian character or 'ethos', both in a positive (conferred by an authority – see Hogan 1984) and interpretive sense (emerging from individual and group interaction – see Donnelly, 2000, 2004), the research team, comprising three experienced researchers, adopted a two pronged process, looking initially for evidence of the nature of Christian distinctiveness – if any – and, subsequently, for evidence of the impact of that particular ethos on the daily life and experience of those involved in their various ways in the life of each Academy.

Visits to the various Academies were arranged in two stages. The first, by a single researcher, comprised one full day of interviews with the Principal, other senior leaders, department heads, subject teachers and support staff. They were designed to gain an understanding of the Academy's value system and its 'ethos' seeking to establish:
- what it is and where it came from;
- what is its distinctiveness;
- what drives it; and
- what delivers it?

Following that initial visit to each Academy, and in the light of any existing relevant documentation, a draft report of the notes/findings was passed to the two researchers comprising the follow-up team. They visited the Academy some time during the week following the initial visit[3] having been briefed about the findings and conclusions drawn about the Academy's stated ethos and value system. Their primary concern was to evaluate the levels and nature of the engagement of the pupils, and the impact upon them, of the

---

[3] While this was the intention, it was not always possible and the time between visits varied. On occasions they were conducted on consecutive days; on others there was a more than a week's gap.

117

Academy's ethos through an analysis of lesson observations and pupil interviews conducted together over one and a half days: one full school day plus the following morning.

Principals/Headteachers had been asked to brief staff in advance about the lesson observations, stressing that:
- the purpose of research was not to evaluate the particular Academy but was concerned with ethos and & engagement within the generality of Church of England Academies;
- the Researchers not watching teachers but what children experience;
- the Researchers may be present for the full or a part of a lesson;
- the availability of the lesson plan was not a requirement but a copy would be helpful;
- lessons would be chosen 'at random', but with sensitivity, in discussion with the Principal/Headteacher;
- all participants and findings would be anonymised.

Observations and Conclusions
We have set out below a selection of the most notable observations and conclusions extracted from the detailed 'thick descriptions' of our field visits. They are concerned with the Christian character and theological underpinning of the Academies and the engagement, experience and understanding of the pupils in the religious mission, their leadership and the religious commitment/adherence of staff.

Of the seven CofE Academies in our sample, only one has been open for more than five years – allowing one full cohort to have completed their compulsory secondary education. However, Northern Community Academy (opened in 2006) had only been fully operational for four years at the time of the first of our Academy field visits in 2010. Of the other academies in our sample, two opened in 2007 (Eastmid and North London Church), one in 2009 (Lower Midshire) and three in 2010 (South Central, Bishopchurch and Nortex). Consequently, none of these could be regarded as fully, or even almost fully established.

Observations – Leadership
The whole of chapter eight of the Dearing Report (2001) had been devoted to the leadership, management and governance of (future) Church of England schools, while a further section (appendix 5) concentrated upon the idea of vocation in teaching and leadership. While acknowledging that there is no single 'right' model for the leadership of a CofE school, Dearing stresses the need for leaders to try and live the Christian values they are trying to embed. From that perspective, the quality of leadership shown by the Principals/Headteachers of all seven Academies was of a very high order. It was recognised as such, not only by the researchers, but also by their colleagues at various levels within the respective institutions.

> **An effusively charismatic Principal ... lead by example to cascade, embed and eternalise those [Christian] values throughout the institution.**

118

> **[The Academy is] energised by the enthusiastic leadership of an
> eternally optimistic, interactive and charismatic Principal,**

Excellent and effective leadership from the Principal/Headteacher was critical to the level of success achieved by the Academies we visited. It is the case, however, that leading this new form of Church of England institution, rooted in the recommendations of the Dearing Report 2001 to be both distinctively Christian (para. 1.6; 1.8) and inclusive (3.28-31; 3.36) required special skills, for which some may not have been prepared and for whom training should be provided (Johnson, 2003). Those responsible for selection and appointments in our sample Academies, sponsors and governors, had clearly recognised that fact, had worked hard to secure the services of high quality people ensure and were not afraid to take swift action if their expectations were not met. Visits to two Academies were cancelled when the respective Principals, in post for just over a year in each case, were suspended from duty and subsequently dismissed. We have no information as to the reasons for the procedures.

Christian Character

In the light of the statement that "all Church [of England] schools must be distinctively and recognisably Christian institutions (Dearing, 2001, 1.6) we considered the extent to which that aspiration had been met in our sample. Six of the seven Academies claimed/stated in documentation, on their website or in conversation (sometime in all three contexts) their Church of England status and character.

> **They [governors] talked eloquently about the nature of the discussions
> and debate that led to their establishment and the importance that
> documents, such as the Dearing Report, made in their initial thinking.**

However, we think it most important to record that, albeit at an early stage in their development, we regarded only one Academy as fully meeting the aspirations of the Church of England has for its new Academies.

> **This is a successful Church of England Academy. [One] of key
> features that make it so [is] a strong commitment from the Principal
> to make a vision of a Church of England school serving its community
> clear; based upon a theological understanding of the mission of the
> Church in the city.**

But we also noted of another Academy that, while it recognises and acknowledges that it is sponsored by the Church of England

> **... [It] does not make any claim to be of itself a Christian institution ...
> [but] certainly has some of the best features of the finest of Christian
> Church schools.**

On the other hand, the development of Christian distinctiveness has been difficult in some institutions.

> **There is recognition of *'a need to be more distinctive regarding our Christian ethos'*, although the Acting Chaplain was unable to articulate what that increased distinctiveness might be.**

Given that the political circumstances and imperatives behind the government's academies programme have been concerned primarily with finding ways of 'improving educational standards' all but one of our Academy sample have been established by converting existing failed or failing schools. It is understandable, therefore, that there is pressure to give priority to improving pupil behaviour and academic performance.

> **Its primary focus has been to raise the expectations of staff, ally fears of change, silence or move on dissenters, increase pace and rigour and monitor progress towards a 'less sloppy, high expectation can-do culture' ... [and] raising expectations and securing [academic] improvement**

Theological Framework

To some extent the difficulties seemed to be connected more with of a lack of theological literacy on behalf of some key members within the various Academies than their actions and aspirations, or with the physical circumstances, location or pupil intake which can militate against the best of intentions.

> **With the exception of the Principal, [the Academy's stated] values although recognisable as 'gospel values') were not specifically couched in Christian terms nor related to the Christian story.**

> **Whilst it seems that governors, the Principal and the Chaplain are attempting to think through the theology that underpins their ethos there was less evidence that they were aware of the nature of the connection between Christian ethos and teaching and learning.**

External factors associated with the school communities prior to conversion, sometimes seen as being 'taken over' however, did make the task even harder for some of the new Academies.

> **There was a failure at the outset to clarify, demythologise and promulgate the community-focussed service mission of the academy to a severely disadvantaged area.**

> **The Academy serves a community traditionally resistant to change which 'is not Christian but has had Christianity thrust upon it'.**

Nevertheless, there are examples of real success, despite the difficulties.

> The Academy is managed by a Team comprising Governors, Principal and Chaplain who appear to have a clear vision for the Christian ethos of the Academy underpinned for most by a personal Christian faith. The principal cited with approbation a comment of the visiting Deputy Diocesan Director of Education in observing ... "this now feels like a Church Academy"

Christian Commitment/Religious Adherence

Working on the, rather crude, assumption that it is particularly difficult to 'pass on what you do not have yourself' we looked at the range of religious commitment and self-identified adherence to a religious world view of the Academy employees. Predictably, none of them were fully staffed with committed, practicing Anglicans in full communion with the Church of England.[4] On the other hand, all the senior leadership teams were committed Christians who saw their work in their respective Academies as part of the Church's educative mission and a personal (religious) vocation, especially in cases where there may be a minority of Christian staff and pupils.

> This is a strongly badged and overtly 'in your face' Christian Academy in terms of its Christian ethos. It displays little truck with a philosophy of 'here for all faiths and none' but makes it clear to students and staff that the Christian ethos is the one they have bought in to. All appear to be well content with the prevailing ethos as synthesised and promulgated by Principal and Chaplain

> The Christian views and beliefs of senior staff inform how they interact with each other and the students. They model well how to treat and value others.

> [The Academy] serves the community in the broadest way possible by actually modelling those Christian values in action

> However, the personal faith commitment of the Head teacher, senior staff and others on the staff does ensure that there is a personal religious commitment that underlies their work and makes itself manifest in the high level of commitment to the students and the moral and ethical framework they are brought up in.

> The Academy is managed by a Team of Governors, Principal and Chaplain who appear to have a clear vision for the Christian ethos of the Academy underpinned for most by a personal Christian faith.

> Christian values are "not seen in how we are badged up, but by their fruits shall ye know them".

---

[4] Interestingly, there were a number of Catholics in senior positions and a wide variety of faith or non-faith perspectives among the teaching and support staff.

However committed the senior staff may be, they depend upon others to help implement the Christian mission of the Academy for the community of pupils (and their parents) since they are the ones who will be most involved in providing the day-to-day experiences that will make Christian education manifest. In most cases staff seemed to have risen to the task, though they have not always, perhaps, fully understood what was being asked of them, or appreciated the theological foundation and purposes of their institution.

> **Whilst Christian ethos is overt, it is not enough 'to frighten the horses' of parents, community and the majority of staff who are not active Christians**

> **Staff are a mixture of a minority of active Christians and a minority of non-believers together with a majority of 'passive Christians'.**
> **The cross-section of staff interviewed represented a variety of faith perspectives amongst such members. They were able to articulate, and to exemplify using a variety of terminologies and examples, the core values of the academy in terms of respect, endurance, service, justice, compassion, trust, forgiveness and a strong sense of koinonia (although they would not necessarily recognise or approve of the term).**

> **There is an acceptance that Christian values do underpin the work of the academy; are 'not in your face' but are rather present in 'an ethos of acceptance' revealed in an open-mindedness 'which respects all faiths and none'.**

> **Sufficient Support Staff have a personal faith commitment or commitment to a school serving a difficult catchment that senior staff can call upon and utilise to make concrete what a Christian church ethos is and how it manifests itself.**

We noted in a number of our sample Academies, a balancing act taking place with various degrees of success in harnessing the good will of staff. There were few objections or outright opposition to the institution's Christian character expressed, though that that does not imply, of course, that everyone adopted or developed a positive attitude.

> **... [the] task is "not to alienate people en route but to take them with us" ... that "some of the details of the route of the journey will need to be revisited" ... but the overall direction of travel as laid down by the sponsors still remains.**

> **This [success] is based on clearly articulated Christian values and that carry all people of faith and no faith.**
> **There is a very strong sense that this remains a 'sponsor-led' school, with the dominant influence on vision and development of ethos residing with the Diocese as the lead sponsor.**

> ... staff of a non-Christian persuasion feel they 'can sign up to the ethos without having to believe in what underpins it.'

> [Official statements such as] this is no 'here for all faiths and none' creed, ... 'the principal aim of Religious Education ... is to affirm, encourage and challenge students on their spiritual journey' ... [enable] senior staff to challenge dissent (for example, over attendance at the specifically formal Christian nature of assemblies) by indicating that 'you knew what you were buying into.'

> There is still some disquiet over the more overt nature of the Christian focus and the role of the sponsors in promulgating it.

Given that, in most instances, the majority of staff would have transferred from their predecessors school(s) under the term of employment legislation existing at the time,[5] it is perhaps not surprising that there was a mixed response to the Christian character of the new Church of England Academies, and that would have an impact on the way in which the pupils responded to, and engaged with, the educative mission they offered.

Pupil Engagement/Understanding

In the main, the Academies in our sample were serving a very mixed population, in the sense that admission criteria are fully inclusive and, consequently, religious activity among a significant proportion of parents and pupils was often non-existent. The lack of any experience of a religious life or world view among pupils made the task of explaining to them what being 'distinctively Christian' meant in such a way that they could appreciate and (choose to) become theologically engaged with the day-to-day educational activities that were provided, extremely difficult, even for the most committed of staff. It is, perhaps, understandable why students were unsure about the Christian character of their Academy.

> Students are well aware that this is a Church school ... they respected the fact ... they attend collective worship ... [but] tended to see being a Church school as being [only] concerned with uniform, behaviour and religious services.

> Students struggled to articulate the meaning of Eucharist practice, or the Christian symbolism that they had been exposed to during collective worship such as the use of incense.
> There was a big gap between what the adults thought a Christian school was like and what the students felt it was about.

---

[5] The Transfer of Undertakings (Protection of Employment) Regulations (TUPE) came into force on 6th April 2006. The regulations protect employees' terms and conditions of employment when a 'business' is transferred from one owner to another: in this case when a Community or Church of England school maintained by the local authority converted to an Academy. Employees of the previous 'owner' automatically become employees of the Academy on conversion on the same terms and conditions as they enjoyed in their previous school.

> Students ... demonstrated that they appeared to lack an understanding of why participation in worship, in particular the Eucharist, was expected or important.

> ... they [students] understood that the diocese was the sponsor but didn't know anything else about it, felt under no compulsion to go to services, knew there was a prayer room but did not feel compelled in any way to attend ... that assemblies always included prayer.

In some instances, the low level of their engagement could be, at least in part, attributed to the inadequacies, not so much in the rhetoric or a lack of Christian iconography, but more in deficiencies in curriculum content and pedagogy.

> ... as yet the Christian ethos has had little impact on the curriculum.

> ... the talk is too abstract and the language of what it is about is unclear to students.

> While there were no overtly Christian positions imposed on students within lessons there is a very strong sense of moral, ethical and generally religious underpinning to the teaching and to aspects of lesson contents.

> In the lessons observed no explicit connections were made between classroom pedagogy, or curriculum and the Christian ethos.

> One student said 'they don't explain what lies behind what is done'.

> Students ... engaged and active participants in the worship but ... this is not uniform practice across all mentor groups, some use the session to talk, to complete administrative tasks or [play] curriculum games.

> The wider ethos did not articulate clearly enough the underlying principles of service to others, commitment to searching for meaning or the development of inner peace/calm that enables students to explore their spiritual side more deeply. Opportunities to explore the implications of faith or non-faith belief [in RE lessons] were few. It helped explain ... their lack of understanding of aspects of worship.

Despite the concerns of a poor level of active engagement there were very few accounts/incidents of which we were made aware where pupils were particularly concerned about or, apparently, actively rejected the Christian character of their Academy.

> They were upset that going up for Eucharist or a blessing was no longer voluntary and that no reason for the change had been given.

> **One female student in year eleven said that she didn't pay attention in RE; she had been to a church primary school and she felt that this did not feel very much like a Christian school in comparison. She explained that at primary school they would sing and worship, 'that showed me it was a Christian school'. She said 'we don't seem to have Christian beliefs shown in the school, for some people who are Christian they can't show it and others could learn from Christians'.**
> **Some year 7 pupils had been reportedly 'rattled by the change' (to a more overtly Christian ethos) and had left the Academy as a consequence.**

What all the students we interviewed seemed to agree on, in all seven academies we visited, was that their teachers (and other staff) were supportive, that they felt safe from bullying and that they were cared for. Given the circumstances in some of the precursor schools, this is no small achievement, though it is our view that to be truly Christian institutions these Academies must find way of emphasising more than care, containment and soft love.

Summary and Conclusions

In this report we have not attempted to test a theory about successful models of Church of England Academy. Rather we have tried to understand the quality, character and purposes of the educational activities in seven number such institutions in the hope that, though working with a small unrepresentative sample, we could produce the sort of richly detailed material that is sometimes termed 'thick description' using the conceptual map below (figure 1) which illustrates our chosen structure for investigating institutional ethos.

Figure 1

Description of Ethos	Dimension of Ethos	Evident in ...	Research Method
Superficial	Aspirational	Documentation & statements from school authorities e.g. governors, sponsors	Review of documents; semi-structured interviews with school authorities
	Outward attachment	School organisational structures; physical environment; observable behaviours of individuals and groups within school	Review of documents; semi-structured interviews with school members (teaching & non-teaching staff/pupils)
Deep	Inward attachment	Individual's deep seated thoughts, feelings, perceptions and attitudes; observable behaviours inside and outside school of individuals and groups; personal beliefs	Review of documents; in-depth formal and informal conversations with school members; long-term observation of personal, organisational interactions and processes

Using these approaches we are trying to go beyond mere fact and surface appearances and present detail, context, emotion and the webs of social relationships that join people to one another. In 'thick description', the voices, feelings, actions and meanings of interacting individuals are heard (Denzin, 1989, p. 83). It evokes emotionality and self-feelings. It inserts history into experience and establishes the significance of an experience, or the sequence of events, for the individuals in question.

The observations and conclusions extracted from the detailed 'thick descriptions' of our field visits are concerned with the Christian character and theological underpinning of the Academies and the engagement, experience and understanding of the pupils in the religious mission, their leadership and the religious commitment/adherence of staff. These, we believe, are crucial to the success or otherwise, of the Academies programme we have been commissioned to review.

While care should be taken before extrapolating from our observations derived from this modelling, our approach can often highlight new ideas or concepts that cast new light on the activity under study, and which might help us understand similar activity elsewhere. This is what we have tried to do with our sample of Church of England Academies; recognising that we will not, and cannot, produce an over-arching model to which all such Academies should aspire. However, that does not mean that there cannot be some generally valid insights to be drawn from our observations which may be of use to those who, in the future, will be considering whether or not to seek to establish new Church of England Academies or convert existing schools to this alternative status.

References
Allder, M. (1993) The meaning of school ethos, Westminster Studies in Education, 16. 59-69.
Anderson, C. S. (1982) The search for school climate: a review of the research, Review of Educational Research, 52. 3. 368-420.
Angelides, P. & Ainscow, M. (2000) Making sense of the role of culture in school improvement, School Effectiveness and School Improvement, 11. 2. 145-163.
Arthur, J. (1995) The Ebbing Tide: policy and principles of Catholic education, Leominster, Gracewing.
Ball, S. J. (1987) The Micro-Politics of the School: towards a theory of school organization, London, Methuen.
Bacon, G. (1979) Through the classroom window, in: Perspectives 1 - The Rutter research, Exeter, Exeter University School of Education, 16-23.
Beare, H., Caldwell, B. J. & Millikan, R. H. (1989) Creating an Excellent School, London, Routledge.
Becker, H. S. & Greer, B. (1960) Latent culture: a note on the theory of latent social roles, Administrative Science Quarterly, 5. 2. 304-313.
Bolman, L. G. & Deal, T. E. (1991) Reframing Organizations: artistry, choice, and leadership, San Francisco, Jossey-Bass.
Bourdieu, P. (1986) The forms of capital, in: J. G. Richardson (ed) Handbook of Theory and Research for the Sociology of Capital, New York, Greenwood Press, pp. 41-58.

Bourdieu, P. (1989) Social space and symbolic power, Sociological Theory, 7. 1. 14-25.

Bourdieu, P. (1998) Practical Reason: on the theory of action, Stanford, Stanford University Press.

Brookover, W. B., Schweitzer, J. H., Schneider, J. M., Beady, C. H., Flood, P. K. & Wisenbaker, J. M. (1979) School Social Systems and Student Achievement: schools can make a difference, New York, Praeger.

Chadwick P. (2001) The Anglican perspective on church schools, Oxford Review of Education, 27. 4. 475-487.

Clegg, A. B. (1962) Social factors, Education, 119. 15-16.

Clegg, A. B. & Megson, B. (1973) Children in Distress, Harmondsworth, Penguin.

Cunningham, W. C. & Gresso, D. W. (1993) Cultural Leadership: the culture of excellence in education, Boston, Allyn & Bacon.

Deal, T. E. (1985). The symbolism of effective schools, The Elementary School Journal, 85. 5. 601-619.

Deal, T. E. (1987) The culture of schools, ASCD Yearbook, Alexandria, ASCD.

Deal. T. E. (1991), Private schools: bridging Mr. Chips and my captain, Teachers College Record, 92. 3. 415-424.

Deal, T. E. & Kennedy, A. A. (1983) Culture and school performance, Educational Leadership, 40. 5. 14-16.

Deal, T., & Peterson, K. (1999) Shaping School Culture: the heart of leadership, San Francisco, Josey-Bass.

Dearing, R. (2001) The Way Ahead: Church of England Schools in the New Millennium, London, Church House Publishing.

Denzin, N. (1989) Interpretive Interactionism, London, Sage.

Department for Children, Schools & Families, (2009) Deprivation and Education: the evidence on pupils in England, foundation stage to key stage 4, London, DCSF.

Donnelly, C. (2000) In pursuit of school ethos, British Journal of Educational Studies, 48. 2. 134-154.

Donnelly, C. (2004) Constructing the ethos of tolerance and respect in an integrated school: the role of teachers, British Journal of Educational Research, 30. 2. 264-278.

Eacott, S. (2010) Bourdieu's strategies and the challenge for educational leadership, International Journal of Leadership in Education, 13. 3. 265-281.

Egan, J. & Francis, L. J. (1986) School ethos in Wales: the impact of non-practising Catholic and non-Catholic pupils on Catholic secondary schools, Lumen Vitae, 41, 2. 159-173.

Evans, J. (1982) After fifteen thousand hours: where do we go from here? School Organisation, 2. 3. 239-253.

Flynn, M. (1993) The Culture of Catholic Schools, New South Wales, St. Pauls.

Fullan, M. G. & Hargreaves, A. (1991) What's Worth Fighting for in Your School? Toronto, Ontario Public School Teachers' Federation.

Furlong, C. (2000) Comprehending culture, school organisation - a cultural perspective in: C. Furlong & L. Monahan (eds) School Culture and Ethos: cracking the code, Dublin, Marino Institute of Education.

Fusarelli, L. D. (2002) Tightly coupled policy in loosely coupled systems: institutional capacity and organisational change, Journal of Educational Administration, 40. 6. 561-575.

Geetz, C. (1973) Interpretation of Cultures, New York, Basic Books.

Glover, D. & Coleman, M. (2005) School culture, climate and ethos: interchangeable or distinctive concepts? Journal of In-Service Education, 31. 2. 251-272.

Goldstein, H. & Sammons, P. (1997) The influence of secondary and junior schools on sixteen year examination performance: a cross-classified multilevel analysis, School Effectiveness and School Improvement, 8. 2. 219-230.

Gorard, S. (2006a) Value-added is of little value, Journal of Education Policy, 21. 2. 235–243.

Gorard, S. (2006b) Is there a school mix effect? Educational Review, 58. 1. 87–94.

Green, E. (2009) Speaking in parables: the responses of students to a bible-based ethos in a Christian City Technology College, Cambridge Journal of Education, 39. 4. 443-456.

Green, E. (2012) Analysing religion and education in Christian academies, British Journal of Sociology of Education, 33. 3. 391-407

Greenfield, T. (1993a) Organisations as talk, chance, action and experience, in: T. Greenfield & P. Ribbens (eds) Greenfield on Education Administration: towards a humane science, London, Routledge, 1-25.

Greenfield, T. (1993b) Theory about organisation: a new perspective and its implications for schools, in: T. Greenfield & P. Ribbens (eds) Greenfield on Education Administration: towards a humane science, London, Routledge, 53-74.

Handy, C. (1976) Understanding Organisations, Harmondsworth, Penguin.

Handy, C. (1988) Cultural forces in schools, in: R. Glatter, M. Preedy, C. Riches & M. Masterton (eds) Understanding School Management, Milton Keynes, Open University, 107-116.

Handy, C. & Aitken, R. (1990) Understanding Schools as Organizations, Harmondsworth, Penguin Books.

Hargreaves, A. (1997), Rethinking educational change: going deeper and wider in the quest for success, ASCD Yearbook, Alexandria, VA, ASCD.

Hill, J. (2010) Speech by Lord Hill of Oareford to the Church of England Academy Family Conference, London, Lambeth Palace, 16 November 2010.

Hill, J. (2011) Speech by Lord Hill of Oareford to the National Conference for Senior Leaders of Catholic Secondary Education, London, Hotel Russell, Russell Square, 27 January 2011.

Hogan, P. (1984) The question of ethos in schools, The Furrow, 35. 11. 693-703.

Johnson, H. (2003) Using a Catholic model: the consequences of the changing strategic purpose of Anglican faith schools and the contrasting interpretations within liberalism, School Leadership & Management, 23. 4. 469-480.

Knight, J. (2009) Visions for Leadership, Speech given to the Catholic Education Service Conference, 31st March, London, Commonwealth Club.

Mead, M. (1928) Coming of Age in Samoa, New York, William Morrow.

Mead, M. (1930) Growing Up in New Guinea, New York, William Morrow.

Mead, M. (1935) Sex and Temperament in Three Primitive Societies, London, Routledge & KeganPaul

Meegan, E. A., Carroll, J. B. & Ciriello, M. J. (2002) Outcomes, in: T. C. Hunt, E. A. Joseph & R. J. Nuzzi (eds) (2002) Catholic Schools Still Make a Difference, Washington, DC, National Catholic Educational Association.

Morris, A. B. (1996) School Ethos and Academic Productivity: the Catholic effect, unpublished PhD thesis, Institute of Education, University of Warwick

Morris, A. B. (2005) Academic standards in Catholic schools in England: indications of causality, London Review of Education, 3. 1. 81–99.

Morris, A. B., & Godfrey, R. (2012) The Application of Public Domain Data to Evaluate the Academic Performance of Eight Church of England Academies, Liverpool, Liverpool Hope University.

Morris, A. B. & Marsh, A. (2002) What motivates newly qualified teachers to work in Catholic schools in England, Networking, 3. 5. 8-13.

Mortimore, P., Sammons, P., Stoll, L., Lewis, D. & Ecob, R. (1988) School Matters: the junior years, Wells, Open Books.

Murgatroyd, S. & Gray, H. L. (1982) Leadership and the effective school, School Organisation, 2. 3. 285-295.

Nias, J. (1989) Refining the cultural perspective, Cambridge Journal of Education, 19. 2. 143-146.

Orton J. D. & Weick K. E. (1990) Loosely coupled systems: a reconceptualization, Academy of Management Review, 15. 2. 203-223.

Ouston, J. (1981) Differences between schools; the implications for school practice, in: B. Gillham (ed) (1981) Problem Behaviour in the Secondary School, London, Croom Helm, 60-70.

Purkey, S. C. & Smith, M. S. (1983) Effective schools: a review, Elementary School Journal, 83. 4. 427-452.

Reynolds D. (1976) The delinquent school, in: M. Hammersley & P. Woods (eds) (1976) The Process of Schooling, London, Routledge & Kegan Paul, 217-229.

Reynolds D. (1982) The search for effective schools, School Organisation, 2. 3. 215-237.

Rutter, M., Maughan, B., Mortimore, P., Ouston, J. and Smith, A. (1979) Fifteen Thousand Hours: secondary schools and their effects on children, London, Open Books.

Saunders, L. (1998) 'Value Added' Measurement of School Effectiveness: an overview, Slough, National Foundation for Educational Research.

Saunders, L. (1999) 'Value Added' Measurement of School Effectiveness, a critical review, Slough, National Foundation for Educational Research.

Schneider, B., Brief, A. P., & Guzzo, R. A. (1996) Creating a climate and culture for sustainable organizational change, Organizational Dynamics, 24. 4. 7-19.

Schultz, M. (1994) On Studying Organizational Cultures, New York, Walter de Gruyter.

Shipman, M. D. (1968) Sociology of the School, London, Longman.

Smith, D. J. & Tomlinson, S. (1989) The School Effect: a study of multi-racial comprehensives, London, Policy Studies Institute.

Solvason, C. (2005) Investigating school ethos...or do you mean culture?, Educational Studies, 31. 1. 85-95.

Strike, K. A. (1999) Can schools be communities? The tension between shared values and inclusion, Education Administrative Quarterly, 35. 1. 46-70.

Strike, K. A. (2000) Schools as communities: four metaphors, three models, and a dilemma or two, Journal of Philosophy of Education, 34. 4. 617-642.

Strivens, J. (1985) School climate: a review of a problematic concept, in: D. Reynolds (ed) (1985) Studying School Effectiveness, London, Falmer Press, 45-58.

Walford, G. (1991) Reflexive accounts of doing educational research, in: G. Walfold, (1991) Doing Educational Research, London, Routledge, 1-18.

Weick, K. E. (1976) Educational organizations as loosely coupled systems, Administrative Science Quarterly, 21. 1. 1-19.

Weick K. E. (1982) Administering education in loosely coupled schools, The Phi Delta Kappan, 63. 10. 673-676.

The Academic Performance of Church of England Academies

Ray Godfrey and Andrew B. Morris

Editor's Note - *Contextualising the Findings*
This is the second of two parallel research projects commissioned from the National Centre for Christian Education by the Church of England Academy Services Ltd. It utilised public domain academic performance data at Key Stage 4 of a small sample of Church of England Academies (n=8) and their precursor schools (n=7). Although the data used was limited to just four examinations, English, Mathematics, Science and a Modern Foreign Language (MFL), the report ran to some one hundred and fourteen A4 pages, necessitating some pruning for inclusion in this book. The full report, however, contains a detailed analysis of each of the eight academies involved. Only one Academy had more than two years' data on its own academic performance. Of the other seven, two had two years and the remaining four a single year's worth of data. After describing the general observations and conclusions that it was possible to draw from the full sample, detailed analyses of three academies are included in this edited account - those for which there is data for more than a single year.

Introduction

The primary concern of this commissioned research report is a focus on the examination performance of pupils attending Church of England (CofE) Academies. In addition, we have looked at, among other things, attendance rates and the extent to which the Academies in our sample have provided effective education for pupils living in areas of social deprivation. At the time the investigation began in 2009 there were relatively few institutions available for study. Consequently, the information we have gathered comes from a small sample of eight CofE Academies. Those data were also limited. With the exception of one case, only one or two years of appropriate public domain data were available. We recognise, therefore, that the findings derived from our opportunistic sample should not be overstated and that great care should be taken before extrapolating from our observations of their academic performance to the CofE sector as a whole.

Church of England Schools and the Research Brief

The National Society for The Education of the Poor in the Principles of the Established Church was founded in 1811 mainly as a result of the efforts of Joshua Watson. The Society's aim was to build a Church of England (CofE) school in every parish. By 1851 there were more than 17,000 CofE schools throughout the country. The Education Act of 1870 introduced state education and divided the country into about 2,500 school districts, each with its own school board. Religious teaching was required in all schools. The 1902 Balfour Education Act allowed church schools to opt for either voluntary aided or voluntary controlled status. Voluntary aided schools kept control of staffing, admissions, buildings and the religious education syllabus. Their governing body was made up of a majority of foundation governors. Voluntary controlled schools gave the control of these things to the Local Education Authority (LEA). Worship in both types of schools continued to be Anglican. Many CofE schools opted to become voluntary controlled as they were unable to raise the money to repair ageing buildings and thus it became the responsibility of the LEA. In most Anglican dioceses today the majority of church schools are controlled.

At the time this research was commissioned the legal framework for church schools remained as enacted by the Education Act 1944. However, the way the Church of England has viewed its schools has varied over that time. In the 1990's there was a resurgence of confidence in the place of its schools within the education system and in readiness for the new millennium the Archbishop's Council commissioned a review, chaired by Lord Dearing. The ensuing report, The Way Ahead: Church of England Schools in the New Millennium was published in 2001 and, it can be argued, re-invigorated the vision for CofE schools by identifying them as standing at the centre of the Church's mission to the nation (Dearing, 2001: xi). The report made seventy-nine recommendations including increasing the number of secondary church schools; the promotion of vocation in teaching; developing a clearer understanding of church school distinctiveness. The Statutory Inspection of Anglican Schools (SIAS) has helped to embed the latter along with the recent development of the christianvalues4schools website.

There has been a growth in secondary church schools and diocesan teams have been expanded to focus on addressing the recommendations. In 2009, however, they found themselves in a very different context. A change of government brought a new system encouraging schools to become self-governing academies directly funded by and accountable to central government, thus breaking the ties with the Local Authorities. This programme of academisation is well under way and is posing challenges for dioceses who seek to maintain a stake in these schools.

There will be a variety of reasons why different Church of England dioceses, and different individual Church of England schools within them, wish to acquire Academy status. It is not the purpose of this research to delve into those reasons, whatever they may be. Rather, the research brief was to investigate of the effectiveness of Church of England academies using qualitative or/and quantitative research methods. In considering how this commission could be best fulfilled, we considered ways to turn it into a discrete set of questions that could be researched. Three discrete, though inter-related, areas were identified (figure 1).

Figure 1

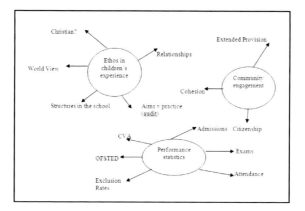

132

This report is only concerned with one of the three areas, namely school performance statistics. Not all of its conceptualised components feature in the final research design which analyses examination and test data already in the public domain of an opportunistic sample of Academies together with that of their associated 'feeder schools' and/or – where applicable - the schools that were replaced at the time of the conversion to Academy status. However, there are some caveats. It was not feasible to meet all CASL's initial aspirations. Changes in the way in which Department for Education (DfE) publishes its examination and test data, and the inevitable variations in the examinations themselves, make year on year inter- and intra-school comparisons problematical. Consequently, it was decided to limit the report to an analysis of the overall school examination record at Key Stage 4, its performance in English, Mathematics, Science and a Modern Foreign Language (MFL). In addition, the examination data were analysed in respect of their Contextualised Value Added (CVA), and related to levels of pupil absence, numbers registered as having Special Educational Needs (SEN) and those achieving the English Baccalaureate (Ebac) qualification.

Assessing School Performance
It has long been recognised that, even where schools may have very similar moral and educational purposes, some have few problems achieving their objectives, while others, drawing pupils from a similar background have many (Clegg, 1962; Shipman, 1968; Clegg & Megson, 1973). It has long been the case that many parents believe some schools to be better than others. They often have decided views that supported their belief and, consequently, a willingness to make sacrifices to ensure their children had access to their preferred school. Nevertheless, it was not until the late 1970s and 1980s that the first significant empirical studies were published in England suggesting that the academic and social backgrounds of pupils were not the sole determining factors in a child's achievement at school in either the secondary (Reynolds, 1976; Rutter et al., 1979; Smith & Tomlinson, 1989) or primary phases (Mortimore et al., 1988).

A government review of more recent research affirms the strength of those early studies, arguing, in particular, that "schools are independently important for deprived pupils' outcomes" (DCSF, 2009, p. 67) and points to a number of institutional factors that may contribute to alleviating some of the pervasive and long-term negative effects of social deprivation. However, it has been argued elsewhere that, together with the level of pupils' prior attainment - itself heavily influenced by socio-economic factors – the overall level of social disadvantage can account for as much as 80% of the apparent difference between schools (Goldstein & Sammons, 1997; Saunders, 1998). On the other hand, researchers in both the UK and USA have cautioned that high correlations between socio-economic status and levels of attainment do not mean they are necessarily causal or that the interaction is straightforward and consistent for every pupil. It is a complex process (Saunders, 1999; Meegan et al., 2002).

Though the school effect may be a relatively small factor in the level of pupils' success at school, that there is some (small) institutional effect has become a focus for central and local government sponsored school improvement programmes and strategies. In 1992 the government began publishing data about the academic outcomes of maintained secondary school. These, so called, Performance Tables were introduced with the aim of informing parents in their choice of school and providing schools with an incentive to raise standards. Initially they recorded only results in the GCSE exams taken by 16 year olds (along with one indicator for A-levels taken by 18 year olds). In 1996 the first tables for primary schools were produced with results for the new Key Stage 2 tests taken by 11 year olds. Over time they have included more indicators, partly as a result of the greater quantity of information available at national level. The first value added scores for all secondary schools were included in 2002, with value added scores for primary schools following a year later.

For many parents, test scores, examination results and 'league tables' may be a suitable measure of a school's apparent level of academic 'success', or 'failure'. In contrast academics argue that examination and test results are not the best criteria for judging the relative effectiveness of a school (see for example, Gray et al, 1986; Goldstein & Cuttance, 1988; Kennedy 1991; Schagen, 1991, McPherson, 1992; Tymms & Dean, 2004), and that a more appropriate mechanism for comparing schools should try to measure the progress pupils make between different stages of their education and take into account those factors known to influence educational outcomes, in particular prior attainment.

However, any choice of procedure for calculating pupil progress is to some extent an arbitrary process, and pupils' actual achievements in test and public examinations are both regarded as a valuable tool by government and have currency in public and political debate. As such, they seem appropriate for use in this study. We would argue that for the purposes of this report, and to meet the concerns of CASL, they should not be the only factors to be considered in assessing the academic performance of Church of England Academies, so we have taken a variety of measures that are freely available in the public domain to apply to those in our sample.

Following a report on value added performance indicators - that is, the progress that pupils make from one key stage to another (School Curriculum & Assessment Authority, 1994) - the Department for Education developed a simple value measure that was added to the published Performance Tables in 1998. Whilst the publication of value added measures in the Performance Tables was generally seen by many as a positive advance on the publication of 'raw results' only, there remained some concerns that pupils' background factors were not taken into account. Consequently, in 2006 a system which provided contextualised value added (CVA) scores was applied to pupils' performance and the first results published in 2006 (for secondary schools) and 2007 for the primary sector. It must be borne in mind that the CVA methodology provides three values, or measures, of overall school performance based around a figure of 1000 for secondary schools (or 100 for primary schools). They are the CVA value itself plus its Upper and Lower Confidence Limits. In the secondary sector, where all three values are above 1000 in the case of secondary schools we can be sure that the school is performing significantly better than could reasonably be expected given its particular circumstances. Conversely, where all three are below 1000, that is evidence of significantly lower than expected performance levels. If the values straddle 1000 then the school is performing as well as can be expected, even if the CVA score is above or below 1000.

All pupils with their details recorded in the Pupil Level Annual Schools Census (PLASC)[1] and having the relevant test or examination scores that can be linked to their previous attainment within their particular schools are included in the CVA calculations. Confidence intervals are calculated using the t test for a confidence level of 95% indicating that there is a 95% probability that the CVA scores of each school fall within their confidence interval range. The confidence intervals are necessary because of the natural fluctuations of a school's results based on the size of the pupil cohort. If the school's confidence interval does not include the CVA centre value of 1000 then that school's CVA score is statistically significantly above or below the national average.

The last fifteen years has seen a period of transition and development in the way examination and test results have been placed in the public domain. As these have become more statistically complex, government has become more sceptical of their effectiveness to the parents and the general public and has returned to earlier more 'crude' form of assessment of school performance. It is likely that discussion on which models to use for various purposes and how to present the results will continue.

Using Secondary Datasets
The decision to use existing datasets as the basis for our comparisons was based on a number of factors. This is a small scale study. As such, attempting to create new and primary evidence would be beyond the financial scope of the NCfCE (or the commissioning body), while using evidence at third-hand, can be distant and distorting. A useful compromise is to use existing data, where it is available, for a new analysis, an approach that is, becoming an increasingly respectable and legitimate methodology in social science research (Gorard, 2012).

The Department for Education has a website full of data on all aspects of school and childhood, including an archive of examination and key stage results for each school up to the current year (http://www.education.gov.uk/performancetables/). Making use of such a valuable resource makes particular sense for small scale studies. It encourages and enables replicability since others can easily use the same methodology.

This particular source of secondary data can help select the sample for a further in-depth study at some future date, and provide the evidence for potentially important hypotheses and stand-alone exploratory analyses to test them. The fact that we are using government data – accepted by policy makers as 'true' – may add weight to our findings, even though, because of our small sample, they can only be indicative rather than over-whelmingly conclusive. We also recognise that, in attempting to compare academic performance of particular institutions, our analysis can only make sense if we use data that are available for all maintained schools

---

[1] Collection of this data began in 2002.

in the locality. Varying local and national conditions might otherwise not be detected as possibly lying behind any observed changes in performance of the newly created Academy compared to that of its precursor school(s). In this case we have used the local authority area as the context for our comparisons.

There are, of course, limitations in using our chosen large-scale dataset, especially when collected by others for another purpose. As a consequence of staying within the public domain, all our data are for schools as a whole rather than for individual pupils. As a result care must be taken to avoid what is known as the ecological fallacy. For example, if a school has an increased number of pupils with high levels of Special Educational Needs (SEN) and a decreased number of pupils reaching, for example, the government defined Level 1 threshold in their examination performance, it is not legitimate to deduce that it is the SEN pupils who are failing to reach the threshold. A particular school might be doing very well for those pupils at the expense of others. Or there might be any number of alternative explanations which are beyond the scope of this investigation.

Sampling and Performance Criteria
Although it might be possible to obtain full confidential data from the Academies that agreed to take part in this part of the research, it would be difficult to obtain such data from every LA maintained school. Without it, comparisons of a particular CofE Academy with its neighbouring schools would be impracticable. Consequently, all data used in this report are from the public domain, which, in turn, has limited the institutions available for study. The sample should, therefore, be regarded being opportunistic rather than representative. While opportunity sampling is the technique most used in many small scale studies, we recognise there are consequent weaknesses in the research when using what might be biased data.

Measures
Using the information in the DfE database we decided to consider seven different factors as the basis for our assessment of comparative performance.

1. Average Points Score
The simplest, and the crudest, method of comparison is provided by schools' average points scores. Each pupil is awarded points for each grade achieved in each General Certificate of Secondary Education examination (GCSE) taken at age 16 at the end of Key Stage 4 of compulsory schooling, with pro rata points for longer or shorter GCSE and other qualifications deemed to be equivalent to GCSEs. Individual pupil totals are averaged for all relevant pupils in a school.

2. Examination Thresholds
These refer to differing key target for pupils taking General Certificate of Secondary Education examinations (GCSE). Tables published by the Department for Education (DfE - formerly DCSF) indicate for each school the percentage of the relevant pupils achieving one of three standards or 'thresholds' defined in terms of the number examinations they have taken and the results they have achieved.

- The **Level 0 Threshold** is set at a single GCSE or equivalent examination pass at Grade A to G.[2]
- The **Level 1 Threshold** is set at five or more (5+) GCSE or equivalent examination passes at Grades A* (formerly Grade A) G.
- The **Level 2 Threshold** is set at 5+ GCSE or equivalent examination passes at Grade A* (formerly Grade A) to C including English and Mathematics

3. Absence

The data used here is the overall absence rates for relevant pupils in each school – the total number of half days missed by pupils divided by the total number of possible half-day attendances. This is equivalent both to the average proportion of pupils missing on any given day and to the average proportion of sessions missed by any particular pupil.

4. High levels of Special Educational Needs

In the context of studies of this type, proportions of pupils with a Statement of Special Educational Need (SEN) in any one institution should be treated with care. They partly depend upon the problems, social, developmental and educational, faced by pupils accepted by the school and partly on the extent to which the school succeeds or fails to adopt a curriculum, ethos and style of organisation that can cope with pupils' difficulties in the normal run of things, rather than listing them as having special requirements.

Thus a child might have a Statement in one school but not in another. At the higher levels, however, outside agencies are involved and, in theory at least, there should be more consistency between schools in a single Local Authority area. Unfortunately the data available are not consistent across the whole time period. In 2004 and 2005 figures were published for pupils with Statements of Special Educational Needs. Later data combine these with pupils at the level of School Action Plus.

It is important therefore not to compare absolute levels of proportions of SEN pupils for the Academy with those of its precursor school(s). The focus should be upon where the schools lie each year in comparison with other schools in the LA, bearing in mind the caveats outlined in the paragraph above.

5. Contextual Value Added (CVA) Scores

Average GCSE points scores are largely predictable on the basis of each pupil's prior attainment and to that extent do not reflect the success of the school. For this reason Value Added Scores (VA) were introduced in 2002 to calculate pupils' points scores measured against different baselines depending on their points scores at earlier Key Stages. In other

---

[2] Pupils who do not achieve this 'lowest' threshold end their compulsory education without any approved academic qualification. Some would argue that for many young people with educational difficulties and/or deprived socio/economic circumstances there is much that they can achieve, educationally and socially, outside the GCSE examination system – though such matters are beyond the scope of this report.

words, to measure the progress of pupils, or the value that had been added since the end of the previous Key Stage.

Additional pupil data from PLASC enabled government to develop more effective tools for analysing the relationships between attainment and a variety of individual and background factors affecting educational outcomes.

Contextualised Value Added (CVA) is a multi-level statistical modelling technique using the actual test and exam results of all pupils in a given year group. It uses a more complex definition of prior attainment than the simple value added model, together with a range of contextual variables known to affect academic outcomes, to predict the attainment of individual pupils. It then compares each individual's actual test or examination results against that prediction. Institutional value added scores are derived from the difference (positive or negative) between the predicted and actual attainment of the school's individual pupils. Adjustments are made to the predicted scores where pupils have particular personal or background characteristics that have a statistical impact on their levels of attainment

Following a successful pilot study in 2005, the first CVA scores for secondary schools were published in 2006 and, it is argued, they give a much fairer statistical measure of the effectiveness of a school and provide a solid basis for comparisons (Ray, 2006).[3] CVA is based on statistical relationships drawn from a national dataset for some 600,000 pupils in each year group in England. However, it has some deficiencies. Only the data that is collected at national level can be included in the model. Some external factors which are commonly thought to have an impact cannot be included because there is no reliable national data available e.g. parental education status/occupation. In addition, the model requires data on pupil's prior attainment test results against which to measure progress. Consequently, to be included in the calculations pupils must have attended an English school some 5 years prior to taking GCSEs. Pupils in KS4 who joined the school from overseas within the previous five years, or for some other reason have no Key Stage 2 test scores on record, cannot therefore be included in the school's CVA measure.

Nevertheless, it is, many have argued, the best mechanism available even though it may be more difficult for a lay person to understand than, for example, a school's average points score per pupil. Nevertheless, no single measure of performance can tell the whole story about a school's effectiveness and CVA must not be viewed in isolation.

Attainment data has an important role in illustrating a school's performance. For example, an improvement in a school's average points score, or the percentage of pupils obtaining five or more examination passes at grade A* - C provides valuable information but may not be reflected in an improved CVA score. If similar pupils elsewhere improve their performance at

---

[3] More details about CVA scores are given in Appendix 2 of the full report while a definitive explanation can be found at: http://www.dcsf.gov.uk/performancetables/schools).

a faster rate, the school's CVA is likely to go down. One must also bear in mind that because a school's CVA score is relative to each year's national picture, their score for one year is not, strictly speaking, comparable with their score the year before, though published CVA Percentiles show where schools are placed nationally compared to other schools, variation in which from year to year can be used to make judgements about a school's own improving (or declining) performance.[4]

6. Regression Analysis

Large secondary datasets can be analysed as simple frequencies and/or percentages, broken down, for example, into categories such as year, sex of student, or geographic region. They can also be modelled using regression techniques and similar. While such sophisticated techniques are not essential and do not represent any kind of definitive test, they can give some useful insights (Gorard, 2012, 84-85). We have utilised a fairly simple approach in an attempt to give some indication of the relationship between levels of school attainment, pupils with high levels of SEN and pupil absence using data available for Local Authority schools for each year separately.

The figures illustrated in these graphs are the 'residuals' for each school – the difference between what was actually achieved by the school and what on average would be expected of any LA school with the same proportion of (say) SEN pupils. Some residuals are positive, some are negative. For simple regression the average (mean) is always zero. Although they will not reflect in detail the complex relationship between SEN, absence and attainment, it is reasonable to assume that any changes made to face-value results by such a simple device would be amplified were it possible to employ more sensitive analytical tools.

7.   English Baccalaureate (Ebac)

This is not a qualification certificated like the International Baccalaureate. Rather it is another threshold combining the indicators that have been gradually introduced over the years and adding a GCSE Grade C or above in a 'humanity' subject. Although the official age-related target for the end of KS4 is for pupils to obtain 5 GCSEs Grade C or above, some schools have responded to the Secretary of State's rhetoric by treating the EBac, with its prescription of which subjects must be included, as if it were a new official target.[5]

Nevertheless, we have compared institutional performance on this qualification using both raw scores (graph12) and regression analysis (graph 13). However, in this case, the lines in the two graphs do not represent the passage of time as only one year of data is displayed.

---

[4] At the time this report was prepared the Contextualised Value Added methodology seemed to have been generally accepted as a suitable tool for comparing institutional performance. However, the current government has decided that CVA scores will not be published after 2010.

[5] It may be the case that schools pursuing the interests of their pupils would already be entering all those who might benefit from studying the range of subjects included in the Ebac and would continue to enter pupils on the same basis in future. Consequently, a marked improvement in Ebac figures in 2011 might not indicate any 'improvement' but reflect badly on a school's commitment to serve the best needs of individual pupils.

8. Comparisons with Local Authority Schools.

Finally, in graphs 14 – 20 we use raw scores and regression analysis to compare CofE Academies with other schools within the Local Authority on four variables, CVA scores, performance at threshold level 2, science and modern foreign languages.

Presentation and Interpretation – Graphs

The format illustrated in the example below (figure 2) is used for all graphs other than those concerned with the English Baccalaureate (as indicated above). Black lines (of three different types) indicate the performance of specific schools of interest. They also have markers to indicate precise data on which the graph is based. Grey lines show the background distribution of all schools in the Local Authority. Dotted lines indicate the maximum and minimum levels achieved each year by any school in the area. The remaining lines indicate percentiles. Five per cent of schools come at or below the 5th percentile; twenty-five per cent of schools at or below the 25th percentile; and so on. This format allows the improvement or otherwise of specific schools to be viewed in two ways simultaneously.

By observing its relation to the graph axis, it is possible to judge performance in absolute terms. By observing its relation to the grey lines, one can judge its performance against other schools in the area. Between 2007 and 2008 the (hypothetical) CofE Academy's average point score rose from about 260 to about 330. Over the same period it also improved in comparison with other local schools, rising from a little above the 5th percentile to just below the 25th. From 2008 to 2009, there was a similar rise to nearly 400 points. The graph, however, shows that other local schools were also improving by about the same amount and, although the CofE Academy improved a little on its previous year's performance, when that of the other Local Authority schools is taken into account it remained closer the 25th percentile than to the 50th. In interpreting percentages, the total number of schools it must be born in mind. In this particular example we have modelled there are approximately fifty LA secondary schools.

Figure 2

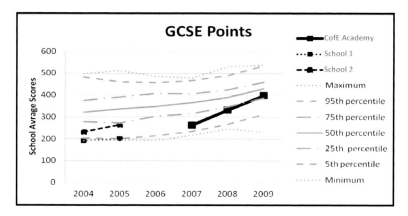

Some Observations and Conclusions
We recognise that academic performance may vary from year to year for reasons beyond the control of the Academy, that a single year's data cannot always be compared to that produced by another cohort, and that one year's data cannot illustrate a trend. To that extent most of our observations will be institution rather sample specific. Nevertheless, there may be some generally valid insights to be drawn from our observations which may be of use to those who, in the future, will be considering whether or not to seek to establish new Church of England Academies or convert existing schools to this alternative status.

Finally, we recognise that measures of academic performance tell only one very small part of the work of a school and, in our view, should not always be the accorded the highest accolades. The value of education to children and the community is much wider than pupils' academic outcomes.

Taking all the caveats into account, and remembering that interpretations of numerical aggregate data need to be checked against real observations and consideration of individual cases, we have set out below a selection of the most notable observations and conclusions extracted from the detailed analyses of the eight academies studied.

Observations - General
We used two measures of overall school performance at Key Stage 4; average GCSE examination points per pupil, and Contextualised Value Added (CVA) scores. Average points scores provide a relatively simple indication of performance that is easily to understand and to compare. CVA scores are much more statistically complex measure, but give the best indication of schools' overall effectiveness and whether that effectiveness is significantly above or below the national average (DfE 2009).

GCSE Average Points Scores
Seven of the eight Academies have precursor schools against which their average points scores in 2010 can be compared. However, when those improved performances were set against the LA average scores only two were at or above the LA norm, albeit starting from a low base. The academy for which there was no precursor school(s) available for comparison was slightly below its LA average points score norm in 2009 and improved to just above the following year.

> **All seven improved on the previous scores achieved by those institutions in the final year before they were replaced by, or converted, to Academies.**

Contextualised Value Added Scores
The CVA scores, in comparison, show the Academies in a much better light, and it is these figures that give a better indicator of the possible impact that a change of status has made.

> Four of the seven have improved CVA scores compared to their precursor school the previous year and also their position in the LA 'league tables'.

One had not improved upon the levels achieved its single precursor school but was still performing better that could be expected, just below the top 5% of schools nationally. One showed little change from the levels achieved by its precursor school; both being well below the LA norm and in the bottom 5% of schools nationally. One (Academy B) while performing as well as could be expected in 2010, its CVA scores straddling 1000, had a lower score that that of its precursor school in 2009.

> The relative performance of Academy B has declined, both in absolute terms and in its ranking in the LA table, below the LA mean. This Academy might usefully be the subject of further study. Its performance is unusual in that it replaced a school which, over the previous four years, has shown a steady increase in its CVA score, and had moved from the bottom of the LA table to above average

Absenteeism Rates

Only Academy F failed to sustain or improve on the levels of their precursor school(s); in four there was little difference either way and in three some measure of improvement, that is a reduction the rate of absenteeism. With that one exception, however, absence in all the Academies was higher than their respective LA norms, for example Academy E, albeit in some cases marginally so.

> Although the very high rates of absence during 2005 and 2006 were reduced in 2008 and 2009 they only matched the previous 'best year' for the Community school in 2004. Academy F's absence rate in its first year of existence increased, putting it at the bottom of the LA table. On this measure there has been no improvement; the position is poorer now than in 2004.

> Academy E has continued and improved upon the trend of its precursor school ... a slow improvement in the absence rate from a high in 2005 and 2006 accelerated in 2009 and 2010 ... from having a high level of absence to a position where it is among the better performing ... in the local authority table.

It could be argued, therefore, that our findings give some support, at least on academic effectiveness grounds, for those advocating the Church of England's Academy programme and give some (tentative) optimism that the modest successes shown by this sample can be replicated in other areas of the country. However, as we have outlined above, the sample is too small to draw to many firm overall conclusions. We suggest, therefore that the greatest value of the available data may lie in us highlighting specific issues of individual Academies. They all have different circumstances in which to operate; all have different advantages and difficulties that contribute to their measured success (or otherwise). Taking all the caveats into account and remembering that all interpretations of numerical aggregate data need to be checked against detailed consideration of individual cases using institutional specific data that is not (currently) in the public domain, the conclusions are the best that can be offered from our a sample.

> **Academy A has achieved considerable academic success and has maintained or improved upon standards prevailing in its precursor schools and the balance of evidence suggests that these improvements are all the more impressive against the background of continuing to serve a disadvantaged population.**

> **Academy E has made improvements in academic attainment at KS4 and in the level of attendance.**

> **Apart from Science, even those pupils with higher levels of attainment at Academy C have not performed particularly well in subjects currently favoured by the government and, therefore emphasised in published school performance tables.**

> **There has not been any noticeable improvement on academic performance in this first year. Academy B appears to be very much an extension of its precursor school and to have performed slightly less successfully, possibly because of reorganisation, possibly for some other reason undetected by the nature of this report. The observed deterioration may even be a simple matter of random variation.**

The examples above have been chosen to illustrate the range of observations and conclusion we believe can be made. A full discussion of the outcomes on all of the measures for the three Academies having data for two or more academic years is set out below.

Institutional Analysis - Academy A
Academy A replaced two small secondary schools: a CofE Voluntary Aided 11-16 High School with approximately 500 pupils (Replaced School 1) and an 11-18 Community School for Boys (Replaced School 2) having slightly fewer than 400 pupils on roll at the time the Academy was established.

Academic Standards
GCSE Average Points Scores
The graph A.1 plots the average points scores for GCSE and equivalent examinations taken by pupils at age 16+ the end of Key Stage 4 for each of the three comparison schools against the background of the general distribution of schools in the LA. Since 2004 these scores have improved for schools generally; so the fact that Academy A has outperformed its precursor schools may not be particularly notable. What is, perhaps, more interesting is that the other

two precursor schools were very low in the LA rankings, but Academy A, starting approximately at the level achieved by those two schools in the last year of their existence, has progressed in comparison with the LA norms and is now just above the median for the Authority.

Graphs A2-A4: Department for Education Attainment Thresholds
Graphs A.2 – A. 4 illustrate comparative institutional performance at the three thresholds defined by the DfE. It is, perhaps, to be expected that all, or nearly all, pupils attending maintained schools achieve at least one GCSE pass grade at the end of Key Stage 4. Such is the case with Academy A.

What is notable, however, is that it has come closer to ensuring 100 per cent of its pupils achieve that minimum standard than either of the two schools it replaced, suggesting that it does, to some extent, support the least able pupils rather more effectively than had previously been the case.

At the higher, more demanding level, the Academy improved on the position which the precursor schools maintained from 2001 to 2005. Its improvement seen here is more notable than that achieved with its average points scores, with the Academy approaching the top of the table in 2008. In 2010 the question that seemed to arise (and which needs to be answered by more sensitive forms of enquiry) was whether it was achieving better average results by focussing on the pupils who appear to have greater potential for Level 2 at the expense of those who need to struggle to reach the lower thresholds. The data suggest that this is not the case since very few pupils are not achieving some success.

Attendance/Absence Rates
There are measures other than the absolute levels of academic attainment that can indicate the effectiveness of schools. One such is the level of pupils' attendance (or absence) rates. The apparent improvement in absence rate at the Academy from 2007-10 may be slightly misleading. Compared to LA norms in the first year of its existence it seems to be at the average level of its two precursor school. There had been little change in the position of those schools in 2005 compared to the previous year, and with the exception of 2010 the Academy has high absence levels near the worst in the LA. Even in 2010, although there is an improvement compared to LA norms, it is marginal.

It is recognised that this form of aggregated pupil data can be a little misleading since the types of absence for which information is available has changed during the period under review (from authorised/unauthorised absence to absence and persistent absence). It is also not possible to assign causes for the absence rate, for example, whether the absence levels are largely due to pupil disaffection or to factors relating to deprivation.

Special Educational Needs
Graph A.6 shows data relating to the level of achievement of pupils with high levels of Special Educational Needs. This is a complex and complicated area and interpreting the data

should be done with care. We would suggest that it would be unwise to draw firm conclusions from the information available. However, relative to other schools in the Authority, it would appear that Academy A has experienced a reducing number of pupils having statements indicating they had high level of Special Educational Needs, and in 2010 those numbers show the Academy was approaching the bottom of the distribution.

A more sensitive form of investigation would be required in order to determine whether this is due to the Academy serving a less disadvantaged population or whether it was serving the same population but more effectively, so reducing the need for SEN statements.

Contextualised Value Added Scores (CVA)
These measures take into account a range of factors known to influence pupil outcomes. They indicate how far each pupil's attainment exceeds or falls short of what would be expected in the light of pupil characteristics, school circumstances and the pupil's prior attainment. CVA data was not available before 2007, so the comparisons in the following graph are with other LA schools rather than Academy A's precursor schools.

On this measure the Academy has improved its academic performance since 2007. In comparison within LA norms, it moves from a position slightly below half way up the table to somewhere near the top in 2010 – this at a time when standards in LA schools generally were also improving. In 2007 its CVA performance indicates that is was not an effective institution, achieving results significantly below that which could be expected.

The 2008 and 2009 cohorts showed an improvement with CVA scores of 1006.8 and 1010.0 respectively, the confidence interval upper and lower limits indicating they were both performing at an appropriate level but its CVA score in 2010 (1028.1) showed a notable improvement on previous performance and compared most favourably with LA and national norms, indicating that it was performing better than one could realistically expect, albeit just below the top five per cent of schools.

Regression Analyses
Graphs 8-11 use a simple regression analysis which has some (limited) ability to compare the performance of the Academy with the schools it replaced and, in the case of some of the newer attainment indicators, to compare it with the generality of LA schools. When the levels of SEN and absence are taken into account, the Academy's average GCSE points scores (graph 8) compare favourably with LA schools and they appear to be consistent with what would be expected from Replaced School 2, if not Replaced School 1.

Still taking levels of SEN and absence into account, graphs 9, 10 and 11 below compare the institutional performance for pupils attaining each of the three DfE examination thresholds. Graph A.9 shows that the proportion of Academy pupils achieving the minimum threshold, that is, at least one GCSE grade, improved in successive years between 2007 and 2009.

However, in 2010 it declined markedly though this is not necessarily significant. The actual numbers of pupils failing to achieve a single grade is so small that one pupil can make a huge difference to positions in the LA table. Graph A.10 shows that Academy A has improved its performance compared to its precursor and other LA schools at level 1. The same pattern can be seen in graph A.11, illustrating performance at the highest threshold level.

English Baccalaureate (Ebac)

The very low proportion of pupils achieving Ebac places the Academy in the bottom half of the LA table even when SEN and absence levels are taken into account.

Comparisons Local Authority Schools – Graphs A.14-A.18

Contextualised Value Added Scores: A good indication of how far schools are dealing with disadvantaged populations is the extent to which their positions in the CVA performance table are better or worse than would otherwise be expected.

On this measure, the school residuals illustrated in graph A.14 show the Academy to be among the institutions that appear to be particularly effective and academically supportive of disadvantaged pupils. Since 2008 it has maintained a position near the top of the LA table.

DfE Thresholds: Given the CVA findings set out in graph A.14 it is not surprising to find that North Town CofE Academy has a rather low proportion of pupils attaining the higher threshold standard of 5+ GCSEs grades A*-C including English and Mathematics. Once SEN and absence are taken into account, the Academy was in the top quarter of the table between 2007 and 2009.

In 2010, the proportion of pupils with this level of attainment did not increase along with other schools in the lower half of the LA table. Furthermore, because the absolute numbers of levels of SEN and Absence declined it would have been expected that its overall performance would have improved. That was not the case.

Science: Graph A.17 shows that, in absolute terms, the proportion of North Town's pupils gaining the standard Science qualification has been improving more than in other LA schools. Once levels of SEN and absence are taken in to account, however (graph A.18), the school residuals move North Town into the top half of the LA table.

Modern Foreign Languages: Data on qualifications in modern foreign languages (MFL) have been published only since 2008 by DfE. Compared to other schools within the LA, North Town CofE Academy had considerably poorer results than average (graph A.19).

When SEN and absence levels re taken into account the Academy's performance in this area of the curriculum is around the LA average but has declined in each successive year relative to other schools (graph A.20). This relative decline in the residual values may be a result of the improvement in its levels of SEN and Absence (graphs, A.5 & A.6).

146

Graph A.1: GCSE Average Points Scores

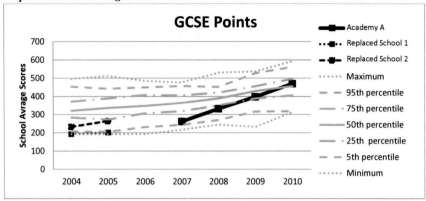

Graph A.2: Attainment at DfE Threshold Level 0

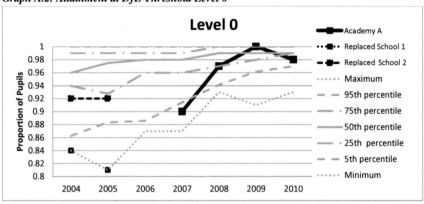

Graph A.3: Attainment at DfE Threshold Level 1

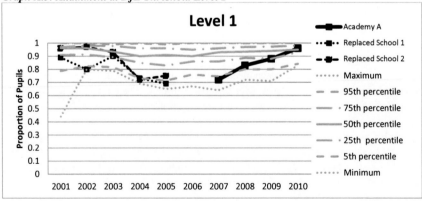

Graph A.4: Attainment at DfE Threshold Level 2

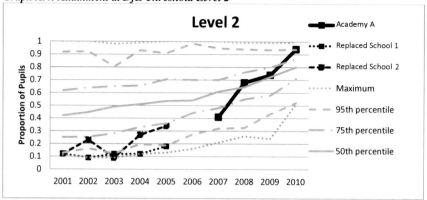

Graph A.5: Pupil Absenteeism Rates

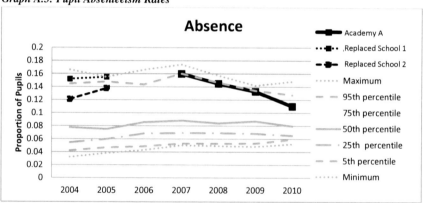

Graph A.6: Proportion of Pupils with SEN Statements

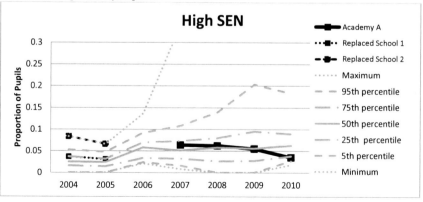

Graph A.7: Contextualised Value Added Scores

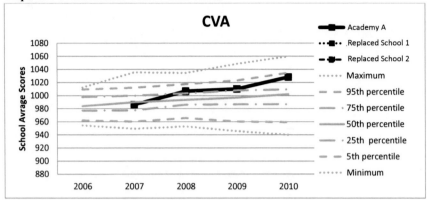

Graph A.8: Regression Analysis – GCSE Average points on SEN and Absence

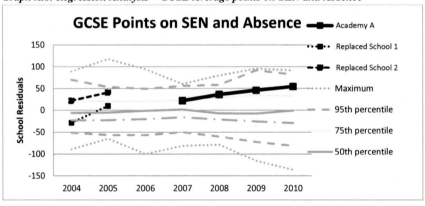

Graph A.9: Regression Analysis – Level 0 on SEN and Absence

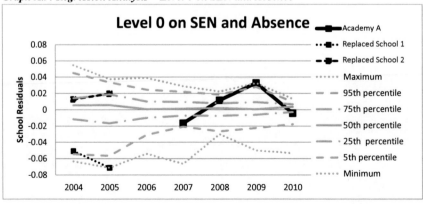

Graph A.10: Regression Analysis – Level 1 on SEN and Absence

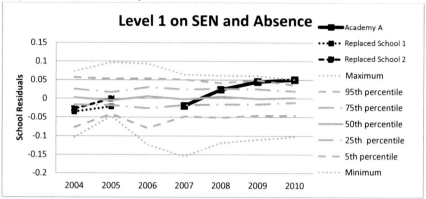

Graph A.11: Regression Analysis – Level 2 on SEN and Absence

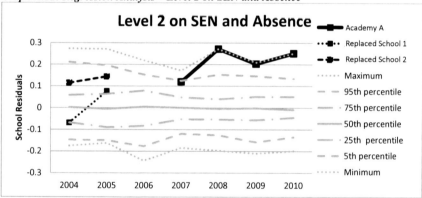

Graph A.12: Attainment in English Baccalaureate

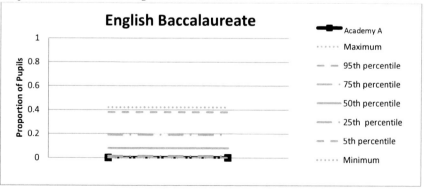

Graph A.13: Regression Analysis - English Baccalaureate on SEN and Absence

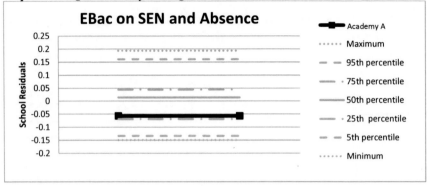

Graph A.14: Regression Analysis – Contextualised Value Added on GCSE Points

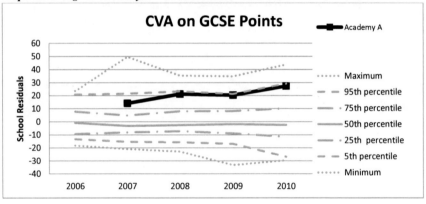

Graph A.15: Regression Analysis – Attainment at Threshold Level 2 (inc. English & mathematics)

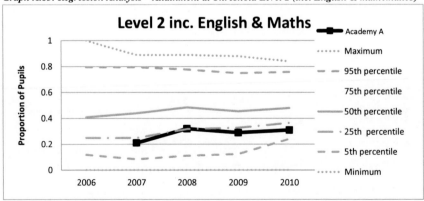

Graph A.16: Regression Analysis – Level 2 (inc. English & mathematics) on SEN and Absence

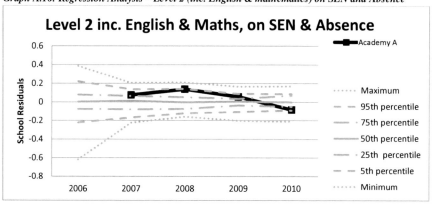

Graph A.17: Attainment of Standard Science Qualification

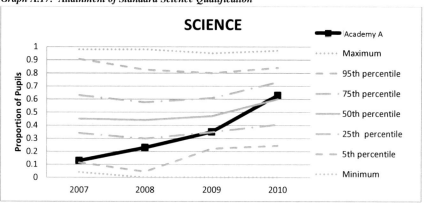

Graph A.18: Regression Analysis – Standard Science Qualification on SEN and Absence

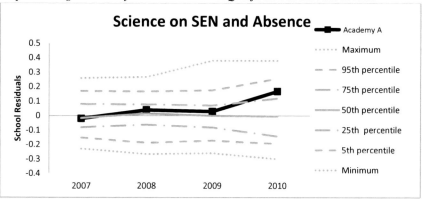

Graph A.19: Attainment in Modern Foreign Languages at Level 2

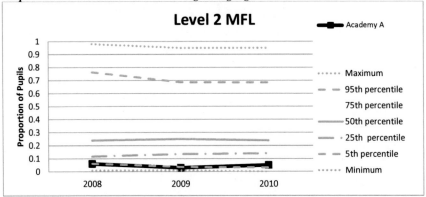

Graph A.20: Regression Analysis – Level 2 Modern Foreign Languages on SEN and Absence

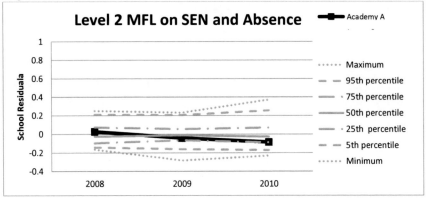

Institutional Analysis - Academy D

No specific predecessor school has been identified relating to Academy D. The first group of pupils attending the Academy who sat public examinations did so in 2009. Consequently, there are two years of data available for analysis. Data for local authority schools for the years 2001 to 2008 are included in the graphs to ensure parity of presentation with the other Academies considered in this report and allow any patterns to emerge. The Academy's performance, as measured by its pupils' **average points score**, shows an improvement from 2009 to 2010. While there has been a slow upward trend in the LA performance since 2004, the Academy has improved its performance at a slightly faster rate than LA schools generally from 2009 to 2010 and is now meeting LA norms.

Attainment Thresholds

The three graphs – D.2, D.3 and D.4 - illustrate comparative institutional performance for the percentage of the pupils achieving a particular standard or 'threshold' defined in terms of the number examinations they have taken and the results they have achieved. The minimum threshold level is set at one examination pass in a GCSE or equivalent examination and the vast majority of pupils attending a mainstream secondary schools should meet this threshold. Within the LA, there has been a gradual improvement of standards since 2008 with nearly all pupils attending LA schools obtained at least one GCSE pass grade in 2010. That pattern is replicated in Academy D. All its pupils achieved that minimum standard in 2010. A reversal can be seen at the higher level 1 threshold (graph D.3) where the Academy was performing slightly better than the LA average in 2009. In 2010 the LA norm increased while that of the performance of the Academy has remained at the same level putting it at the LA median – indicating a small relative decline. With so few pupils failing to achieve this level, most of the fluctuation will be random variation rather than a significant indication of things needing attention. On the other hand, there is a noticeable increase in the proportion of the Academy pupils attaining 5 or more GCSEs pass Grades at C or above, which takes it from below the median level to (almost) equalling the average performance of LA schools.

Attendance/Absence Rates
In common with all schools in the Local Authority, Academy D has successfully reduced absence rates in 2009-10 matching the trend of recent years

Special Educational Needs
The proportion of SEN pupils attending Academy D has been higher than the local authority average in both 2009 and 2010.

Contextualised Value Added Scores (CVA)
After taking into account those factors which are known to affect pupil's levels of attainment, there has been a noticeable improvement in the performance of pupils attending the Academy (graph D.7). While its average points scores suggest that it has improved its performance but only to the LA norm, this more accurate measure of comparative effectiveness shows the it moving from the LA average level in 2009 to a position very close to the top of the authority league table in 2010. Its CVA scores in 2009 (CVA = 1004.5; upper limit = 1017.5; lower limit = 991.6) indicate that it was performing as well as expected, all things being equal. In 2010 it was performing much better than expected on this measure (CVA = 1029.3; upper limit = 1042.1; lower limit = 1016.6).

Regression Analyses
While the published information allows a relatively simple form of data analysis care should be taken in interpreting the results. And in the particular instance of the Academy D, since there is no predecessor school, the results illustrated below in graphs D8 to D11 have less value than for some of the other Academies in the report but are included here to maintain uniformity of presentation.

English Baccalaureate (Ebac)
Graphs D.12 and D.13 show results for 2010 only. The numbers achieving the Ebac qualification places the Academy at the bottom of the table, a position that changes only

marginally when SEN and absence is taken into account (graph D.13). In the current political debate this might be a case where the Academy could be seen as improving GCSE results at the expense of 'traditional academic' subjects.

Comparisons with Local Authority Schools
Analysis of Academy D'S's pupils **contextualised value added** and average examination scores suggest that the Academy is among the institutions that appear to be most supportive of disadvantaged pupils. It performed well in 2009 and has improved that position relative to other schools in the local authority in 2010

The proportion of Academy D's pupils attaining **threshold level 2** (5+ GCSEs grades A*-C including English and Mathematics) is low and below LA norms in 2009. In 2010 it has improved and is about average for area. When taking levels of SEN and absence rates into account (graph D.16) the comparative improvement is more marked, moving to just above the LA average from near the bottom of the table. Even so, in the current political climate 'being average' or just above may be something needing further attention.

The raw **science** results suggest that this area of the curriculum should be of concern. The results (graph D.17) show that in 2009 attainment in this area was well below the average in the local authority area and deteriorated the following year. However, when taking SEN and absence rates into account (graph D.18) the picture improves somewhat with the Academy improving its relative position to near the LA average.

Comparisons of the **Modern Foreign Language** examination results of pupils reaching the level 2 threshold show the Academy moving from about the LA average in 2009 to well below in 2010. That pattern of deteriorating performance is even more marked when SEN and absence rates are taken into account (graph D.20).

Graph D.1: GCSE Average Points Scores

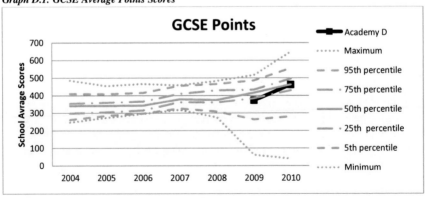

Graph D.2: Attainment at DfE Threshold Level 0

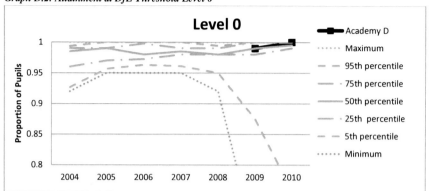

Graph D.3: Attainment at DfE Threshold Level 1

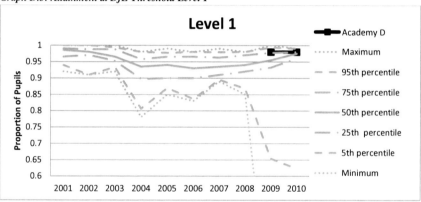

Graph D.4: Attainment at DfE Threshold Level 2

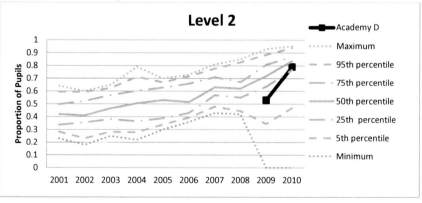

Graph D.5: Pupil Absenteeism Rates

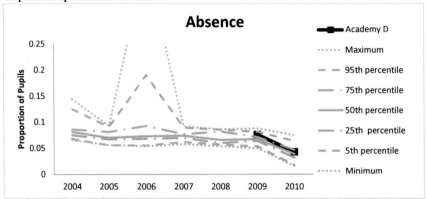

Graph D.6: Proportion of Pupils with SEN Statements

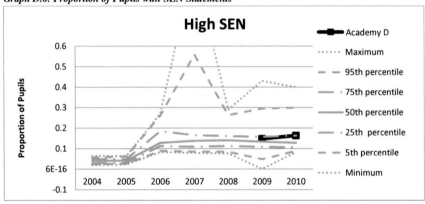

Graph D.7: Contextualised Value Added Scores

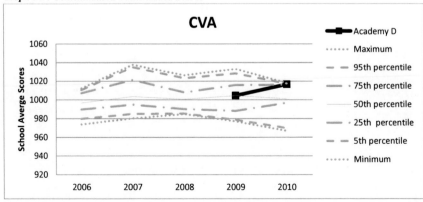

Graph D.8: Regression Analysis – GCSE Average points on SEN and Absence

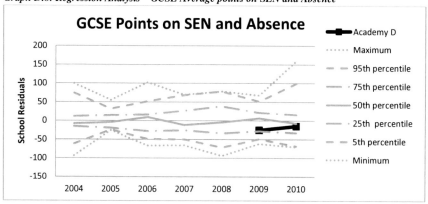

Graph D.9: Regression Analysis – Level 0 on SEN and Absence

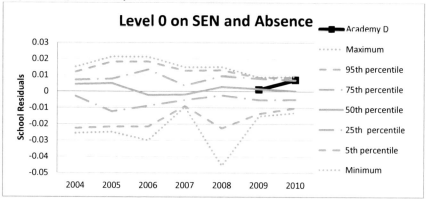

Graph D.10: Regression Analysis – Level 1 on SEN and Absence

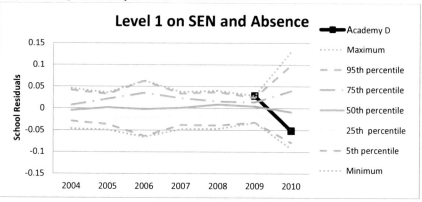

Graph D.11: Regression Analysis – Level 2 on SEN and Absence

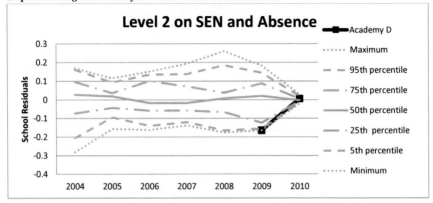

Graph D.12: Attainment in English Baccalaureate

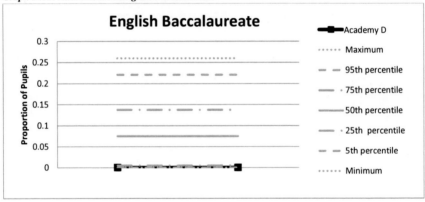

Graph D.13: Regression Analysis - English Baccalaureate on SEN and Absence

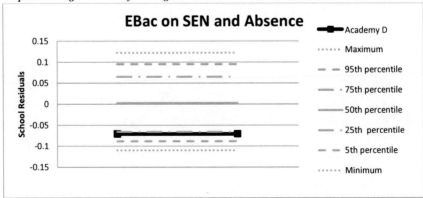

Graph D.14: Regression Analysis – Contextualised Value Added on GCSE Points

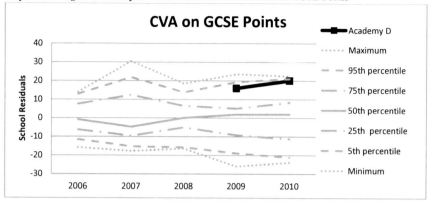

Graph D.15: Regression Analysis – Attainment at Threshold Level 2 (inc. English & mathematics)

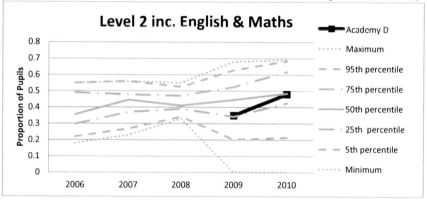

Graph D.16: Regression Analysis – Level 2 (inc. English & mathematics) on SEN and Absence

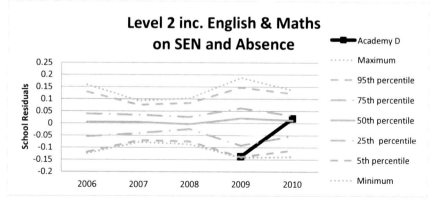

Graph D.17: Attainment of Standard Science Qualification

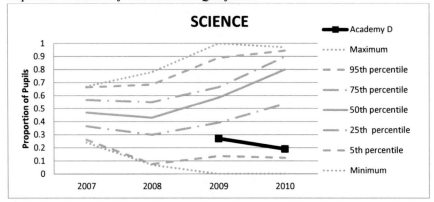

Graph D.18: Regression Analysis – Standard Science Qualification on SEN and Absence

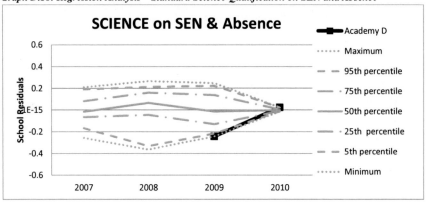

Graph D.19: Attainment in Modern Foreign Languages at Level 2

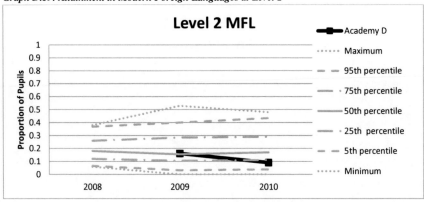

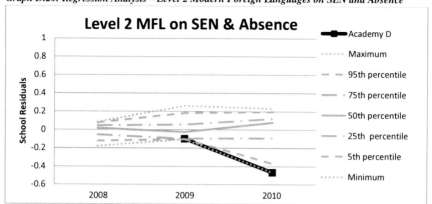

Institutional Analysis - Academy E

The public domain data relating to Academy E is compared to that of the single school which it replaced.

GCSE average points score achieved by Academy and its precursor school is plotted against the background of the general distribution of schools in Nottinghamshire. Since 2004 the average points scores of schools generally within the LA have been increasing, so the fact that that the Academy has continued the upward trend of its precursor to just below the median average points score is not surprising. The Academy is now performing just below the median for the local authority as a whole.

Attainment Thresholds

Across the local authority nearly all pupils in all schools of whatever type or status achieve at least one GCSE pass at grade G or above – the lowest of the three threshold levels. On this measure the pupils attending the Academy's precursor school were steadily improving their performance from a low base in 2005.

The first cohort of pupils at the Academy taking examinations in 2009 equalled the performance of the previous year in the precursor school while the second cohort have improved slightly again, with 98% of pupils achieving the minimum standard (graph E.2). The Academy's precursor school, though on an upward trend since 2005, remained below the LA median level on all three performance thresholds.

The graphs for threshold 0 and 1 indicate that in the first two years of its existence how the Academy, while improving on that previous performance, was still slightly below the median of LA schools. It is at the highest performance threshold (Level 2), however, that the comparative performance of the Academy shows the greatest improvement over its precursor school, with an attainment about the average for the authority.

Attendance/Absence Rates

On this measure Academy E has, again, continued and improved upon the trend of its precursor school. What was a slow improvement in the absence rate from a high in 2005 and 2006 accelerated in 2009 and 2010, moving the Academy from having a high level of absence to being among the better performing schools in the LA.

Special Educational Needs

The improvements in attendance noted above have been achieved while the proportion of pupils registered as having high levels of special needs (SEN) has remained high compared to the mean level across the local authority, and similar to those recorded at the precursor school. However, the numbers should be treated with caution, bearing in mind the complexities involved in identifying and registering such pupils.

Contextual Values Added Scores

Taking pupil and background characteristics into account, Contextual Value Added Scores (CVA) indicate that the Academy's precursor school was performing consistently below the LA mean. While its CVA score in 2006 indicates that it was not particularly effective, however, its scores in 2007 and 2008, though below the median level, indicate that, all other things being equal, the school was performing much as would be expected.

On becoming an Academy the CVA scores increase, moving above the LA mean in 2010. However, while the 2009 CVA score show the Academy was not performing below the levels that would be expected (CVA = 987.1; upper limit = 997.2; lower = 976.9), the improved performance in 2010 (CVA = 1005.3; lower = 995.5; upper = 1015.2) show that it is simply performing as one would expect even though it moved into the top half of the LA table.

Regression Analysis

Resources and the availability of data allow only the simplest forms of statistical analysis. Care should be taken in interpreting the results, since absence rates and SEN rates are only proxy indicators of the challenges a school may face.

Though the Academy has improved pupil attendance and reduced SEN registration, GCSE average points scores have declined a little compared with other schools when these two factors are taken into account. In contrast, the proportion of pupils achieving the Level 2 threshold has improved more, even when SEN and absence levels have been accounted for.

However, the picture at Level 1 and Level 0 is less favourable, showing a decline in absolute terms and in comparison with LA norms. The extent to which the average points scores improve or decline - once the factors affecting pupil outcomes are taken into account (CVA) – provides an indication of how effectively schools are overcoming the performance inhibitors those factors impose.

On this measure, Academy E has moved to near the top of the LA table in 2010.

English Baccalaureate

The Academy's Ebac performance (near the bottom of the LA performance table before levels of SEN and absence are taken into account) when compared to other curriculum areas could be seen as an indication that the improving results are at the expense of what could be termed the 'traditional academic' subjects.

Comparison with Local Authority Schools

The proportion of Academy pupils attaining 5 GCSEs grades A*-C including English and Mathematics, remains well within the lower half of the LA table, though it is higher than the cohorts who attended the precursor school, and is improving. However, its performance is still below the LA norm. When levels of SEN and the absence rate are taken into account, the data show a different picture. While the Academy's performance, in comparison with LA schools, shows that it is improving its relative position and, in 2010 no longer in the bottom half of the table but very close to the norm, its performance is poorer than that of its precursor school from 2006-2008, albeit on a downward trajectory. How important this is, will be, perhaps, a matter for political as well as educational debate within the county.

In terms of those with the standard **science** qualification, Academy E has continued the upward trend of its precursor school. Once SEN and Absence are taken into account, the Academy is close to the top of the LA table.

In contrast with its pupils' performance in science examinations, the proportion gaining the standard **Modern Foreign Language** qualification at the Academy is low, both relatively and absolutely. However, given the limited data currently available, the extent to which this may be a true reflection of the Academy's long-term strategy, and whether it may or may not be desirable, are matters for observation and discussion both within the Academy itself and, perhaps, in the wider community of schools within the area, especially since it might appear to be a feature of the DfE's future examination policy.

Graph E1: GCSE Average Points Scores

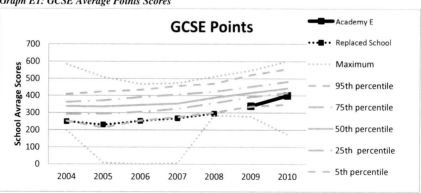

164

Graph E.2: Attainment at DfE Threshold Level 0

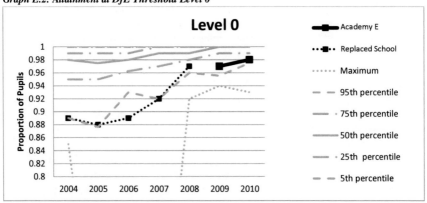

Graph E.3: Attainment at DfE Threshold Level 1

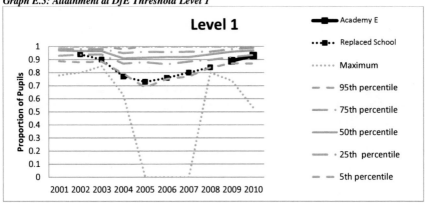

Graph E.4: Attainment at DfE Threshold Level 2

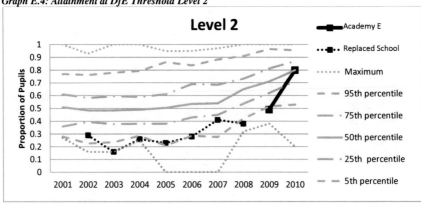

Graph E5: Pupil Absenteeism Rates

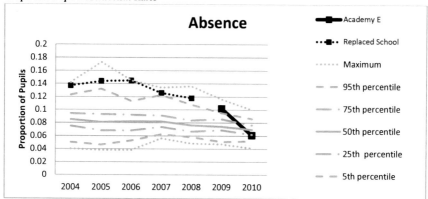

Graph E6: Proportion of Pupils with SEN Statements

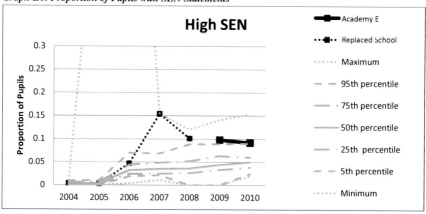

Graph E.7: Contextualised Value Added Scores

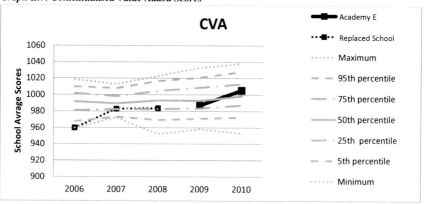

Graph E.8: Regression Analysis – GCSE Average points on SEN and Absence

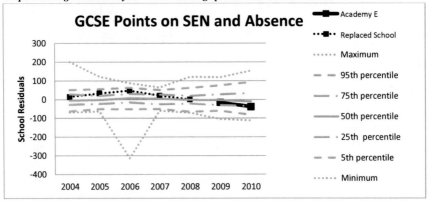

Graph E.9: Regression Analysis – Level 0 on SEN and Absence

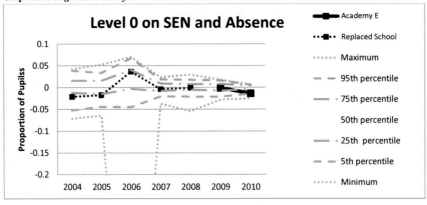

Graph E.10: Regression Analysis – Level 1 on SEN and Absence

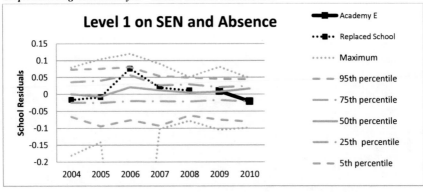

Graph E.11: Regression Analysis – Level 2 on SEN and Absence

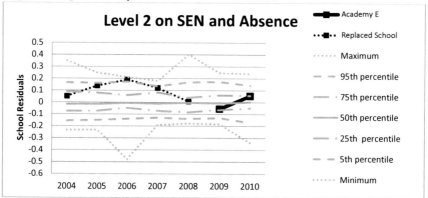

Graph E.12: Attainment in English Baccalaureate

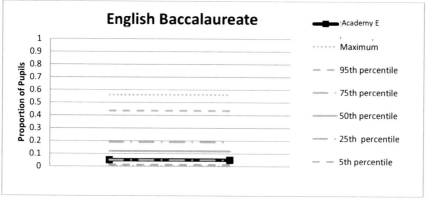

Graph E.13: Regression Analysis - English Baccalaureate on SEN and Absence

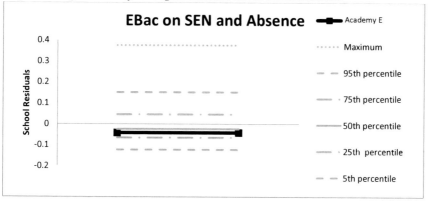

Graph E.14: Regression Analysis – Contextualised Value Added on GCSE Points

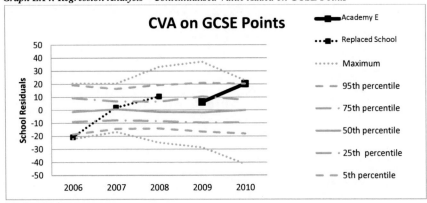

Graph E.15: Regression Analysis – Attainment at Threshold Level 2 (inc. English & mathematics)

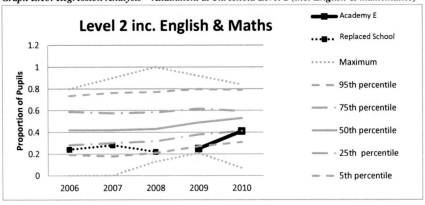

Graph E.16: Regression Analysis – Level 2 (inc. English & mathematics) on SEN and Absence

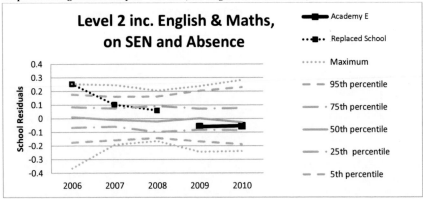

Graph E.17: Attainment of Standard Science Qualification

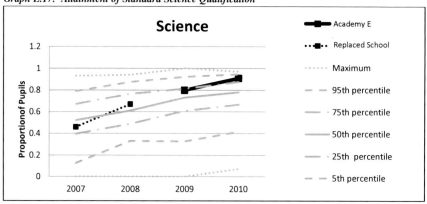

Graph E.18: Regression Analysis – Standard Science Qualification on SEN and Absence

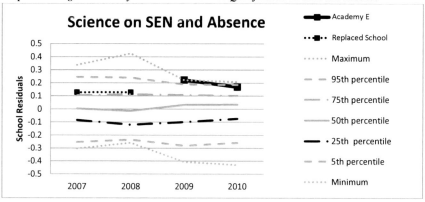

Graph E.19: Attainment in Modern Foreign Languages at Level 2

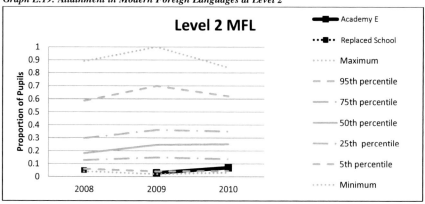

Graph D.20: Regression Analysis – Level 2 Modern Foreign Languages on SEN and Absence

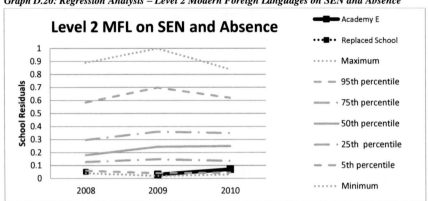

References

Clegg, A. B. (1962) Social factors, Education, 119. 15-16.

Clegg, A. B. & Megson, B. (1973) Children in Distress, Harmondsworth, Penguin.

Dearing, R. (2001) The Way Ahead: Church of England Schools in the New Millennium, London, Church House Publishing.

Department for Children, Schools & Families (2009) Deprivation and Education: The evidence on pupils in England, Foundation Stage to Key Stage 4. London: DCSF

Goldstein, H. & Cuttance, P. (1988) A note on national assessment and school comparisons, Journal of Educational Policy, 3. 2. 197-202.

Goldstein, H. & Sammons, P. (1997) The influence of secondary and junior schools on sixteen year examination performance: a cross-classified multilevel analysis, School Effectiveness and School Improvement, 8. 2. 219-230.

Gorard, S. (2012) The increasing availability of official datasets: methods, limitations and opportunities for studies of education, British Journal of Educational Studies, 60. 1. 77-92.

Gray, J., Jesson, D. & Jones, B. (1986) The search for a fairer way of comparing schools' examination results, Research Papers in Education, 1. 2. 91-118.

Kennedy, J. (1991) Adding value to raw scores, Managing Schools Today, 1. 4. 13-14.

McPherson, A. (1992) Measuring Added Value in Schools, National Commission on Education, Briefing No. 1.

Meegan, E. A., Carroll, J. B. & Ciriello, M. J. (2002) Outcomes, in: T.C. Hunt, E. A. Ellis & R. J. Nuzzi (eds) Catholic Schools Still Make a Difference: ten years of research 1991-2000, Washington DC, National Catholic Education Association, 43-53.

Mortimore, P., Sammons, P., Stoll, L., Lewis, D. & Ecob, R. (1988) School Matters: the junior years, Wells, Open Books.

Ray, A. (2006) School Value-Added Measures in England, a paper for the OECD Project on the Development of Value-Added Models in Education Systems, London, Department for Education and Skills.

Reynolds D. (1976) The Delinquent School, in: M. Hammersley & P. Woods (eds) The Process of Schooling, London, Routledge & Kegan Paul, 217-229.

Rutter, M., Maughan, B., Mortimore, P. & Oustan, J. (1979) Fifteen Thousand Hours, London, Open Books.

Saunders, L. (1998) 'Value-Added' Measurement of School Effectiveness: an overview, Slough, National Foundation for Educational Research.

Saunders, L. (1999) 'Value-Added' Measurement of School Effectiveness: a critical review, Slough, National Foundation for Educational Research.

School Curriculum & Assessment Authority (1994) Value-added Performance Indicators for Schools, London, SCAA.

Schagen, I. (1991) Beyond league tables: how modern statistical methods can give a truer picture of the effect of schools, Educational Research, 33. 3. 216-222.

Shipman, M. D. (1968) Sociology of the School, London, Longman.

Smith, D. J. & Tomlinson, S. (1989) The School Effect: a study of multi-racial comprehensives, London, Policy Studies Institute.

Tymms, P. & Dean, C. (2004) Value-Added in the Primary School League Tables, National Association of Head Teachers, London, NAHT.

The Translation of Ethos in Joint Church Academies
Elizabeth Green

Editor's Note
This two year research project, from 2009 to 2011, was funded by the Jerusalem Trust. It was the first major investigation undertaken by the National Centre for Christian Education at Liverpool Hope University and, given the joint church foundation status of the University, was particularly appropriate. It aimed to increase understanding of the processes that can help and hinder how joint church sponsored institutions can implement an ecumenically based vision of Christian education. Most of the work contained in this report was subsequently incorporated into a peer reviewed paper published in Research Papers in Education in 2014 (Volume 29. 3. 285-299).

Introduction
[*At the time of writing this report - Ed*], with one hundred and forty-four academies, the Church of England is the biggest provider of such institutions in England.[1] The Roman Catholic Church had fifty-one academies in 2011.[2] Writing in the Times Educational Supplement, Marley (2011) argues that as local authority powers dwindle 'the Church of England is poised to step into the breach' and become a driving force in education. This is despite well articulated opposition to the presence of religion in education and to the academies policy in the research literature.

In several locations the Church of England and the Roman Catholic Church have worked together to secure the expansion of church school places by jointly sponsoring academies. Little empirical research has been carried out within this field and so this paper contributes to a much needed mapping of the field and to our understanding of these new academic institutions. The research comprised an interview based study and was carried out in three joint Church academies during the academic years 2009/10 and 2010/11. It summarises the key findings in relation to the positioning, ethos and culture of jointly sponsored church academies by addressing two key questions: how do jointly sponsored academies articulate their objectives and Christian ethos and, what is the relationship between school structures and the ethos of the academy? This paper will first introduce the policy context of academies and briefly outline the dual system before exploring the literature around joint church schools, church schools and academies. It will then account for the methodology and theoretical framework of the study before presenting three key findings.

Contextualising the Field
There are currently three academies sponsored jointly by the Church of England and the Roman Catholic Church. Whilst few in number they may, in time, be joined by a small but

---

[1] Source: Church of England and Catholic Education Service. Figures correct at January 2012.
[2] Catholic Education Service Annual Census of Schools & Colleges 2011.

distinct group of joint church schools within the maintained state sector who have not taken up academy status (approximately twenty[3]). Set against the backdrop of the expansion of the academies programme, the persistence of the dual system in the United Kingdom which supports state funding for religious schools and the sense that the landscape of education in England is undergoing considerable transition, the experience of this small group of joint church academies is worth considering, especially at a time when the very notion of Church provided schools is coming under scrutiny.

Whilst this perspective may under-estimate the historic legacy of the church Marley (2011) raises an important question about the relationship of the church to education in a time of transition; how do joint church academies relate to the system? Traditional settlements have the potential to be completely unpicked by the current trend back to a private system (Ball, 2007) and this is happening without much public consultation about those wider issues.

Policy Context
Schools provided by Churches pre-date state funded universal education in this country and have played a significant role in the fabric of the state system since it formally began in 1870 (DfEE, 1995). Today, the presence of such schools in the state funded education system is commonly presented as an anachronism, out of touch with modern times and the liberal secular state (Copson, 2011). This perspective typically ignores the historic legacy of the dual system in England, although to be fair, it is complex and not always well understood. It fails to acknowledge that the creation of a state funded system of education in England and Wales was to a large extent made possible because both the Church of England and the Roman Catholic Church had taken seriously their responsibility to provide an education for the poor. This was before the principle of universal education had been widely accepted. Chadwick (1997) writes that when the Newcastle Commission of 1861 recommended a national system of schools it recognised how essential the existing church voluntary schools would be to the extension of elementary education to all social classes. Pillay (2009) writes that the church in the West, 'through its cathedral schools, was the progenitor of education and schooling' (p.10).

The dual system of state and church schools was formalised by the 1944 Butler Education Act which Chadwick (1997) writes 'finally approved a national system of free primary, secondary and further education to be administered through the local authority and supported by the rates and central government grants' (p. 33-34). Church schools were affirmed alongside county schools as integral to provision but offered a choice of status either to be 'Voluntary Aided' (VA) or 'Controlled' (VC). In VA schools the governing body employs the staff, the school sets its own admission arrangements, and buildings and land are owned by a charitable foundation; in VC schools, the local education authorities (LEAs) remain in control of staffing and admissions. In VC schools denominational religious instruction was

---

[3] Source English ARC, http://www.cte.org.uk/Articles/190991/ ... /Joint_Anglican_Roman.aspx> Accessed 01/09/2012. Accurate figures are hard to obtain since the Church of England and the Catholic Education Service list different numbers of joint church schools in their documentation.

guaranteed if parents specifically requested it, otherwise religious education (RE) is taught according to the locally agreed syllabus. Whilst these designations remain today the picture has become even more complex with the creation of new designations such as academies, trust and foundation schools.

The academies programme in England dates back to a Conservative government initiative of the early 1980's. City Technology Colleges (CTC's) were established in 1985 (DES, 1986) to serve areas of urban social and economic deprivation. At the time CTC's were seen by commentators and researchers as a significant step towards the privatisation of education which underpinned the subsequent legislative agenda of the 1980's Thatcher government (Walford & Miller, 1991, Whitty et al., 1993). CTC's were sponsored by private business, philanthropists and Christian churches and foundations that originally had to invest two million pounds; CTCs received per capita funding but had independent school status. This model of sponsorship was adopted by the 'New Labour' government who extended the City Academy policy as it became known, despite having pledged to reverse it when they were in opposition (Tomlinson, 2001).

'New Labour' was committed to opening 400 new academies by 2010 (Gillie & Bolton, 2010). In the academic year 2009/10 (in England the academic year runs from September to July) there were 200 academies open, 53 of these were designated as having religious character, all Christian (Department for Education (DfE), 2011). The Church of England sponsored nineteen academies; the Roman Catholic Church sponsored two and one academy was jointly sponsored by the Church of England and the Roman Catholic Church. The remainder were sponsored by Christian charitable foundations such as Oasis, the Grace Foundation and the Emmanuel Schools Foundation. The acceptance by New Labour of what Tomlinson describes as 'Conservative faith in choice and competition' preserved the principle of recruiting private sponsorship for schools and extending it to faith-based groups (2001, p.85).

The subsequent Coalition government continued to support the expansion of academies and their sponsorship by religious groups. The extension of the policy to include primary schools quickly increased the number of academies open. In November 2011 there were one thousand, four hundred and nineteen, academies open in England. (Scotland, Wales and Northern Ireland set their own education policy because of devolved government and they do not have academies).

Every school which is rated as outstanding by the English inspection system the Office for Standards in Education (OfSTED) may convert to academy status and these are known as 'converter' academies, new academies are known as 'sponsored'. Sixty eight of the academies open in January 2011 were designated as having religious character (DfE, 2011). The requirement to be in an area of low socio-economic deprivation has been dropped as has the requirement for sponsors to put in an initial financial investment. Schools judged by OfSTED to be failing may be converted into academies and run by sponsors of existing successful academies. The policy has generated fierce public and academic debate. General questions about equity, funding and the decline of the common school have been as controversial as the more specific concern about state funding for religious schools in view of the perceived rise in religious terrorism and sectarianism.

Literature

Joint Church Academies stand at an intersection of competing fields of education and this is reflected in the research literature. Broadly three areas are relevant for understanding their context and for establishing a rigorous framework of analysis:

i)   the research into joint church schools carried out by Chadwick (1994) and which remains the only major investigation in this field;

ii) research into Church of England schools and Catholic schools in their own right; and -

iii) research carried out in the academies.

There are some key differences in the way that Roman Catholic and Church of England schools understand their educational mission and purpose and, it could be argued, there is probably no such thing as a generic Church of England or Roman Catholic school. The geography, history and politics of archdiocese, diocese, religious orders and parish mean that no two Roman Catholic or Church of England schools are the same. A detailed discussion of the history and evolution of Anglican and Catholic education in England is beyond the realms of this paper; nevertheless some broad characteristics can be identified and are widely used within the literature as points of comparison. The Roman Catholic Church school has traditionally regarded the responsibility to educate children of the Catholic faith as its primary purpose. Bryk's (1993) commonly used but helpful illustration of the three-legged stool helps us to see the place of the Catholic school alongside the parish church and home.

Historically, in England, the Catholic school offered security and social mobility to a poor, ethnic and religious minority which suffered from sectarian prejudice. Morris & Godfrey (2006) argue that today parents are more likely to seek the high educational standards and human values associated with Catholic education over a commitment to the formal practice of Catholicism and they suggest that this might help to explain the increasing popularity of Catholic schools with non-Catholic parents. Nevertheless there remains a sense of connectedness to a community of faith, expressed in a particular Christian ethos which underpins approaches to Catholic education in maintained schools in England which Grace (2002) refers to as 'Catholicity'.

The Church of England has traditionally conceptualised its task as the general education of the children of the parish. As the established church the parish includes all children whether or not they or their families regularly attend church. A significant review of the Church of England's education provision was undertaken in 2001 and it extended, or perhaps re-stated, the centrality of church schools to the Church of England's mission to the nation (Dearing, 2001). *The Way Ahead* report argued that Church of England schools were in danger of losing their distinctiveness and the review set out what it regarded as the fundamental characteristics of a Church school. They recommended that Church of England schools should be led by a head teacher committed to the Christian character of the school. This stops short of requiring head teachers to be members of the Anglican Church; head teachers of Catholic schools, however, are required to be baptised Catholics. The review also recommended that the school should 'engage meaningfully in a real act of Christian worship every day'; offer a school life incorporating Christian values, devote 5% of curriculum time to RE; observe the major Christian festivals; maintain an active relationship with a parish church and make explicit use of Christian symbols in the fabric and furnishings of the school (Dearing, 2001, section 4.6).

Since *The Way Ahead* was commissioned in 2001 over one hundred new Church of England schools have been opened, much of this rapid expansion is a response to the review's recommendation that the Church of England should open more secondary schools (its primary provision considerably out-numbered its secondary provision when *The Way Ahead* was commissioned); this has been achieved partly through the creation of Church of England academies. Between them, the Church of England and the Roman Catholic Church account for around a third of state maintained provision.

Having recognised that there are some differences in how the two churches understand their educational mission and purpose we need to consider how joint church schools in England came to be and how they fit into the ecumenical landscape. This paper will not review the history of integrated schools in the rest of the United Kingdom but it does draw heavily on the work of Chadwick (1994). Chadwick's book *Schools of Reconciliation* reflects on an integrated school in Belfast - and is worth further reading for those interested in the particular context of Ireland. Chadwick (2011) argues that the ecumenical movement in this country underwent three distinct phases in the twentieth century. Within the Church of England the influence of Tractarian theology at the beginning of the century and its emphasis on the one visible body of the church and the Eucharist was significant for reminding Anglicans of their shared common heritage with Roman Catholics (Chadwick, 1994). In 1962 the Second Vatican Council resulted in a decree on Ecumenism which placed it firmly onto the agenda. The Council established a Secretariat for Christian Unity and after a visit of the Archbishop of Canterbury, Michael Ramsey, to Rome in 1966 the first Anglican/Roman Catholic International Commission (ARCIC) was established. In 1982 a common declaration was signed by Pope John Paul II and Archbishop Runcie, Chadwick argues that this would have been unthinkable at the beginning of the Century. The end of this first phase was marked by what ecumenists regard as a disappointing response to the ARCIC report on behalf of the Vatican council and Chadwick argues that phase two, from the mid 1980's through to the late 1990's, was marked by a reassertion of Catholic orthodoxy with ecumenism struggling to get onto the radar. Phase three from the turn of the century to the present has been marked by a renewed interest in churches working together but living with difference, the goal of complete unity has perhaps been postponed in favour of cooperation in the present around projects such as education, community work and local fellowship. Joint Church schools in England have opened throughout these phases with a cluster in the late 1970's and early 80's and another group more recently including the academies which are the focus of this research. Chadwick's (1994) research confirms that the reasons for creating a joint church school are various and often depend as much, if not more, on a range of local factors such as the availability of church school places, the motivations of the clergy and the resources of schools than they do on a commitment to ecumenical education. Nevertheless Chadwick (1994) argues that there remains within the joint church school movement a determination to work in partnership to educate 'young people in shared Christian values' (p. 58).

Using the story of St Bede's Joint Anglican/Roman Catholic School in Redhill where she worked as the Head of RE, Chadwick (1994) discusses a range of issues common to the creation and development of joint church schools. It is important to briefly identify these issues as they were used in the theoretical framework for this study into joint church academies. Chadwick (1994) poses a number of questions which may rightly be asked of all Christian schools but which joint church schools have to explore from the perspectives of two traditions with their attendant concepts of parish, different theologies and different cultural norms and assumptions; all of which can create points of conflict. These questions are: how does the Christian school explicitly nurture the faith of its pupils, while educating them to be intellectually critical? What should be the relationship between the Christian school and the nearby parish communities? In what ways, if any, will the ethos or community spirit of a Christian school be distinguished from that of a county school? To what extent will that ethos affect the teaching of non-religious subjects in the curriculum and the way in which members of the school relate to each other?

Chadwick's research shows that although there are issues particularly pertinent to the joint church school context (such as if and how to celebrate Eucharist or how to teach RE in a joint church school) joint church schools also wrestle with many of the same questions that other Church schools do when working out their role in an increasingly secularised society. As school communities (staff and students) become less familiar with the church and its teachings, issues around theological and spiritual literacy, what constitutes distinctive Christian school leadership, how to relate rightly to the expectations of parents and how to respond to the pressures of government policy become more difficult to resolve. These themes are more fully examined in a review of the research evidence on the impact of schools with a Christian ethos, including church schools and academies, by Green & Cooling (2009). They argue that there does not appear to be a common language for talking about values, spirituality or ethos and a lack of consensus regarding the purpose of, and contribution to be made by, Christian distinctiveness in education (Green & Cooling, 2009, p. 77). The research that they reviewed found that head teachers and school leaders were often ill-equipped to articulate the mission and purpose of their schools in theological or spiritual terms (see for example Street, 2007 and Johnson & McCreery, 2007). Jelfs, (2008), Green (2009a) and Deakin-Crick (2002) found that when Christian ethos and values do not underpin the wider curriculum, beyond RE, their impact on students is relatively limited. Whilst schools like St Bede's in Redhill addressed some of these questions, particularly in relation to curriculum approaches and integrating the teaching of values when they were founded, the advent of the national curriculum, a lack of confidence amongst teachers when talking about matters of faith (see Revell & Walters, 2010) and the pressures of achieving national standards and operating in a market system would suggest that such approaches are not so widespread in joint church and church schools today. The joint church academy project afforded a unique opportunity to chronicle the process of creating two new joint academies and observe sponsors and senior leaders attempting to address these questions and issues; in this sense it builds directly on Chadwick's work updated for our contemporary educational context.

To date there has been little empirical research available in relation to academies and none published in relation to those sponsored by the Catholic Church or the Church of England. A number of authors write about academies at a policy level particularly in relation to the issues of democratic models for both education and social policy. For example Ball (2005, 2007) has written extensively about the relationship between the academies programme and what he sees as an anti-democratic re-shaping of the public sector through the participation of unaccountable modern philanthropists and businessmen. Gunter, Woods, & Woods (2009) carried out a case study of a secular academy with a specialism in business and enterprise. They used the case study to test out a typology of entrepreneurialism and have argued that traditionally individualistic business models rather than those based on collective democracy still dominate conceptions of enterprise in academies (Woods, Woods, & Gunter 2007; Gunter, Woods, & Woods 2009). Similarly, Hatcher & Jones (2006) raise questions about local democratic processes with their research into the consultation procedures surrounding the establishment of new academies. They argued that the process of creating academies fails to take seriously local opposition to the loss of their community schools and threatens parental and community rights. Gorard (2005) used the DfES own figures on school performance between 1997 and 2003/04 to contest the policy discourse that academies improve standards in education. He found that there was no evidence that CTCs and academies were performing any better than the schools they replaced.

Two research studies explore the Christian ethos and core values of academies sponsored by a non-denominational Christian foundation. Pike (2009) has investigated the relationship between the core values of the sponsor and the aspirations of pupils at Trinity Academy in Thorne near Doncaster. Trinity Academy was designated the most improved academy nationally in 2007 and is sponsored by the Emmanuel Schools Foundation (ESF). Pike (2009) concluded that the combination of business sponsorship, seven core values (honourable purpose, humility, compassion, integrity, accountability, courage and determination) and Christian ethos played a significant role in transforming opportunities for academy students. This author's ethnographic study of a CTC and two academies sponsored by ESF was the first to be carried out in the UK (Green, 2009a). Green (2009a) found that although students demonstrated good biblical knowledge and valued being informed about religion, there was little evidence that the core values and Christian ethos were a strong enough vehicle to radically reshape their worldview. Whilst both Green (2009b) and Pike (2009) agree that the use of core values in the ethos creates a consensual space where different conceptions of the origins of values and morality can coalesce, Green (200b) argues that the practical effect is a dilution of the Christian basis of the ethos being communicated to students. Whilst this research was not carried out in church academies, Green (2012) has raised pertinent questions about how ethos is perceived by students, how it is embedded or not embedded in structures, pedagogy and curriculum, and whether it effectively communicates the distinctive Christian educational experience intended by sponsors. These questions overlap with those raised by

Chadwick (1994) in the context of joint church schools and form the context for this research into joint church academies.

Methodology and Theoretical Framework

Data collection and analysis was carried out during the academic years 2009/10 and 2010/11. There were two primary research questions: 1) how do jointly sponsored academies articulate their objectives and Christian ethos? In particular how do they manage this in predecessor schools during the transition phase and 2) what is the relationship between school structures and the ethos of the (proposed) academy?

These questions were investigated through data collection in three joint church academies. Two were in the process of development and officially opened in September 2011 and one had been open for over a decade. One academy amalgamated two predecessor schools, one academy replaced a Roman Catholic Church school and one academy was a new school. One of the academies was located in a large metropolitan city, one in a former spa town and one in a former manufacturing town; all three were located in areas of relatively low socio-economic status with a predominantly white working class population. Data was collected through documentary analysis and interview. Documentary analysis comprised documents available in the public domain such as prospectuses, consultation documents, expressions of interest from sponsors as part of the academy bid and other material which had been lodged with the Department of Education. Interviews were semi-structured, with topics and prompt questions organised around the following themes: background (this refers to context and the nature of participants' connection with the academy); sponsors and core values, and transition (transition from predecessor schools where relevant).

The participants comprised a purposive sample chosen because of their role in relation to the academy. These roles included: principals and vice principals, diocesan education officials, governors, representatives of management consultancy and building management companies, clergy and sponsors. In all three academies access was gained via a letter of introduction using a known contact wherever this was possible. The interviews snowballed in that participants would recommend other people to interview and so further contacts were then followed up. A total of fifteen interviews were carried out. Interviews were digitally recorded and transcribed by the researcher (this author was the sole researcher). All participants were sent a copy of the transcript and offered the chance to amend the record if they wanted to, no amendments were made. All of the participants were over the age of 18 and able to give written informed consent, they were given written information as to the aims of the study, how the material would be used and how to withdraw; participants have the right to withdraw from the study at any point and without giving a reason. Participant data has been fully anonymised but due to the small size of the sample it may be possible to identify the academies themselves even though they are not named in any writing about the research. As a result no one academy is reported on individually in this research and participants were informed that this would be the case. The gender of participants is not given nor their specific job title in order to further protect their anonymity, in addition a delay of at least one year has been built in to the publication of this research so that no material appeared at the same time as the new academies opened.

The theoretical framework used for analysis in this research draws on the approach developed by Grace (2002) in his research into Catholic school mission in the context of the marketisation and secularisation of the English education system. This is one of the studies in which Grace utilises the concept of 'Catholicity' referred to earlier in this paper. Grace employs Bourdieu's concepts of field, habitus and capital to investigate what forms of capital Catholic leaders have to draw on in the contested field of Catholic education. Catholicity refers to the spiritual and religious sense of pupils and staff expressed in things like attendance at mass or the number of religious vocations amongst school leavers. Grace (2002) concluded that Catholicity can operate as a form of spiritual capital which Catholic school leaders can draw on in the face of secular challenges to traditional concepts of Catholic mission and education. This spiritual capital stems from their religious identity and heritage, Bourdieu would term this habitus and he used the term to refer to deep-seated dispositions and cultural assumptions which are held sub-consciously because of things like our religion, class and gender. Grace (2004) has consistently argued that we routinely analyse class and gender in sociology of education research but have failed to take religion seriously as a space for analysis. Grace used Bourdieu's work to frame a set of theoretical questions around identity, hierarchy, power and competition which he used to interrogate his data. This author has developed a theoretical framework of analysis which builds on Grace's approach using Bourdieu's tools and developing sets of questions which take seriously the beliefs of academy sponsors and research participants yet opens up religion as a space for the analysis of structures and processes in Christian academies (Green, 2012). This approach uses Bourdieu's concepts as organising categories for qualitative coding and then uses questions developed from these and from themes in the literature together with grounded themes from the research questions as a way of creating windows onto the data. It has the advantage of setting up distinct chains of evidence and analysis which clearly relate back to the research questions, theory and literature in the field.

In this study of joint church academies a set of theoretical questions was developed using Bourdieu's concepts along with the questions posed by Chadwick (1994). A full list of the questions can be found in the appendix, but broadly they can be grouped as follows:
   i)   questions for structural analysis, including questions like do joint academies constitute a 'field' or are two separate fields in operation (Catholic and Anglican) if so what is the relationship;
   ii) theological questions, such as what theological understanding underpins concepts of education and ethos and
   iii) Church school questions, these comprised the questions posed by Chadwick and an additional question: what is the relationship of academies to the dual system?

Discussion
This paper discusses three intersecting findings from the joint church academies research project. Namely that joint church academies are sites of intersecting and competing fields of

181

education; that they are relatively isolated from other joint church schools and that there is considerable potential for the aims of the sponsors to be diluted at critical points in the creation of a new academy. Ball (1990) has written about the ways in which national policies are interpreted and often reinterpreted at a local level. The greater the number of stakeholders involved, the greater the potential is for competing understandings of the nature and purpose of education. Whilst academies are designed to be independent, innovative and relatively free from the politics of local education provision the number of sponsors involved, complex consultation processes and stringent levels of national accountability may in fact create a very complex web of competing interests (see Ball, 2005; Hatcher & Jones, 2006). With respect to the joint church academies these interests may be grouped under the following headings: denominational, socio-economic and political.

Discussion in this paper primarily focuses on competing denominational interests and will seek to illustrate how these are overlaid with perspectives that stem from class or from status and positioning e.g. clergy and laity. All three of the academies in the research sample had multiple sponsors. In addition to the Church of England and the Roman Catholic Church this included a variety of organisations such as universities, and other independent schools.

All three of the schools were located in areas of relatively low social and economic status where middle class parents educated their children predominantly out of area. In two instances predecessor schools were perceived as failing or in decline which placed the new academies under considerable pressure nationally and locally to demonstrate improvement. In both of those instances there was some opposition from Catholic parents to the perceived loss of 'their' Catholic school and this is an important theme to explore further as an example of competing denominational interests in the field overlaid with social, economic and political factors.

Grace's (2002) work around 'Catholicity' and the historic legacy of Catholic schools being closely connected to their respective communities helps to account for the strong current of feelings associated with the closure of two Catholic schools in this sample; but so too does the social-economic context and political (with a small p) identity of the communities involved. Bourdieu's conceptual tools help to reveal the inter-play between religious beliefs/assumptions and those associated with class and regional identity. Participants who lived and worked in the areas surrounding the predecessor schools pointed out that they constituted relatively insular communities.

In one instance a Catholic school served a pocket of lower socio-economic status bounded by very wealthy communities in the rest of the town. The school roll had been falling and one Catholic participant articulated some frustration that wealthier Catholic families tended to educate their children out of area. There remained a strong perception that the Catholic school served the poorer community and hadn't received the proper credit or support for hanging in there and offering a Catholic education to local Catholic families. The view of another participant who attended a protestant Free Church was that this was an area of town that simply needed a good school of its own and that Christian values would support that:

'I'm in my role and in this job to provide outstanding education but also to share God and to share faith with young people and I don't mind where they end up going to church.'

(Interview Transcript, D2).

From the perspective of diocesan officials Catholic places in all three locations needed to be secured in the context of falling rolls. One of these interpretations is not necessarily right and the other wrong, the point is that they co-existed as narratives within the same space and they illustrate competing assumptions about the nature and purpose of religious faith and education. One of the dividing lines is undoubtedly denominational. In all three sites participants who identified as Catholic expressed some uncertainty about how the Church of England understands its educational mission and ethos, in some cases this was expressed as outright scepticism. This can partly be accounted for by the fact that there had not been a Church of England secondary school in any of the three locations. There was an assumption that Catholic education was somehow stronger with a more clearly understood vision. Of even more interest was that this view was articulated by both Catholic and Church of England participants. For example one Anglican participant described the presence of the two churches in one location as follows:

'... the Catholic church is very evident and powerful and structured, the Anglican Church less so. But of course there's a weighting factor in that because the Catholic Church was strongly connected through [name of predecessor school removed to preserve anonymity]. And of course what this gave rise to as we moved forward into consultations was that the Catholic Church were better mobilised. And what really did emerge was, I don't know what you'd call it really, vicarious religiosity ... the Anglicans were new on the block in that sense, and our structures and processes were less well formed.'

[Interview Transcript, I2]

From the perspective of the sponsors it seemed that Anglican participants in the research acknowledged that *The Way Ahead* (Dearing, 2001) had asserted a clearer vision for distinctive Anglican schooling but also that joint church academies could benefit from the clarity of purpose associated with existing forms of Catholic education.

In both of the locations where a new academy replaced a Catholic predecessor school the local opposition from Catholic parents was interpreted by Anglican participants as having more to do with class than religion. One participant argued that local parents whose children attended a community school:

'... were so thrilled by the fact their kids were going to have the opportunity to be in a new school they weren't worried about the fact that it was going to be a church school. They just wanted their children to have a chance. But the Catholic parents were very outspoken and the bottom line was they didn't want

their kids mixing with [name of community school removed to preserve anonymity] kids.'

[Interview Transcript, I1].

This research project did not interview parents and so the validity of this interpretation cannot be established; it has been included as an example of where the competing perspectives lie and how issues of religion and class intersect. It illustrates the positioning of 'other' denominational groups in the field as the problem and it may also reflect misconceptions about how Catholic parents understand the place of the school in the community. Another line that intersects with denominational difference in the field is the distinction between Catholic clergy and laity. Those members of the clergy who were interviewed regarded parents and students as part of the community of the church whereas lay participants pointed out that many families were un-churched and saw the community of the joint academy as distinct from that of the church. One Catholic lay participant, reflecting on his experience of working with the Church of England for the first time in the creation of a new joint church Academy, felt that the Church of England was more realistic about this and commented:

'This is just what I got from the Church of England whereby there's no assumption that they [pupils] will necessarily have been churched...So even though they're coming to a, you know, it's not a joint faith, a Church of England school it's a recognition of where they're starting from, you know in terms of any journey that they have. Now I think with Catholic, you've got your primary schools. It's still, I suppose, how can one put it, there's still hope that people would have gone to a church, should be churched. And it's more 'they've never been to church isn't that awful' sort of approach rather than an acceptance of young people's lives or family life today and what the nature of the mission is.'

[Interview Transcript, I7]

The point here is definitely not to argue in any sense that Church of England schools are better attuned to the needs of a secular pupil population; rather this is evidence of the existence of different perspectives regarding the purpose of education and the nature of the community in a church school which all have to find a way to co-exist in a joint church academy. In this particular instance it is interesting that working with a different denomination enabled this participant to articulate a level of frustration with the approach of some Catholic clergy and to be confronted with different ways of representing the community of the school. Having identified this arena of denominational struggle the key question is to what extent is a new cultural understanding (Bourdieu would call this 'habitus') being formed in the site, how is this negotiated, who are the key spokespersons i.e where does the power lie in the construction of ethos? To link this to the questions that Chadwick (1994) poses: in what ways, if any, will the ethos or spirit of the joint church academy be distinguished from its predecessor school(s)? These questions will be explored further as we discuss the relationship of joint church academies to joint church schools and the translation of sponsors' aims into practice.

Using Chadwick's (1994) research as a point of comparison the study found that all three joint church academies had faced a very similar set of issues to those encountered by St Bede's Redhill as it was established. Bringing two church communities together for worship, wrestling with identity as a church school, and deciding on an RE curriculum are all identified by Chadwick (1994) as issues that joint church schools routinely face. Due to the lack of empirical research in this area it is not clear whether they are resolved in similar ways across the joint church school sector. They were not addressed in the same ways in the three joint church academies. Two out of the three joint church academies had decided not to celebrate joint Eucharist in order to side step an issue deemed too controversial to tackle in their particular diocesan context. In one of these academies attendance at services in the chapel was voluntary and in any case the chapel was a tiny room tucked away to the rear of the building and not the kind of focal point often found in church schools. In all three joint church academies the RE curriculum had been an issue of significant concern for Catholic parents and sponsors. Catholic sponsors had been adamant that RE should have 10% of curriculum time; one participant explained that not achieving this would have been deal breaker in the creation of one of the academies:

> 'In think if we'd said well actually it's only going to be 9.5% I think the whole thing would have gone into halt.'

[Interview Transcript, I4]

In her work Chadwick (1994) acknowledges that resolving potentially contentious issues around worship, religious identity and RE can be painful but argues that in order for ecumenical partnership to be real and meaningful they need to be openly discussed with the whole school community before decisions are reached. Furthermore she argues that these kinds of discussions are a significant part of the process for bringing two church communities together and becoming secure in their identity. A participant involved in the opening of two joint church academies explained how important it had been for the sponsors to work together to drive through their vision. When asked how issues of disagreement had been handled this participant seemed to think it was better that such challenges be resolved by sponsors and if necessary dealt with behind closed doors:

> 'There were different ideas around the table but at the end everyone wanted to achieve the same thing and I think these sponsors are the same and I think that is part of the journey that they've had...working together I think things get ironed out in the end and get sorted out.'

[Interview Transcript, I3]

This contrasts with the experience Chadwick (1994) writes about at St Bede's where staff from the amalgamating schools were encouraged by the head teacher to meet regularly in departments and working parties to discuss all aspects of schools life from discipline to curriculum and report to on what their contribution could be. Well-attended staff prayer meetings continued weekly for up to two years at St Bede's after the joint church school opened. A significant area of difference for the joint church academies of course is that they were opening as new schools. In two cases the previous schools, and by association their staff, were deemed by the government to be failing. The academies were going through a stressful and painful process of TUPE and in one case staff coming from a community school were anxiously waiting to find out what working in a church school was going to be like. When asked to comment on whether staff had been consulted and included in discussions about the new academy, its ethos, its curriculum and its new building one participant argued that this was difficult to do without raising people's expectations around what their own jobs might be. It was considered important by participants that the joint church academies be seen as completely new schools and that, what were perceived as, poor teaching practices and low standards were not simply transferred across:

> 'You do want to consult with staff and engage with them but that's also tricky because things will be different in the new academy, people might not be in the same role that they're in now when they transfer across... And we're going to start coming to a tricky part now with starting the TUPE process because I'm not sure if some staff realise that and I'm wondering if some staff just think yeah, I'll transfer across and I'll just do what I do now: which defeats the object of the Academy.'

[Interview Transcript, J3]

This is potentially one of the critical areas where the aims of the sponsors carefully written into the education brief and other planning documents may be lost in translation. The process of tackling potentially divisive issues and taking a position on the nature of worship, RE and determining the core values of the ethos happens separately from the appointment of staff and often before the recruitment of Principals and senior leaders. What is interesting is that although these issues have also been contentious for other joint church schools the research found no evidence that sponsors had talked to the governors or diocesan teams involved in their creation. There had been some consultation with other academies and a sharing of experienced personnel, local authority and diocesan expertise during the planning stages. For example, participants who held posts in other established academies served on committees or offered advice, but the bulk of their contribution was to areas not considered 'religious' such as legal matters, finance and project management. The prevailing view was that the joint church school identity and Christian ethos was really a matter for the sponsors. This is partly explained by the fact that the academy policy has deliberately created a sector which does not have to operate in relation to other schools. Government policy actively encourages sponsors to take on chains of academies and to build on their experience of running them. Green (2009a) has argued that this encourages academies to adopt structures and operating processes uncritically without considering whether they support or undermine the Christian ethos of the institution. Furthermore, Green (2009a) argued that academy models were very hierarchical with top down systems of decision making and she found that this was also compounded by a theological hierarchy. In other words staff who shared the religious habitus of the sponsors were more visible in the academies both in relation to decision making processes but also as spokespersons for the Christian ethos (Green, 2009a).

More research is needed, but Grace's argument about the nature of 'catholicity' as a form of spiritual capital together with the perception that Catholic education has a stronger more visible identity suggests that Catholic sponsors may be the more dominant partners in the creation of joint church academies and hence more influential in the construction of ethos. The rhetoric around Christian ethos in the documentation of the academies researched will often portray a community built around a shared set of values but in practice sponsors assume that ethos can be 'created' in a new school with a top down delivery model. This model is often dependent on explicit ethos statements, teaching in RE and assemblies and in the pastoral care structure (Green, 2009b). Donnelly (2000) describes this as a positivist model arguing that the true nature of a school ethos needs to be researched in the gap between what is imposed top down and what is generated from the bottom up. Green's (2009a) research in this gap found that structures and processes, curriculum and pedagogy communicate ethos to students often more powerfully than explicit teaching about Christian values in RE and collective worship.

In one of the regions in the sample there was a considerable history of the Roman Catholic and Church of England dioceses working together in partnership; this is not necessarily the same as affirming a theological commitment to the kind of ecumenical goals espoused by ARCIC. It was not possible to thoroughly examine the theological frameworks written into the education briefs for the joint academies in the sample since they were not all publicly available. Analysis of the interviews carried out with key participants who had been involved in writing the briefs and closely involved in the bid process for the two new academies suggested that the framework largely relied on the language of 'shared values' and articulated a commitment to be faithful to both traditions and welcoming to those of 'other faiths and none'. Some participants talked of sharing 'gospel values' and contributing to the mission of the church. The majority were frustratingly vague about the theological basis for the mission and ethos in the joint church academy that they were involved in. The exceptions two Catholic participants who were able to clearly articulate a theology of Catholic education but who were very frustrated with the experience of working on the creation of a joint church academy: twelve months later they were no longer working on the project.

As discussed in the literature review the wider research around church schools in England suggests that school leaders lack theological literacy and are not confident about articulating the ethos and mission of their schools in these terms. One of the participants argued that appointing a head teacher and leadership team to take ownership of the sponsors' ethos and to mobilise it in the institution was a critical point at which a sponsor's mission and ethos might be lost in translation:

> 'The question for academies... is who is the guardian of the mission? Is the mission clearly identified? Is it owned, is it checked on, is it in the heart of the place or is it in the mind of one person? So I've seen academies I have to say produce great responses but along comes the head teacher: I'm going to do it this way. That's the autonomy of the profession.'
>
> [Interview Transcript, I2]

This reflects contemporary discourse in which school leaders, in particular Principals, shoulder almost sole responsibility for the success or otherwise of their schools. Within the academy model Principals effectively function as Chief Executive Officers. In a church academy, let alone a joint church academy, this places considerable trust in their ability to lead a faith community and yet this will have been addressed only briefly, if at all, in their training. With the caveat that a detailed analysis of the education briefs has not been carried out the findings from this research suggest that a clear theological rationale for the distinctive identity of a joint church school may not have been handed on to senior leadership teams in the first place. Chadwick's (1994), Donnelly's (2000) and Green's (2009a) research all suggest that ethos is not something that can be worked out in advance and handed on. If theological difference, religious identity and Christian ethos are formed through negotiation within a community, as Chadwick (1994) argues, then this model would appear to be fundamentally flawed.

Conclusion
This research project sought to investigate how joint church academies are situated within the field, how they relate to existing academies and the maintained joint church school sector and how they articulate their vision and ethos. Little empirical research has been carried out within academies and so this study contributes to a much needed mapping of the field and to our understanding of the culture and positioning of individual academies.

It found that joint academies are sites of intersecting and competing fields of education, operating in relative isolation from the wider joint church school sector. Whilst sponsors may have been relatively clear about their aims and objectives it did not seem that the creation of joint church academies was rooted in a robust framework of ecumenical theology. There was not much evidence that a good understanding of ecumenical mission and ethos was handed on to Principals and senior leadership teams and the research concluded that this was a critical point where aims and objectives were lost in translation. Potentially divisive denominational issues such as the Eucharist, collective worship and RE were discussed and resolved by the sponsors, often before teaching staff had been appointed. This contrasts with the nature of collaborative working recommended by Chadwick (1994) as an essential component of establishing a joint church school committed to meaningful ecumenical partnership.

Academies are subject to a highly pressured policy discourse around results and standards. The academy policy has provided the church with a way to continue to partner the state in providing education but the speed with which success and improvement must be demonstrated appeared to supersede theological reflection in these cases. The research concluded that this had the potential to dilute the distinctive aims of joint church school education.

References
Ball, S. J. (1990) Politics and Policy Making in Education: explorations in policy sociology, London, Routledge.

Ball, S.J. (2005) Radical policies, progressive modernization and deepening democracy: the Academies programme in action, Forum 47. 2 & 3. 215-22.

Ball, S. J. (2007) Education PLC: understanding private sector participation in public sector education, London, Routledge.

Bryk, A.S. (1993) Catholic Schools and the Common Good, Cambridge, MA, Harvard University Press.

Chadwick, P. (1994) Schools of Reconciliation: issues in Joint Roman Catholic Anglican education, London, Cassell.

Chadwick, P. (1997) Shifting Alliances: church & state in English education, London, Cassell.

Chadwick, P. (2011) untitled paper presented at the Joint Church Schools Conference, Ely, October 2011.

Copson, A. (2011) 1 in 10 English Secondary Schools are now Academies: The BHA continues to warn of the potential dangers of religious Academies, http://www.humanism.org.uk/news/view/725, accessed 13 January, 2011.

Deakin Crick, R. (2002) Transforming Vision: managing values in schools, London, Middlesex University Press.

Dearing, R (2001) The Way Ahead: Church of England schools in the new millennium, The National Society for Promoting Religious Education, www.churchofengland.org, [Accessed 17 August, 2012].

Department for Education & Science (1986) A New Choice of School, London, Her Majesty's Stationery Office.

Department for Education & Employment (1995) Consultation Paper on Self-government for Voluntary-Aided Schools, London: DFEE

Department for Education (2011) Faith Schools: Faith Academies, www.education.gov.uk/b0066996/faith-schools/faith, [Accessed May 14, 2011].

Donnelly, C. (2000) In pursuit of school ethos, British Journal of Educational Studies, 48. 2. 134-154.

Gillie, C & Bolton, P. (2010) Academies Bill Research Paper, London, Her Majesty's Stationery Office.

Gorard, S. (2005) Academies as the 'future of schooling': Is this an evidence-based policy? Journal of Education Policy, 20. 3. 369–77.

Grace, G. (2002) Catholic Schools: mission, markets and morality, London, RoutledgeFalmer.

Grace, G. (2004) Making connections for future directions: taking religion seriously in the sociology of education, International Studies in Sociology of Education, 14. 1. 47–56.

Green, E. & Cooling, T. (2009) Mapping the field: a review of the current research evidence on the impact of schools with a Christian ethos, London, Theos.

Green, E. (2009a) An ethnographic study of a CTC with a Bible-based ethos, unpublished DPhil thesis, University of Oxford.

Green, E. (2009b) Speaking in parables: the responses of students to a Bible-based ethos in a Christian City Technology College, Cambridge Journal of Education, 39. 4. 443–56.

Green, E. (2012) Analysing religion and education in Christian academies, British Journal of Sociology of Education, http://dx.doi.org/10.1080/01425692.2012 [Accessed 11 April 2012].

Gunter, H., Woods, P. A. & Woods, G. J. (2009) Testing a typology of enterpreneuralism: emerging findings from an Academy with an enterprise specialism, Management in Education, 23. 3. 125–9.

Hatcher, R., & K. Jones, K. (2006) Researching Resistance: campaigns against academies in England, British Journal of Educational Studies, 54. 3. 329–51.

Jelfs, H. (2008) 'Is it the dance of life, Miss?' An exploration of educational paradigm and pedagogical practice in Church of England schools, unpublished PhD thesis, University of Bristol.

Johnson, H. & McCreery, E. (1999) The Church of England head: the responsibility for spiritual development and transmission in a multi-cultural setting, International Journal of Children's Spirituality, 4. 2. 165-170.

Marley, D. (2011) An answer from above? Times Educational Supplement, 23rd December, http://www.tes.co.uk/article.aspx?storycode=6158763 [accessed 29th December 2011].

Morris, A. B. & Godfrey, R. (2006) A statistical survey of attainment in Catholic schools in England with particular reference to secondary schools operating under the trust deed of the Archdiocese of Birmingham, Canterbury, National Institute for Christian Education Research.

Pike, M. A. (2009) The Emmanuel Schools Foundation: sponsoring and leading transformation at England's most improved academy, Management in Education, 23. 3. 139–43.

Pillay, G. (2009) Preface, in: E. Green & T. Cooling (2009) Mapping the Field: a review of the current research evidence on the impact of schools with a Christian ethos, London, Theos.

Revell, L. & Walters, R. (2010) Christian Student RE Teachers, Objectivity and Professionalism, Canterbury, Canterbury Christ Church University.

Street, R. W. (2007) The impact of The Way Ahead on headteachers of Anglican voluntary-aided secondary schools, Journal of Beliefs and Values, 28. 2. 137-150.

Tomlinson, S. (2001) Education in a Post-Welfare Society, Buckingham, Open University Press.

Walford, G., & Miller, H. (1991) City Technology College, Milton Keynes, Open University Press.

Whitty, G., Edwards, T. & Gewirtz, S. (1993) Specialisation and Choice in Urban Education, London, Routledge.

Woods, P.A., Woods, G. J. & Gunter, H. M. (2007) Academy schools and entrepreneurialism in education, Journal of Education Policy, 22. 2. 263–85.

Academies: Unity of Purpose?
The Catholic Educational Dilemma Revisited

Geraldine Bradbury

Editor's Note

Geraldine's research analyses the development of Catholic education since the 19th century, with special reference to the response of the Catholic sector to the challenges and opportunities presented by various Education Acts, its ability to influence legislative changes, and the context within which the internal deliberations about its educative policies took place. The dilemma facing the bishops in the run up to the Education Act 1944 was financial (Beck, 1955). Could the Church meet the costs of securing voluntary aided status for its schools which would guarantee their Catholic character? Today, Geraldine argues, it is structural. This extract is taken, mainly, from chapter 5 of her thesis, and is concerned with the response of the Catholic sector, particularly in the Diocese of Salford, to the Academies Act 2010.

Introduction

Each of us is a synthesis of our stories, either that of our own life or our family or the community in which we live and with which we identify ourselves, creating our world view from within the context of this story. Education has a vital role to play in transmitting those stories and that cultural identity from one generation to the next, providing not just 'the story' itself but the literacy skills necessary to access the story - the language required to listen and/or read and understand and the wisdom to discern in order to live the story authentically and retell it to the next generation.

For the Catholic[1] sector in England this has been set within the context of at times almost overwhelming challenge, occasionally self-inflicted, but more obviously externally imposed as a consequence of the destruction and persecution which followed, for instance the Reformation. That the Catholic religion survived and Catholic education continued in some form is a testament to the sacrifice and personal determination of many. Support came through schools and seminaries still existing in Europe and a gradually restored tolerance was given further impetus by the sympathy of British people towards exiles fleeing the consequences of the French Revolution who settled in England bringing their Catholic religion and schools[2] with them.

---

[1] I use the word 'Catholic' to denote those Catholics who belong to the Roman Catholic tradition and 'Church' to the religious organisation of Roman Catholics. 'Catholic' means a person who has been baptised into the Roman Catholic Church or received into the full communion of the Roman Catholic Church having been baptised in another Church or ecclesial community.

[2] 'School' refers to maintained & independent schools & colleges providing education to pupils at primary and secondary levels.

The Irish potato famine started in 1845 and between then and 1852 an estimated one million people emigrated from Ireland transforming the English Catholic community '... *into an overwhelmingly poor and ignorant group'* (Arthur, 1995, p. 13). Many settled, along with their clergy, in the emerging industrial cities of the North, in the Midlands and in London.

Catholic Education: Its Current Context

Despite the social and financial challenges, the unity of purpose displayed in public by the bishops across the years following the restoration of the hierarchy in 1850 – and especially leading up to the enactment of the 1944 Act - ensured that a viable and distinctive Catholic sector was established and consolidated as an important element within the state maintained education system. However, in recent years the burgeoning cost of education to the state and questions being raised about school outcomes have led to wide-ranging legislative changes in the national education system which the Catholic sector has tried to accommodate whilst preserving the advantages gained in 1944 by adopting the expensive Voluntary Aided status for its schools.

Responses to the Academies Act 2010 suggest that Catholic sector unity is in disarray with potentially dire consequences for the ecclesial character and purpose of the sector. The question of whether or not schools could or should become academies has reignited discussion about the purpose of Catholic schools and whether a change of status could affect their mission. In particular, there has been a great deal of debate as to whether it is possible for Catholic schools to convert to academy status without losing the hard-won protections afforded by the 1944 Education Act. Regional differences are marked. Of the 145 Catholic Academy schools open at the time of the Catholic Education Service (CES) Census in 2013 only 13 were in the North West, and none at all in the Dioceses of Salford and Lancaster.

Contextualising the Debate

Unlike the Church of England which readily embraced Academy status, it seemed that the Catholic sector was unable to respond with any coherence to the 2010 Academies Act and embarked on internal and, at the time of writing, still unresolved discussions about the fundamental purpose of Catholic schools. In addition, the ability of the bishops and indeed anyone else, to affect policy is limited by the fact that the government increasingly consults through issuing papers rather than by providing opportunities for discussion. One risk is that the Church sector, both Catholic and Church of England, could become marginalised, or treated as an irrelevance. In October 2013, for instance, a rapid response had to be made to a consultation paper on 'School Organisation' which, whilst seeking to streamline bureaucracy omitted any specific reference to Bishops or their dioceses. The paper advised governing bodies that, when considering changes to the status of their school, they should consult with their local authority (specifically mentioned in the consultation document) and 'any other body or person that they think appropriate'.[3]

---

[3] While this phrase would include the appropriate Bishop and Diocesan Trustees, the lack of specificity suggests there was little understanding by officials of the legal ownership and governance of Catholic schools.

Had the proposals been allowed to go through unchallenged the possibility of governors attempting to make decisions without the strategic overview of the diocese or the religious body, and without a clear understanding of the legal implications of their already existing Trust status could have had confusing consequences to say the least.

The decision of the Bishops to opt for Voluntary Aided status for its schools in accordance with the provisions of the Education Act 1944 ensured that the Church has been able to protect their Catholic character through Trustee ownership of the school premises and Trustee appointment of foundation governors who are in the majority on the governing body. The Governing Body are the employer and admissions authority; they control the use of premises and are entitled to give preference in employment to communicant Catholics where this is a genuine occupational requirement.[4]

The Academies Act 2010

The Education Reform Act 1988 made it possible for the government to act in partnership with the private sector to provide education, an addition to historical partnerships with the voluntary sector. By the time of the Learning and Skills Act 2000 the concept of City Academies had been introduced, later to be designated simply as 'Academies.' The Academies Act 2010 (UK Parliament, 2010) continued the fundamental realignment of educational structures, strategies and practices building upon the previous (Labour) government's concept of converting schools to academies where that school was perceived to be failing its pupils.

The coalition government which assumed power in 2010 first proposed that in addition, secondary schools which had been judged to be 'outstanding' by Ofsted be invited to become an Academy,[5] with eventually all schools being entitled to convert, and arrangements being put in place to convert schools which were deemed to be failing to provide an adequate standard of education[6]. This led to two types of academy – a 'sponsored academy' which results from government intervention, and a 'converter academy' which has voluntarily adopted this status and is not required to have a sponsor. In 2012 the option to seek academy status was made available to primary schools.

Academies are independent schools, which receive funding directly from the government, in effect establishing a business contract between the school and the Secretary of State, and by doing so remove the school from the current statutory framework, effectively reducing the amount of funding available to the local authority and other schools within the boundary.

---

[4] School Standards and Framework Act 1998 (amended) Section 60
[5] Reference is made to academy in the singular, whilst recognising in practice that Catholic academies are probably working together in a multi-academy company, referred to as a MAC or a MAT (multi-academy trust company) depending on the diocese in question. Essentially a MAC and a MAT are companies not trusts since they are set up using Articles of Association and are registered at Companies House.
[6] Academies Act 2010, s.4§ 4(b)

The Academies Act 2010 was a hastily conceived document[7] with academy proposals built on secular commercial grounds. The complications for the voluntary sector were exacerbated during the earliest days of the coalition government by changes in personnel within the Department for Education (Barber, 2013) and apparent ignorance of the complexities of the existing 'dual system'; the legal consequences of changing status; and the complex combination of charity and education legislation[8]. Account had to be taken of the fact that Catholic schools were already part of a Charitable Trust under the terms of which the school must operate as a Catholic school, and the question of land ownership, as Catholic schools are built on land owned by their Diocesan Trust[9]. Consequently in May 2010 the Catholic Education Service (CES) issued guidance to dioceses advising caution and suggesting that 'it is unlikely that Catholic schools will be able to become Academies.' (CES, 2010)

However, the Department for Education (DFE) was taking account of Church sector lobbying[10] and in an unprecedented development, the enacted legislation stated:

> *The governing body of a foundation or voluntary school that has a foundation may make an application under this section only with the consent of –*
>> *The trustees of the school, and*
>> *The person or persons by whom the foundation governors are appointed.*[11]

The continued willingness of the department to negotiate with the voluntary sector with respect to academy legislation has resulted in an agreed suite of documents which are available from the CES. Since Local Authorities are not a feature of this provision the department has also worked with and through the CES as the agent for the diocesan Bishops.

Further guidance for Diocesan Schools Commissions (DSC) from the CES in June 2010 referred in general terms to the specific implications for Catholic schools. This document acknowledged that some schools had expressed an interest in exploring the possibilities of seeking Academy status but that many schools had expressed their desire to maintain the special relationships which existed within a network of diocesan schools, under the trusteeship of their Bishop, or the network of schools held together within the trusteeship of a religious organisation.[12] In 5 October 2010, Dr Oona Stannard[13] informed dioceses of a working group set up to explore the matter of Academies in the Catholic sector. She referred to two questions – the more practical problem of whether Catholic schools **could** pursue

---

[7] 'We passed the Academies Act within 100 days of taking office' §5:9 *The Importance of Teaching* November 2010.

[8] An example of the *reduced visibility of the voluntary school as a distinct (and distinctive) entity* to which Paul Barber referred (Barber, 2013).

[9] From personal unpublished meeting notes.

[10] As providers of a third of schools, Church school support would be important.

[11] Academies Act 2010, s3: § 3 & 4.

[12] Information taken from my unpublished personal notes.

[13] Director of the CES at the time.

Academy status given their legal position as part of a charitable Trust and whether the protections afforded by voluntary aided status could be retained; and the much more fundamental issue of whether in fact a Catholic school **should** become an Academy.[14] Deliberating on these two issues is complicated by the autonomy of individual Bishops, and their right to decide on the schooling which takes place within their diocese, and the local geographical and demographic factors which have an implication for the viability of each school. The CES continued to negotiate with the DFE about these specific concerns as Dr Stannard reported to a symposium held in Westminster in April 2011, but she warned that,

> *'If as Catholics we continue to concentrate our energies on only critiquing the concept of this policy we will be left behind and our influence on the wellbeing of education nationally, our place in the debate, the openness of politicians to listen to us etc., may all be diminished. The more other schools become Academies, **the weaker would be our position if we continue to look backwards rather than forwards**.*'[15] *[author's emphasis – Ed]*

I argue, however, that 'looking backwards' can inform decisions, and that there is an inherent danger in not acknowledging and learning from the narrative of the past, as Archbishop Malcolm McMahon told his listeners at a recent conference.[16]

The Symposium in April 2011 which included Bishops, Diocesan Directors of Education and Diocesan Financial Secretaries was hosted by the CES to provide an opportunity for dioceses to share information and responses to the Act. It was at this meeting that differences became apparent, with dioceses in the south of the country reporting schools showing a much greater interest in pursuing academy status than that being noted in the North West.[17] One Diocesan Director expressed a concern that the different perceptions were indicative of a growing lack of cohesion, and voiced the belief that the Catholic community had preserved its schools over the years by presenting a united front and that the current difference of opinion only served to weaken the sector.[18]

The initial, very negative, response from the CES, that no Catholic school could move to Academy status has subsequently been overturned in a statement from Bishop Malcolm McMahon, Chairman of CES, in January 2011 in which he said:

> *'We should make conversion to Academies a ready possibility for Catholic schools, subject to the wishes of their Bishop, Trustees and Governing Body.'*

---

[14] Taken from my unpublished personal notes.

[15] Ibid

[16] See p. 6: 'We can only look forward to the future if we can understand how we have reached the present.'

[17] In a total of one hundred and forty-five Catholic Academies, thirteen are located in the North West, with none in the Dioceses of Salford and Lancaster – CES Data 2013.

[18] Information taken from unpublished personal notes

In order for this to happen a suite of Single and Multi-Academy Models has been developed, negotiated and agreed, which offer protection for the Voluntary Aided status of the schools, and a stated readiness by the DFE for schools to convert 'as is' with Voluntary Aided schools retaining that status, and 'Catholic' schools continuing to be called 'Catholic'.[19] Barber,[20] however, has warned of potential dangers in changing from 'a statutory system guaranteed by the Legislature to a series of contractual agreements with the Executive' (Barber, 2013, p. 21), citing the ease with which policy in respect of such contracts can be changed without national scrutiny, whilst also acknowledging that careful use of the new framework could lead to a stronger position for some.

The picture of Catholic Academy provision has varied across the country with the most recent figures from the CES 2013 Census showing that there were:

> '1,006 primary academies in January 2013, constituting about 6% of all primary schools; and 1,638 secondary academies, about half of all secondary schools. At the same date the Catholic sector had 74 primary academies, 4% of all Catholic primary schools, and 71 secondary academies, 21% of Catholic secondary schools. Almost all the Catholic academies were 'converter' academies, rather than 'sponsor-led' academies. Dioceses varied greatly in how far they had embraced the initiative: six had no academies; eight had fewer than 10, five between 10 and 20 while in the Nottingham diocese nearly half the schools had become academies: 35 in total.'[21]

(CES, 2013)

Of the dioceses that do embrace academy status for their schools there are variations in their approach with some only allowing Multi-Academy Trusts rather than single school academies; and others developing diocesan-wide co-operative strategies. It is significant, and indicative of his support for academy status, that at this time the Chairman of the Catholic Education Service, Bishop Malcolm McMahon was Bishop of Nottingham, which has the highest number of academies in any Catholic Diocese. The Diocese of Salford meanwhile is one of the six dioceses that to date have no academies. The Ordinary at that time, Bishop Terence Brain, took a very specific view of Academy status, writing a letter in December 2012[22] in which he stated his opposition and his reasons.

> 'Our strength is in the diocesan "family" concept: we have always seen ourselves holistically, striving to offer every child in whatever school the opportunity to know themselves as 'loved by God' and with talents that can be developed to enable each and every one of them to live as someone with a unique value in the sight of God. I cannot see Academies bringing anything extra to this ideal: in fact I see that there is a real risk that this diocesan

---

[19] Code of Canon Law (1983), Can. 80. 3. §3. 'Even if it is in fact Catholic, no school is to bear the name Catholic school without the consent of competent ecclesiastical authority.'

[20] Director of the CES from May 2013

[21] CES Digest of 2013 Census § 9

[22] Private letter to Salford Diocesan Schools Commission 19 December 2012

strength could be undermined if we venture along the road to Academy status.'

(Brain, 2012)

He also expressed his conviction that the Diocese of Salford will be able to supplement the greatly reduced role of the local authorities within its boundaries reasoning that there is already a successful system of *'collaboration and inter-school supports* making *the need to seek an alternative to the Local Authority support ... less necessary than in other dioceses.'* (Brain, 2012). In contrast Bishop McMahon argued that working with the DFE rather than against it had beneficial results, such as:

> *'Excellent conversion policies and documentation, including memorandums of understanding ... which satisfy the requirements of the Bishops and the Government and which have been found useful by most dioceses who have considered or are considering conversion to academy status. These policies, for example, protect the Bishop's role in the appointment of directors of academies and members of local governing bodies in multi-academy trusts, the teaching of religious education, the appointment of practising Catholics to certain positions, and admissions.'* (McMahon, 2012, p. 6)

Providing that these legal safeguards are in place new academies can offer opportunities for the Catholic sector with the chance to replace the role of local authorities with a stronger role for the Diocesan Schools Commissions, providing that the diocese concerned has the resources available, both in terms of suitably qualified staff, office accommodation and administrative support to make it successful.

In an article published in the Catholic newspaper *The Tablet* a Catholic school governor and an enthusiastic supporter of the academy concept pointed out that, in his view, Academy status changes the relationship between the school and the state, not between the school and the Church (Craven, 2012). At a local level the practicalities of having a range of academy schools in addition to their maintained schools could put a considerable strain on the ability of a diocesan education team to service the needs of all its schools. The broadening of the role will bring other challenges in terms of securing school standards and improvement sufficiently successfully to meet ethical as well as state requirements. When Grace wrote about the academy debate within the Catholic educational community, he pointed out that many people see this as an opportunity to *strengthen Catholic education in various ways* but he also identified some of the issues, in particular focussing on those concerned with 'mission'. He recommended revisiting the statement about Catholic values expressed in 'The Common Good in Education' published by the Bishops in 1997 and ensuring that any pursuit of academy status is preceded by prayer, reflection and discernment (Grace, 2012, p. 28).

The Mission Dilemma

How the educative mission of the Catholic Church is interpreted depends on the country or the era which provides the context:

'Yet the diverse situations and legal systems in which the Catholic school has to function in Christian and non-Christian countries demand that local problems be faced and solved by each Church within its own social-cultural context.' (Congregation for Catholic Education, 1977, §2)

As the educational landscape has changed in recent years searching for an adequate response to both the secular and the sacred has presented new dilemmas. At a conference in 1996 the Catholic Bishops had issued a statement reminding schools that education in a Catholic school is *'based on the belief that the human and the divine are inseparable'* and must affirm that each person is a unique gift from God (CBCEW, 2013). There are, however, difficulties in making the Church relevant in the eyes of some families.

'We have to acknowledge the fact that, unpalatable as it may be for us, very many Catholics are, for the most part, untouched by the Church and have little knowledge of Catholic beliefs and practice. In our consumer society, the Church is seen as one stall in a large market place, and to many it is not a very attractive one. We should not conclude from this, however, that people are in no way religious or in no way hungry for the spiritual, though they may, from our point of view, have different ways of showing and expressing it . . . we have to face our particular situation and seek new ways of education to and in the faith, new ways of taking up the call.' (Gallagher, 2001, p. 39)

Bishop Sherrington, Auxiliary Bishop of Westminster and Chairman of the Diocesan Education Commission recognised that this indifference is couched in the changing social environment in which we now work and the challenges which this affords Catholic educators.

'In seeking to communicate the faith, we are faced with different understandings of human life and the ethical values that flow from the particular narratives. The cultural context tends to maximise freedom and values these different lifestyles equally. In the education of students, there is need to make a critique of these various world-views with their underlying vision and values in the light of Catholic religious education with a focus on anthropology and personhood. We teach not only values but also virtues of prudence, justice, temperance and courage and provide a vision founded on the theological virtues of faith and hope and love.' (Sherrington, 2013)[23]

Legislative Challenges
Following the restoration of the Catholic hierarchy in 1850, the Bishops sought to establish Catholic schools, and the policy of having a place at a Catholic school available to every Catholic child was increasingly articulated as a fundamental principle. Attempts to comply with recent government legislation have, however, made this a difficult thing to achieve,

---

[23] Address to the conference of the Catholic Association of Teachers, Schools & Colleges (CATSC) in January 2013

illustrating the disjunction between the government's priorities and vision for education and those of the Catholic Church; and between the Bishops themselves and some of their schools:

> *'If institutional requirements dominate community, rather than serve it, then mission is likely to be obscured, the legal will be mistaken for the moral, hierarchy will be assumed too readily to be the sole source of authority.'*
>
> (Sullivan, 2000, p. 139)

The inability to define an agreed and consistent purpose for Catholic education has underpinned many of the dilemmas facing the system today. The initial focus of the Bishops in the 19th and early 20th centuries of providing education for baptised Catholic children, when faced with the challenges of a pluralist society of the 1950's onwards, led to questions from both outside and within the Church as to their purpose(s) (Rodger, 1999) and whether there might be a 'tipping point' in which the Catholic character of a school is defined and determined by the percentage of baptised Catholic pupils who attend it (Adams, 2011).[24]

An alternative perspective has been given by the Schools Commissioner for the Plymouth Diocese stating:

> *'In relation to our schools, we do not define 'Catholic' by those who attend but by the provision that is made for those who attend. That is, first and foremost a Catholic school is about making a specific educational offering to children and families, regardless of their faith background.'*[25]

The removal of 'surplus' school places in the 1980s led to the closure of some schools, the amalgamation of others and in some luckier instances (because they could be re-opened if required), classrooms or areas of a school being temporarily closed. Dioceses worked closely with their local authorities to comply but nevertheless such drastic changes could not be made without a great deal of controversy and upset as staffing needs were realigned and much-loved schools closed or amalgamated.

A further challenge came in 1998 when the regulations in the Schools Standards and Frameworks Act invoked an upper limit of 30 pupils in any Key Stage 1 class taught by a single teacher[26]. Since most classes in this phase do have just one teacher in effect this legislation applied to the vast majority of schools. The combination of the two changes has meant that in some areas there are simply not enough school places available to accommodate all of the baptised Catholic pupils who apply for a place in the reception class and nor is there an accessible alternative Catholic school able to provide for them. Thus one of the key principles of Catholic education over many years - that of a place in a Catholic school for every Catholic child - becomes impossible to achieve.

Other changes in admission regulations have also proved to be a challenge for schools which are not oversubscribed. During Bishop Patrick Kelly's tenure in the Diocese of Salford the

---

[24] *The Tablet* 15th October 2011, pp. 6-7.
[25] Taken from private personal notes
[26] School Standards and Framework Act §1: 1-6

expectation was that Catholic schools would have a 100% Catholic intake in order that the faith life of all pupils could be met with integrity. In Voluntary Aided schools, where governors are the admissions authority as defined in statutory regulations, they have gradually had to change their admissions criteria to comply with government legislation so that, whilst they still give priority to baptised Catholic children, if there are places available once all are accommodated, then they must offer places to other children who have applied.

For many schools this has meant a growing number of admissions of children of other faiths or none whose beliefs have to be catered for whilst still preserving the distinctive Catholic ethos. Whilst this move has meant a departure from what some would perceive to be a 'ghetto' mentality and an embracing of the diversity present in the local community, in the Diocese of Salford this has also meant that there are some Catholic schools where, because of changing demographics, Catholic pupils are now in the minority. In May 2014 it was decided, controversially, that a primary school with a 99% Muslim intake would henceforth be handed to an academy trust set up by the Anglican Diocese of Blackburn, on the basis that the diocese was unable to fulfil its Trust Deed to provide Catholic education, a move which led to fundamental questions being raised:

> 'What does this say about the purpose of Catholic education establishments in general? Do they exist primarily to educate Catholic young people, and lose their raison d'être when there are not enough of them around? If the much-vaunted "Catholic ethos" makes such a distinctive contribution, on what basis is it justified to withdraw that benefit from non-Catholic students? Fundamentally, what makes a school or college Catholic?'
>
> (The Tablet, 2014)[27]

If the school is to take seriously the responsibility of providing for the spiritual and faith life of all and at the same time offer a distinctively Catholic ethos, then the challenges in such schools and their staff face are many and varied. Cardinal Vincent Nichols reminded schools:

> 'In admitting children of other faiths, a Catholic school surely takes on the responsibility of helping those pupils to integrate their faith and life, just as it seeks to do for Catholic children.'
>
> (Nichols, 1997a, p. 46)

In January 2014[28] a Catholic Academy principal discussed her experience of working in a school with changing demographics, and her belief that, as part of a Multi-Academy Trust she was actually in a better position to provide for a diverse intake because she could draw on other schools in the Trust for support to maintain Catholic mission and ethos. More recently, possible changes to admissions legislation have jeopardised the potential involvement of the Catholic sector in providing new Academies and Free Schools. It is proposed that such

---

[27] Editorial, 'End of an Ethos', *The Tablet*, 17 May 2014, p. 2.
[28] Unpublished research interview notes, eventually to be incorporated into CES/NCTL Catholic Faith Leader module

institutions must offer 50% of their places to pupils of other faiths or none even if they are oversubscribed with applications from Catholic families.[29]

In November 2013, concerned about the implications of this new regulation, the Catholic Bishops' Conference of England and Wales (CBCEW) issued a statement reaffirming its commitment to Catholic education as central to the mission of the Catholic Church and stating that *'the imposition of a 50% cap on the control of admissions is not a secure basis for the provision of a Catholic school and urges dioceses to resist any pressure to establish a school on that basis.'* A move which appears to signify that there is in fact a 'tipping point.'

The CES has met regularly with Ministers and until this cap is removed has stated on behalf of the CBCEW that there will be no new Catholic Academies. Mark Hoban, a Catholic MP, sought to explain to a Commons Committee the reasons for the objection in a debate on 4 February 2014,

> *'There is a requirement on bishops to decide that where there is a demand for Catholic education, that this is satisfied. They feel it would be a breach of canon law to support a school that then turned away Catholic children. There is a broader point too about ethos. There is something very different about a Catholic school and its values. There are aspects of school life which are bound up in the sacramental life of the school - the participation in mass, a set of shared values, and the reference points that relate to the church and its teaching. It is hard to see how you can maintain that shared set of values and ethos if half the pupils are unable to relate to the practice of the Catholic faith. That is not to say that these schools should be exclusively Catholic, and indeed three in 10 children at Catholic schools are not Catholic. But the point comes where the dilution of a school's Catholicity means it loses its ethos and it loses parental support. The faith-based admissions cap is a disincentive to Catholic Church and separate faith schools as it dilutes their ethos.'*

> (Hansard, 2014)

Philosophical Challenges

The perception that people were becoming less altruistic was given further credence by the words of the then Prime Minister, Margaret Thatcher that, *there is no such thing as society. There are individual men and women, and there are families. And no government can do anything except through people, and people must look to themselves first.*[30] Not a sentiment that was going to endear itself to the Christian mission of the Catholic Church. The CBCEW responded by publishing *The Common Good* in which they directly address this statement:

> *'There exists a set of ideas that tries to answer questions like these. They are based on firm Christian principles. But they are just as likely to appeal to*

---

[29] Including such a requirement in the details of any contract for a new Academy or Free School is illustrative of one of the dangers pointed out by Barber (2013) – see above.

[30] Interview given to *Women's Own* magazine, October 31 1987

people with no belief. They come from the Roman Catholic Church, which is why we call them Catholic Social Teaching.'

(CBCEW, 1997)

In contrast to the historical quest for universal education, the focus on offering 'Choice and Diversity' begun in 1992[31] successfully placed education in the market place, seeing education as a commodity which can be won or purchased. This governmental approach to the problem of meeting the escalating costs of providing effective schools began with the Education Reform Act 1988 and the institution of grant maintained schools, together with a rise in private sector involvement in the funding of schools and the competitive element which was a consequence of published 'league tables'. There is a clear dilemma.

'Can a legitimate balance be found between Catholic values and market values or will market forces in education begin to compromise the integrity of the special mission of Catholic schooling? Can Gospel values survive in the face of a more direct relationship with the market place and education?'

(Grace, 2002a, p. 7)

The Role of Parents

Bishop Malcolm McMahon[32] referred to a 'disconnection' between parish and school in that there are so few of the families who espouse the Catholic faith in terms of education actually attending Church on a Sunday:

'Yet both our schools and our parishes are Catholic, and a big question for all of us concerns how we can reconnect the two in such a way that our schools and parishes don't become parallels, since parallels never meet. So we do have to remind schools that, in the midst of their other academic studies, they must remember their mission to hand on the Deposit of Faith.'

(McMahon, 2012, p. 6)

This echoes the conviction of the Bishops in 1854, that building schools which could serve as a church was an effective way of engaging with their people, but the expectation then must be that the staff are willing and able to carry out the inherent evangelical role, and that there is an equal recognition of responsibility from the parishes. Catholic school leaders are likely to take this aspect of their work seriously and constantly seek ways to involve apparently disaffected families in the life of the parish, but there is much to be done both strategically and practically if full participation is to become a reality.

While he was Bishop of Salford, Patrick Kelly, recognised a growing dependence on school rather than parish for the sacramental development of young people and linked his concern about this to his review of arrangements for the reception of children into full communion with the Church. His 'Sacramental Programme' structure would be parish based thus

---

[31] 'White Paper' July 1992, which led to the Education Act 1993
[32] Inaugurated as Archbishop of Liverpool 1 May 2014

widening responsibility for and participation in the educative mission. In reality, in many parishes, this has still involved the school in much of the preparation and organisational work, sharing the wealth of experience already available there.

Families more readily select their local parish primary school but the selection of a high school is far more complex. Parents are now faced with making educational choices from a multiplicity of options, and the question has to be faced of how they exercise this choice, and what criteria do they use? Information about individual schools is readily available in Ofsted and media reports, and on diocesan websites, but the imperative to actively seek a Catholic education is only one among many, making the warning of Bishop Turner, to make Catholic schools *as tempting as possible* as relevant now as it ever was.

Excommunication is no longer offered as a threat to those choosing other schools, but the financial pressures of withdrawn transport subsidies together with lack of church attendance provide other stresses.

In order to establish a priority list for admissions it is the case that some church schools expect families to provide proof of parish involvement and church attendance in order to demonstrate that their child deserves to be allocated a place.

The Catholic Bishops however have always maintained that the Sacrament of Baptism welcomes the baptised into membership of the Church, and have resisted any other definition in terms of school admissions, so that over-subscribed Catholic schools are dissuaded from including in their admission criteria any reference to or expectation of church attendance. On the other hand, criticisms have been made from within the Church that, despite the vast resources of time, effort and finance poured into education over the years the numbers attending Mass at the weekend are falling and that therefore the education system has failed.

The Role of Teachers
The Church continues to place great emphasis on the role of teachers in terms of religious education and the mission of the church. They have to fulfil the dual roles of excellence in secular pedagogy together with witness to the sacred, mediated through the particular doctrines of the Catholic Church, but the strategies to train, support and develop them in their vocation are inconsistent. In their study of induction of teachers new to Catholic education in Canada (but equally relevant to the situation in the UK) Chatlain and Noonan conclude that:

> *'If new teachers are not equipped to fulfil their role as the heart of the school, then the ability of the Catholic school to fulfil its mission will be compromised and the distinctive nature of Catholic schools may be placed in doubt.'*
>
> (Chatlain & Noonan, 2005, p. 511)

As well as the impact on the schools, I would argue that by not supporting teachers throughout their career in Catholic education the consequent lack of confidence also results in stress and a disinclination to seek leadership roles. An additional factor is that of ensuring that the 46% of teachers[33] in Catholic schools who are not Catholic are well informed and supported in their work; an educative role that involves among other things a responsibility to assist parents in nurturing their children. The importance of the task is evident in the papal address to pupils from Catholic schools in September 2010.

> 'What God wants most of all for each one of you is that you should become holy. He loves you much more than you could ever begin to imagine, and he wants the very best for you. And by far the best thing for you is to grow in holiness.'

> (Pope Benedict XVI, 2010)

The Authority Dilemma

Changes in the way our society functions have led to changing perceptions of the role of 'authority' and questioning of how authority is exercised and by whom. This is as true within the Catholic Church as it is elsewhere, posing fundamental problems for a hierarchical organisation which had historically demanded obedience from its followers,

> 'An authority which seeks to base itself on power is rejected by young people today. They have perhaps forced us to accept the hypocrisy which was all too often found in this. "Do as I say, not as I do." Their revolt forces us back to the roots of Christianity: Christ's authority depended on a personal relationship, not on any form of power.'

> (Konstant, 1997a, p. 113)

One example of a change in the deference shown to the leadership of the Bishops can be seen in the controversy surrounding the potential to change the legal status of diocesan schools arising from the provisions of the Education Reform Act 1988. The Bishops had been clear about their opposition to grant maintained (GM) status for its schools but compliance with their wishes by school governors and parents was becoming far more difficult to achieve as over one hundred Catholic schools abandoned their existing Voluntary Aided status to become became grant maintained. A group of Catholic parents were prepared to take Cardinal Hume to court for his continued resistance to GM status at one school while the Cardinal threatened to place himself in contempt of the courts on this issue (Grace, 2001, p. 496).

Organisational Control

Power and authority vested in dioceses and recognised by LAs resulted from the 1944 Education Act and subsequently increased as schools looked to them for support with capital, legal and planning issues. The role of Diocesan Schools Commissioner was introduced and incumbents have become adept at working in partnership with local authorities developing overall policy strategies for Church schools. Although at first this was often a clerical role these positions have increasingly been taken by laypeople and at present 52% of Schools Commissioners are lay men, 33% are lay women and only 14% are clerics although most

---

[33] Figures taken from CES School Census 2013. The Diocese of Salford has over 64% Catholic teachers.

dioceses have a senior cleric with overall responsibility. This is further complicated by the fact that many dioceses have amalgamated their RE departments and Schools Commissions, which may strengthen the support given to schools but could potentially weaken the focus that Schools Commissioners have on policy strategy, at a time when informed negotiation is crucial.

It has been argued that Government policy since the 1980s has gradually eroded the legal rights of voluntary aided status and the powers of trustees (Arthur, 1995, p. 251) as has been seen in the issues concerning admissions, class size etc., and was a particular concern in addressing grant maintained policy development. The 'policy loop' (identified by Fitz and Halpin, 1991) has had an effect, as Barber explains.

> 'All of this reduced the visibility of the voluntary school as a distinct (and distinctive) entity to the extent that, in the main, they escape the notice of newer officials altogether. The result is that almost every new government initiative is designed without taking account of the voluntary sector.'
>
> (Barber, 2013, pp. 12-13)

Barber cites instances of government policy and, on a local level, personal experience of working with Local Authorities (LA) and Interim Executive Boards (IEBs) reveals the effect of this 'invisibility.' Without legal safeguards, a Board of Directors (governors) could be replaced if the school is deemed not to be achieving the expected standards as can happen now if a local authority deems it necessary for an IEB to be put in place in a Voluntary Aided school. Replacement governors nominated by the DFE, (or in the case of an IEB, by the Local Authority) are not necessarily chosen to support the Catholic nature of a school and 'control', or at least the ability to influence the school, can very easily pass out of the realm of the local diocese. Archbishop Malcolm McMahon is certain that the Academy policies which have been agreed offer the required protection for Bishops in the appointment of governors and Academy directors; the teaching of RE; certain staff appointments; and school admissions.

Teachers: Training, Formation and Development
The then Secretary of State for Education, Michael Gove, highlighted the significance of teachers when he wrote that *at the heart of our plan is a vision of the teacher as our society's most valuable asset* (Department for Education, 2010, p. 7). Arguably, the greatest source of direct influence in terms of the educative mission of the Church are the teachers and governors themselves, as the concluding remarks in 'Lay Catholics in Schools' indicates:

> 'Lay Catholic educators in schools . . . must never have any doubts about the fact that they constitute an element of great hope for the Church . . . it has entrusted them with the integral human formation and the faith education of young people. These young people are the ones who will determine whether the world of tomorrow is more closely or more loosely bound to Christ.'
>
> (Congregation for Catholic Education, 1982, §81)

From the earliest years following the restored hierarchy, the necessity of having trained Catholic teachers to supplement religious order and clerical involvement was recognised and the opening of Catholic Training Colleges quickly followed. Allies impressed upon the hierarchy the now urgent need for trained teachers, the short sightedness of using any untrained teachers because they were cheap, the obligation to keep the schools efficient, and the need for a national Catholic policy (Beales, 1950, p. 376).

A network of Catholic Training Colleges gradually developed, providing qualified teachers for the growing number of Catholic schools. In Liverpool the Notre Dame order continued to train Catholic women teachers until 1980 when the college amalgamated with Christ College and St Katherine's to form what has become Liverpool Hope University. Other training colleges have amalgamated or closed in the past thirty years so that of the remaining colleges there is now a lack of Higher Education Institutes which specifically train Catholic teachers. In itself this could have a positive influence if it were not for the fact that the proportion of teachers who are baptised Catholics is slowly decreasing[34] and the young Catholic teachers coming into our schools now are often a product of that 'disconnection' between school and parish to which Archbishop McMahon referred. It has been argued that they emerge from a Church context which is diverse and confusing rather than from the ecclesial environment of a generation ago which was clear, distinct and sure of every answer and practice (Duminuco, 1999, p. 136).

As a headteacher interviewing and employing young staff, and as a Diocesan Officer working with trainee and Newly Qualified Teachers (NQTs), I have encountered many enthusiastic and capable people who are baptised Catholics and want to work in a Catholic school, but many tell the same story – experience at a Catholic primary school, followed by a Community High School, often for reasons of convenience[35]; and with limited involvement with their local parish.

In other words, their experience of their faith came to a halt at the age of 10. We would not expect someone with such limited knowledge of any subject to suddenly be able to teach it in all its complexity. How much more difficult is it then for someone to achieve the wisdom and experience to accompany a pupil on their faith journey? Even those young teachers who are regular communicants deserve the support, development and formation which we give to other aspects of their progress as we accompany them too.

The Catholic Bishops' Conference of England and Wales (CBCEW) Religious Education (RE) Curriculum Directory reminds teachers that they should:

> 'Be prepared to give living witness to what they teach;
> recognise that they share in the teaching office of the Church exercised in the
> person of the local bishop and enshrined in the trust deed of the school; and -

---

[34] Falling from 55% in 2011 to 54.4% in 2013 (CES, 2013)
[35] A situation which is likely to increase as more Local Authorities seek to save money by withdrawing the transport subsidy which enabled children from less advantaged backgrounds to travel to Catholic schools

fulfil their professional responsibilities with regard to all that develops and enhances the life of the Catholic school.' (CBCEW, 2012, p. 5)

It remains to be seen how this can be achieved without consistent, high quality professional and personal development and formation from a church which takes the provision of Catholic teachers to the schools as seriously as did Allies in 1870. Teachers are also told in the RE Directory that they should:

> *'Take care continually to deepen their own knowledge and understanding of the Catholic faith;*
>
> *take seriously the duty of every Catholic to form his or her conscience; and*
>
> **be given opportunities for their own spiritual and professional development as Catholic educators.'** (ibid) [author's emphasis - Ed]

Research undertaken by the Heythrop Institute confirmed the *pressing need* for recruitment *and formation* of leaders able to fulfil the vocation of leading a Catholic school (Hanvey & Stannard, 2009, p. 22) and I would argue that this formational development must be life-long and professional in order to be successful. The interpretation of how to deliver this entitlement is in the hands of individual dioceses and the limited resources available to their officers, so that whilst some teachers can access some excellent developmental and formational programmes, other areas are less well served.

There has been a developing commitment to Continuing Professional Development (CPD) for teachers, some of which does include formation. Bishop David Konstant spoke of this broader entitlement and the responsibility of the Catholic educational community towards the adults working in the schools:

> *'Catholic teachers must not only have opportunities for professional development but also time to reflect on the purpose of their work, and on their own spiritual development.'*
>
> (Konstant, 1997b, p. 40)

The response to the loss of the Catholic Training Colleges lacks cohesion or any expectation on behalf of the system, or governors as the employers, that their teaching staff will be able to provide evidence of at least a minimum amount of knowledge about their faith. The Catholic Certificate of Religious Studies (CCRS) has an important role to play, not least because it is the only recognised national programme which can offer any assurance of knowledge and understanding of the Catholic faith. However, it is not a requirement for any teacher and although it is regularly listed as a 'desirable' prerequisite on the Person Specification for an aspiring Catholic deputy or headteacher, it is not compulsory. There is, therefore, nothing which reliably enables school leaders to judge, before appointment, the ability of a teacher to fulfil the role of guiding and developing the faith life and knowledge of their pupils, and no national programme which addresses the formational needs of school staff. Robinson explored existing research into Catholic CPD and the introduction of the CCRS to fill the 'knowledge gap' left by 'the swing from a traditional catechism-based approach of rote learning to a post-Vatican II emphasis on personal experience and faith journeys often not rooted in any connection to theology' (Robinson, 2002, p. 144). She considers the organisational and structural issues which have led to a poor uptake in some areas and suggests improvement to the current CCRS as well as extending provision to enable continuing study opportunities.

The Diocese of Salford offers the CCRS as an 'in-house' course, with schools collaborating to make the course more accessible and a realistic offer to all staff. Liverpool Hope meanwhile offers the CCRS as an on-line course, with students participating from across the country. In both instances numbers of participants are growing rapidly, pointing to an acknowledgement of need from both the schools and the teachers. According to the most recent figures available from the CES only three dioceses have more than 20% of teachers who have the CCRS and all of these are in the North West.[36] Catholic school leaders face their own particular challenges, including the specific responsibility of school leaders for developing ministry as an aspect of the teacher's role (Boylan, 2013). However, implementing such a responsibility may differ depending upon the specific religious character of the institution. For example, it has been argued about headteachers of Church of England schools that, as leaders of a more ambivalent faith tradition they are better able to respond to the local context, whereas Catholic leaders 'functioned with the certainty of centrally determined moral absolutes and with a strong, easily recognised culture that places its emphasis on building a faith community' (Johnson, 2003, p. 476). Further to her argument she suggested that, in comparison with Church of England schools:

> *'The question would seem to be whether the role expected of headteachers and their choices of approaches to value and cultural transmission will be sufficient to survive the more insidious and oblique attack of the fragmenting post-traditional society. The Catholic school, in fortress mode or not, could be prepared for, if not entirely protected from, that attack.'*
>
> (Johnson, 2003, p. 476)

Recognising the need for a formational and developmental programme for aspiring and serving school leaders of the Diocese of Salford developed the 'Salford Catholic Leadership Programme' which set out to supplement, rather than replicate local or national provision, providing an opportunity for exploration of personal and professional mission within the context of the Catholic education system within the diocese. A particular strength of the programme lay in accessing the experience and expertise of senior leaders in diocesan schools who volunteered to act as personal mentors to the participants, encouraging participants to visit a variety of settings. Participants are challenged throughout the programme to reflect deeply on their own knowledge and understanding of their faith, and provided with opportunities to engage with the dialogue and language so that they are able to articulate their personal values and mission, and have a better understanding of the distinctive mission of Catholic schools. There are pockets of provision, including CCRS which people access at various stages of their career and several diocesan programmes most notably for

---

[36] Archdiocese of Liverpool 28%; Diocese of Salford 24%: Diocese of Lancaster 20%

aspiring school leaders, but there is further need to address the issue of providing high quality continuing professional development (CPD) which does not assume a deep knowledge, or even great experience of the faith even from those young teachers who present themselves as baptised Catholics suitable for employment in a Catholic school. Widespread, consistent and 'effective' CPD should be offered as career development for all staff and increasingly for governors too as Bishop Konstant confirmed:

> 'It is important for us, as members of the Christian community, to know and develop the strengths of the teaching profession.'
>
> (Konstant, 1997b, p. 35)

Religious Education

Archbishop Malcolm McMahon has spoken about the essential role which he feels that Religious Education has in promoting *a tolerant and understanding* society. He emphasised the potential impact of government policy on Catholic schools in particular, in loss of funding and properly trained teachers reminding his listeners:

> 'The Bishops' Conference reaffirms that Religious Education is the core subject in Catholic schools and academies requiring 10% of curriculum time. In view of the recent reallocation of resources in initial teacher training to English Baccalaureate subjects in England, the Bishops' Conference seeks assurances that the supply **of highly qualified religious education teachers** [author's emphasis – Ed] will be ensured as a matter of government policy. If RE is taught well, in both style and content, it will go a long way to addressing the disconnection between many pupils & their parishes to which I have already referred; it will also ensure that RE is seen as a subject which is not only at the heart of Catholic schools but also, I hope, included in the English Baccalaureate as being worthy of study in its own right.'
>
> (McMahon, 2012, p. 8)

In language which repeated the claims for equitable provision for Catholic children which were such a basis for the argument presented by Bishop Turner and others, in 2012 the CBCEW issued four resolutions regarding Religious Education, pointing out that a policy which effectively demotes Religious Education encroaches on the ability of Catholic parents to fulfil their obligations:

> 'The Bishops' Conference recognises that all parents and legal guardians have the right and duty to educate their children. Catholic parents have an additional duty and right to choose those schools and academies which best promote the Catholic education of their children[37]. Mindful that religious education is at the very heart of the curriculum in Catholic schools and academies, its exclusion from the core academic subjects as defined by the English Baccalaureate effectively limits the ability of parents to choose

---

[37] Vatican (1983) Code of Canon Law for the Latin Rite, Canon. 793, §1

schools and academies, and their right to ensure the education of their children is conducted in conformity with their own religious and philosophical convictions (cf. European Convention on Human Rights, Protocol 2, Article 1). The Bishops' Conference therefore requests the government to uphold parents' rights in this regard.'

(CBCEW, 2012)

Religious Education has exercised minds and hearts over the years, from early disputes about which translation of the Bible was to be used, through the arguments against the Cowper-Temple clause and into modern considerations of curriculum development. When the work of the 'National Project of Catechesis and Religious Education' resulted in an RE Framework 'Weaving the Web' in 1988, the Diocese of Salford judged it to be too liberal in content and developed their own (Arthur, 1995, p. 65). Bishop Vincent Nichols referred to the Salford RE programme when he spoke about how Catholic RE teaching should speak of *the common* human quest and provide opportunities for laying the foundation of an appreciation of other faiths (Nichols, 1997, p. 49). He quoted from programmes of study being piloted in Salford, which included that pupils at key stage three should be encouraged to recognise the order, magnitude and intricacy of creation and be given the opportunity to share their own feelings about creation with other pupils (ibid).

The lack of unity and the struggle for control over what is taught continued and this programme, REVision 2000 was itself withdrawn in 2010 because it too was considered by some of the diocesan clergy to be insufficiently doctrinal. Meanwhile, the National Board of Religious Inspectors and Advisers (NBRIA) has developed guidelines for the RE Curriculum upon which the Section 48 Inspection[38] is based, and many dioceses, including Salford, have chosen commercial schemes which are based on these guidelines. The wider debate about the status of Religious Education in all maintained schools continues, particularly since 1988, which was when the subject became designated as 'Education' rather than 'Instruction' - the study *of* religion rather than *in* religion (Bennett, 2014).

Bennett argued for the retention of religious education in all schools rather than making education completely secular, arguing that doing so enables pupils to learn about a range of religions, which would not be the case if religion was only to be learned about at home. He suggested that a potential consequence of secularising schools could be greater opportunities for fundamentalism and misunderstanding. He also pointed to the influence of faith within the whole cultural experience – as he says ignore belief in the human story and you've deliberately ignored one of its pillars.

Standards
The focus on standards in schools has gradually sharpened since the Schools Standards and Framework Act 1998, and accountability for standards rests with school governors or, in the

---

[38] Schools 'of a religious character' are inspected under both Section 5 (by Ofsted) and Section 48 (by the appropriate diocese)

case of an academy, the Board of Directors. Inspections under Section 5 and Section 48 of the Act provide an external assessment of standards in the school.

A maintained Catholic school can expect challenge and support if required from the local authority, although the capacity of a local authority to offer extensive support to a school in difficulties is seriously undermined in many areas, as funding is redistributed. In the case of an academy, the directors can either seek school improvement services from the local authority or from another provider if they so choose.

The Secretary of State has assumed punitive powers under which failing schools could be considered to be in breach of contract. Pring (2012a) responded to Mike Craven's enthusiastic advocacy of academy schools by stating that 'this is the most centralised system of education in Western Europe since Germany in the 1930s'.[39]

Barber also draws attention to the startling degree of centralisation inherent in academy contracts (Barber, 2013, p. 23). Unless there is careful consideration of the legal documents under which an Academy Trust or Company is formed there is a danger that failing to meet standards could result in the directors being replaced, and not necessarily by foundation directors, as we have already considered. Recent alleged events in Birmingham schools[40] have highlighted further issues which can be attributed to centralised control, as the Local Government Association's Children and Young People Board, stated:

> *'This has been an unsettling time for parents and children and it is vital they are at the forefront of any action taken in response to these investigations. Parents need to know who is accountable for their local school, but under the current system accountability is confusing and fragmented. It is clear that effective oversight of standards and finance in schools across the UK cannot be exercised from Whitehall, and the jumble of regimes risks leaving mums and dads unsure where to go for help when they have concerns. Local authorities know their schools and the communities they serve and strong local oversight by local authorities is needed to spot warning signs where schools are beginning to cause concern and tackle problems before it is too late. Councils need powers to intervene in all underperforming schools quickly and effectively without the need to ask permission from Whitehall.'*
>
> (Local Government Association 2014)[41]

---

[39] Pring R. (2012a) Perils of Academy Status, *The Tablet* Feb 18th 2012. For a more extensive review of the increasing centralisation of the national educational service, see also, Pring, R. (2012b) 60 Years On: The Changing Role of Government, British Journal of Educational Studies, 60. 1. 29-38.

[40] In November 2013 an anonymous letter was sent to Birmingham City Council suggesting a clandestine ('Trojan Horse') infiltration of some schools by Islamic extremists. Investigations (Clarke, 2014) found no evidence of violent extremism but clear evidence that there are a number of people, associated with each other and in positions of influence in schools and governing bodies, who espouse, sympathise with or fail to challenge extremist views.

[41] Press release, 9 June 2014

The quest for excellence is one which the Catholic Bishops have enshrined in a statement of principles for Catholic Education:

'The search for excellence is seen as an integral part of the spiritual quest. Christians are called to seek perfection in all aspects of their lives. In Catholic education, pupils and students are therefore, given every opportunity to develop their talents to the full.'

(CBCEW, 1996)

But in the following year Bishop David Konstant took up this same theme and warned of the possible negative effect of seeking to achieve excellence within the competitive culture which was a consequence of the governments developing educational philosophy:

'If the league tables mean that a school is encouraged to raise its standards, they are to be welcomed – provided that the criteria on which they are based are valid. The search for excellence is a profoundly Christian quest, since it means striving to make the best possible use of God's gifts. That is the search for excellence is seen as a means of weakening or destroying others, then it is morally evil.'

(Konstant, 1997c, p. 67)

The Community Dilemma

The challenge of aligning any decisions about education with Catholic Social teaching has continued into discussions about academy structures and diocesan preferences. Craven, a supporter of academisation, warned of the consequences of sacrificing potential gains by not engaging, and Bishop McMahon expressed the subsequent dilemma:

'On one level, canon law supports such an approach, enshrining parental choice, high standards in education and subsidiarity. But this language sits uneasily with the interpretation of Catholic Social Teaching by some dioceses, which prefer the language of solidarity, community, the "family of Catholic schools" and the preferential option for the poor. And there is a clear if unstated concern that the best schools will "declare UDI" at the expense of the rest of the diocese. For Catholics, it is clearly important not to overemphasise parental choice at the expense of solidarity. But the reverse also applies and, clearly, it would not be right to use the argument of Catholic Social Teaching as an excuse for doing nothing, and trying to preserve a structure of schools that is withering week by week in the state sector.

(Craven, 2012)

'We had to base our judgment firmly in the Magisterium, in particular Catholic social teaching and the importance of doing what is right for the common good, the wider community, and the poor and marginalised.'

(McMahon, 2012, p. 5)

Over twenty years ago the Congregation for Catholic Education accepted that society had become more pluralistic and resolutely advocated respect for all; it also articulated the dilemma which many schools face:

> 'On the other hand, a Catholic school cannot relinquish its own freedom to proclaim the Gospel and to offer a formation based on the values to be found in a Christian education; this is its right and its duty. To proclaim or to offer is not to impose, however; the latter suggests a moral violence which is strictly forbidden, by the Gospel and by Church Law.'
>
> (Congregation for Catholic Education, 1988, §6)

When the Catholic Church continued to insist on the distinctive ethos offered by their schools it became a target for criticism in England despite the fact that even parents who were not Catholic continued to choose Catholic schools for their children:

> 'The vision which sustains Catholic education has to be fashioned and lived in the specific details of each school day, and in the social and cultural setting of contemporary Britain. Neither is an easy setting.'
>
> (Nichols, 1997a, p. 46)

This complexity requires local responses to episcopal guidance which would be as relevant for a 3-form entry primary school in the leafy suburbs of south Manchester with a 100% Catholic intake, as it is for a small 1-form entry urban school with a 99% Muslim intake. Carmody (2011) cites the work of Lonergan to argue for an empirically based contemporary philosophy for Catholic education which could lead to renewal and re-invigoration, but also requires a deeper commitment to educating for as well as in a diverse society:

> 'For Lonergan, community is primordial. It coheres or divides where the common field of experience, understanding, judgement and commitments begin and end. To ensure proper inclusion, the person needs to be able to affirm him or herself as being both like and different from the other. Such authentic affirmation is recognised by Lonergan as being no easy achievement personally or socially. It entails intellectual, moral, religious as well as, if the critics are right, social, even psychic conversions.'
>
> (Carmody, 2011, p. 114)

Meanwhile schools have to navigate the new funding streams and search for local agreements about relative needs and abilities in order that they can work towards the 'common good' as well as secure the best provision for their own individual community.

One academic writing in a Catholic newspaper argued: 'no school or college is 'an island entire of itself.' It means that no governing body, no individual group of parents has the right to disregard the good of another institution, while promoting the good of its own school or college.' (Grace, 2012)

Leadership[42] Challenges

Regarding education as a commodity to be 'bought and sold' sets particular challenges for Catholic leaders encountering the 'immediate practical realities of market forces ... and the challenges of survival, success and mission integrity' (Grace, 2002a, p.183). Grace argues further that the moral and professional dilemma:

> '... currently facing Catholic head teachers (primary and secondary) in England is the recognition that a competitive market culture in schooling is making it much more difficult to be in the service of the poor, the troublesome, the alienated and the powerless.'
>
> (Grace, 2002b, p. 8)

As leaders of a faith community they embody a Catholic vision, and are the human interface where Catholic values are witnessed. The way in which they work with other schools is particularly significant, whether it is as leaders of an academy supporting other schools in the Academy Trust; with diocesan networks; or in the broader school-led, self-improving system embodied in National College for Teaching and Leadership-led strategies such as 'Teaching Schools' and 'Licensed Provider' schools.

Catholic schools with Teaching School status have professional contractual duties and obligations to the State, which have in the past been fulfilled by local authorities and Higher Education Institutes (HEI). The CES has responded by supporting the development of the Catholic Education Alliance (CEA), which aims to bring together all Catholic Teaching Schools to provide a single unified Catholic professional voice of practice on a range of issues including: the curriculum; teaching and learning; teacher training; professional development; school improvement; leadership formation; succession planning; governance; and research and development from distinctively Catholic roots.

Local Responses

Dioceses in the North West of England meet regularly to explore strategies for continuing to support the schools in an area which includes some of the larger and therefore more viable Local Authorities, as well as some of the smaller, more vulnerable ones. They have surveyed schools to ascertain which Local Authority support services are valued most highly, and approached various bodies to secure favourable rates from the many privatised sources available, in an effort to ensure that all schools have access to the best available provision.

The Finance Dilemma

There has long been a struggle for the Catholic sector to secure and maintain funding for schools. In the context of the current economic climate, and falling church attendance with the consequent diminishing returns from the parishes this has resulted in genuine difficulties. It is little wonder that the reaction of one diocesan financial Secretary to the possibility of

---

[42] 'Leadership' is used here to denote senior leaders and governors, although many of the challenges are faced by all staff in Catholic schools

academy status for their schools was that "at least we won't have to find the 10%" [*of the total building and maintenance costs – Ed*].

Compared to the vigorous response made during Bishop Turner and Cardinal Manning's time when, without state aid, they succeeded in expanding the number of schools from 350 – 892 (Gillard, 2014) this seems inadequate to say the least. The potential consequences of not exploring in greater depth the impact that a change of school designation could have on the mission and vision of the church are vast.

Retrenchment is an undeniable feature of Catholic life - convents and parish churches have closed, congregations have been absorbed into neighbouring parishes, and the remaining church services are often poorly attended. Some question the continued financial support for schools when this support appears not to be mutual. However, a concerned parent wrote about his fear that principles will be sacrificed in the quest to solve financial difficulties through for academy funding:

> '*It is apparent that with the current financial difficulties a "dash for short-term cash" is replacing a rigorous examination of principle, and has become the defining principle for all schools going through this process. My question is straightforward: how is Catholic identity and autonomy preserved in the face of 100 per cent funding from central government, and are we simply relying on assurances from ministers rather than having legislative safeguards?*'

(Pycroft, 2011)

Pycroft closed his letter by saying '*it appears that the Bishops have acquiesced to pressure from government and have not given sufficient moral leadership to ensure long-term viability.*' In contrast, it could be argued that academisation provides the Catholic sector with a way of ensuring financial viability. Though its underpinning philosophy means '*reducing education to the status of one commodity among others competing for public funding,*' in a suggestion reminiscent of the 51 annual subscribers referred to by Bishop Turner,[43] it also opened the way for '*wealthy Catholic entrepreneurs who could be induced to come together to sponsor academies and free schools, particularly in disadvantaged areas.*' (Bayldon, 2012)

In November 2011 the Bishops issued a statement reiterating the requirement for equitable funding:

> '*At a time of great change, and as we consider how our schools can best serve the Common Good, the Bishops are grateful for the continued support of the Secretary of State for Education for Voluntary Aided schools. However we strongly urge HM Government to ensure that children being educated in Voluntary Aided schools are not disadvantaged, financially or otherwise, compared with other categories of schools. The Bishops' Conference instructs*

---

[43] Salford Diocese - Pastoral Letter 9 December 1862

the CES to strive to obtain from the Secretary of State an assurance that Fair Funding principles will continue to apply to all Catholic Schools in the state sector.'

(CBCEW, 2011)[44]

Catholic schools draw from a wider geographical area than their community counterparts, and pupils therefore have greater distances to travel. But, as Local Authorities have had to find ways to work within reduced budgets, many have opted to withdraw some or all of the subsidies offered for transport to these schools[45].

In this case the CES have been pro-active, creating a 'Toolkit'[46] which draws on legal precedents and offers information and guidance on how to lobby local MPs and Councillors in an effort to protect this important subsidy. In Lancashire for instance, where many Diocese of Salford schools are situated, this will mean that parents have to find £495 every year for each child attending a Catholic High school from September 2014, and the CES website quotes *'one area where the local authority has removed all subsidies, the cost of school transport will be up to £1379 per year.'* Catholic schools await with trepidation the impact on their admission numbers, but the effect on the church's mission of the potential loss of contact with these families is even more concerning.

Summary

The educational policies of the coalition government have done little to alleviate the dilemmas posed for the Catholic sector by Conservative and Labour governments since the 1980s. Societal changes occurring during the same period have only served to highlight the confused allegiances of the Catholic population, and the dilemmas which individual families face in choosing a school for their children.

Schools themselves, and the people who staff and lead them, are products of this same society and without clear guidance nevertheless are attempting to define and lead educational faith communities. Mixed messages about what defines a Catholic school and whether they can legitimately comply with government policy and yet retain their distinctive identity only add to the confusion. Meanwhile many school leaders are faced with the daily task of defending distinctiveness to a pluralistic community where the demands for a unifying force are only too real.

Diocesan schools are predominantly staffed by lay teachers, who are expected to combine the sacred and the secular in their work, to support and promote the Catholic ethos of the school in which they work. Yet they are often underprepared for such a vital task, and we lack a

---

[44] Statement available on CES website

[45] The Education and Inspections Act 2006 improved and extended the offer of free school transport first set out in the 1944 Education Act, containing a duty on local authorities to provide free transport for some of the most disadvantaged pupils to attend a secondary school selected on the grounds of religion or belief where that school is more than 2 and less than 15 miles from their home and there is no nearer suitable school.

[46] http://www.catholiceducation.org.uk/campaigns/transport-toolkit

cohesive package of developmental, formational training which would support them throughout their career.

Developments at the CES offer the possibility of strong and informed dialogue with government bodies, and the support for the CEA bodes well for the future development of distinctive programmes for schools. The strong support of the Bishops and the co-operation of diocesan officers will be essential however if this venture is to succeed since the CES, as an agency of the Bishops Conference can only operate through dioceses and not directly with schools themselves.

References

Adams, S. (2011) Keeping the faith, The Tablet, 15th October, pp. 6-7.

Arthur, J. (1995) The Ebbing Tide: policy and principles of Catholic education, Leominster, Fowler Wright Books.

Barber, P. (2013) 1944 and All That: Christian schools and the political settlement, in: A. B. Morris, (ed) Re-Imagining Christian Education for the Twenty-First Century, Chelmsford, Matthew James Publishing, 9-28.

Bayldon, M. (2012) The academy definition and Catholic schooling, Networking, September, 33.

Beales, A. C. F. (1950) The struggle for the schools, in: G. A. Beck, (ed) The English Catholics 1850-195, London, Burns and Oates, 365-409.

Beck, G. A. (1955) The Cost of Catholic Schools, London, Catholic Truth Society.

Bennett, T. (2014) I don't believe in God but teaching children about religion is one of the most important things I will ever do, Times Educational Supplement, 21 March, 24-28.

Brain, T. (2012) Letter to the Salford Diocesan Schools Commission, 19th September.

Boylan, P. (2013) Formation of Christian teachers - a role for the school community, in: A. B. Morris (ed) Re-Imagining Christian Education for the 21st Century, Chelmsford, Matthew James Publishing, 173-182.

Carmody, B. (2011) Towards a contemporary Catholic philosophy of education, International Studies in Catholic Education, 3. 2. 106-119.

Catholic Education Service, 2010. The Catholic Education Service. [Online] Available at http://www.catholiceducation.org.uk/ [Accessed 10 March 2014].

Catholic Education Service (2013) Digest of Census Data for Schools and Colleges in England, London, CES.

CBCEW (1996) Principles, Practices and Concerns, Manchester, Gabriel Communications.

CBCEW (1997) The Common Good and the Catholic Church's Social Teaching, Manchester, Gabriel Communications.

CBCEW (2011) Statement on Fair Funding for Schools, Catholic Education Service [Online] http://www.catholiceducation.org.uk/ [Accessed 10 March 2014].

CBCEW (2012) Religious Education Directory, London, Catholic Bishops Conference of England and Wales.

CBCEW (2013) The History of Catholic Schools. [Online] Available at: files.meetup.com/13055/The_history_of_catholic_schools.htm [Accessed 7 January 2014].

Chatlain, G. & Noonan, B. (2005) Teacher induction in Catholic Schools, Catholic Education, 8. 4. 499-512.

Clarke, P., 2014. Report Into Allegations Concerning Birmingham Schools Arising from the 'Trojan Horse' Letter, London, Her Majesty's Stationery Office.

Congregation for Catholic Education (1977) The Catholic School, Vatican City, Libreria Editrice Vaticana.

Congregation for Catholic Education (1982) Lay Catholics in Schools - Witnesses to Faith, Vatican City, Libreria Editrice Vaticana.

Congregation for Catholic Education (1988) The Religious Dimension of Education in a Catholic School, Vatican City, Libreria Editrice Vaticana.

Craven, M. (2012) Bring on Catholic academies, The Tablet, 4 February, p. 33.

Department for Education (2010) The Importance of Teaching, London, Her Majesty's Stationery Office.

Duminuco, V. J. (1999) Towards the millennium, in: J. C. Conroy, (ed) Catholic Education. Inside-Out/Outside-In, Dublin, Lindisfarne Press, 135-159.

Fitz, J. & Halpin, D. (1991) From a 'sketchy policy' to a 'workable scheme': the DES and Grant Maintained Schools, International Studies in Sociology of Education, 1. 129-151.

Gallagher, J. (2001) Soil For The Seed, Great Wakering, Essex, McCrimmons.

Gillard, D. (2014) Education England. [Online] http://www.educationengland.org.uk [Accessed 8 January 2014].

Grace, G. (2001) The state and Catholic schooling in England and Wales, Oxford Review of Education, 27. 4. 489-500.

Grace, G. (2002a) Catholic Schools: mission, markets & morality, Abingdon, Routledge Falmer.

Grace, G. (2002b) Catholic education in England and Wales, in: M. A. Hayes &. L. Gearon (eds), Contemporary Catholic Education. Leominster: Gracewing, 3-16.

Grace, G. (2012) Moving forwards or stepping backwards?, The Universe, 15 July, 28.

Chatlain, G. & Noonan, B. (2005) Teacher induction in Catholic schools, Catholic Education, 8. 4. 499-512.

Hansard (2014) Parliament. [Online] Available at: http://www.publications.parliament.uk/ [Accessed 22 March 2014].

Hanvey, J. & Stannard O. (2009) Mapping the future, in: Visions for Leadership, London: Heythrop Institute for Religion, Ethics & Public Life, 13-28.

Johnson, H. (2003) Using a Catholic model, School Leadership and Management, 23. 4. 469-480.

Konstant, B. D., 1997. Education and the common good, in: Partners in Mission, London, Matthew James Publishing, 72-82.

Konstant, B. D. (1997a) The curriculum and cultural and moral values, in: Partners in Mission, London, Matthew James Publishing, 108-113.

Konstant, B. D. (1997b) 'Master builders': the role of catholic teachers, in: Partners in Mission, London, Matthew James Publishing, 34-44.

Konstant, B. D. (1997c) The Church and Catholic independent schools, in: Partners in Mission, London, Matthew James Publishing, 59-71.

McMahon, B. M. (2012) The Future of Catholic Education, www.catholicvoices.org.uk, [Accessed 12 February 2014].

Nichols, B. V. (1997) The Church's Mission in Education in a Multi-Faith Society, in: Partners in Mission, London, Matthew James, pp. 44-59.

Pope Benedict XVI (2010) Address to Pupils, Sports Arena of St Mary's University College Twickenham, Friday, 17th September.

Pring, R. (2012a) Perils of Academy status, Letters to the Editor, The Tablet, February 18th, p. 17.

Pring, R. (2012b) 60 years on: the changing role of government, British Journal of Educational Studies, 60. 1. 29-38.

Pycroft, A. (2011) Cash at the cost of ethos, The Tablet, 16th April, p. 19.

Robinson, M. (2002) Continuing professional development, in: M. H. &. L. Gearon (eds) Contemporary Catholic Education, Leominster, Gracewing, pp. 139-154.

Rodger, A. R. (1999) Catholic education: authority and engagement, in: J. C. Conroy (ed) Catholic Education: Inside-Out/Outside-In, Dublin, Lindisfarne Books, pp. 302-323.

Sherrington, J. (2013) Address to the Conference of the Catholic Association of Teachers, Schools & Colleges (CATSC), January 2013.

Sullivan, J. (2000) Catholic Schools in Contention, Dublin, Lindisfarne Books.

United Kingdom Parliament (2010) Academies Act 2010, London, Office of Public Sector Information.

Vatican (1983) Code of Canon Law for the Latin Rite, Vatican City, Libreria Editrice Vaticana.

Mediating the Mission: Teachers in Catholic Primary Schools in Ireland

Fiona Mary Dineen

Editor's Note
The prime purpose of Fiona's EdD thesis was to explore how Primary school teachers understand their role in relation to the Church defined mission of the Catholic school in the contemporary Irish Republic, (always referred to as Ireland in the text). This edited extract includes two of the ten sections of chapter four (entitled 'Presentation of Research Findings') covering the respondents' understanding of the 'ideal' or 'aspirational' ethos of Catholic schools and the challenges involved in generating and sustaining those aspirations, together with one of the six sections of chapter five which provides a synthesis of the 'habitus' of Catholics schools that emerge from the thesis.

Introduction

Ireland occupies a unique situation in the historical relationship that exists between Church and State in the development of the primary phase. However, over recent decades, Ireland as a nation state has undergone significant socio-cultural, economic, political and religious change. At the same time the nature and purpose of Primary education in Ireland has been an area of intense public debate, particularly the role of schools that provide an education within a religious ethos and informed by religious values – often (mis)called 'faith schools'. That there is a tension between competing perspectives of the primary purposes of education is increasingly evident. These contrasting views could be presented as the 'tension between a view of an accountability driven system of education; and one inspired by values and the idea that education is a force for personal and social liberation.'[1]

At the primary level, the tensions between these worldviews manifest themselves in debates about Catholic school management; their religious ethos; inclusion; religious education and faith formation; curriculum content, and sacramental preparation,[2] encouraging a much needed reflection on the nature and purpose of faith schooling in contemporary Ireland at a time when, it can be argued, its contemporary cultural context has directly contributed to an educational system in which pragmatic and utilitarian philosophies pervade that, in turn, regard education as a commodity, driven by measured outcomes.

Such a perspective does not sit easily with the Catholic view of education as an essentially humanising endeavour characterised by the values of love, hope and justice. Consequently, Catholic primary school educators face the lived reality of trying to mediate the mission of the Catholic school and negotiate this ever changing landscape of contrasting worldviews and values.

---

[1] This characterisation is taken from McGettrick, B. (2014) Being Open to Others: Proceedings from the Association of Catholic Institutes for the Study of Education (ACISE) Conference, Liverpool Hope University, April 2014.

[2] See evidence from report on *Forum on Patronage and Pluralism in the Primary Sector*, Department of Education (2014).

Using a positivist paradigm the study explores how teachers ascribe meaning to a Catholic ethos amidst a variety of competing educational, political and cultural agendas. The complex inter-relationship of these agendas and their impact on the role of the teacher is the primary focus of this study. These relationships are reflected in figure 1 below:

Figure 1

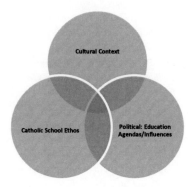

While describing the personal experience of individual teachers is critical for this study, the socio-cultural context of this lived reality must always be part of the discourse, as must the theoretical literature on Catholic education. Hence, while this study seeks to explore and describe the perspective of the teacher, it also seeks to understand how this perspective is related to the particular context of a school and the theoretical assumptions of Catholic education since '… fieldwork material cannot simply be read in the 'vivid present' or it becomes [just] another form … of 'abstracted empiricism'. It has to be read and interpreted against a theoretical framework, a historical set of relations and a cultural configuration of which it is a part' (Grace, 2002: 14). For the purposes of this research I will make use of concepts of 'habitus' and 'field' (Bourdieu, 1967, 1992) and apply them to Catholic primary schools/education in Ireland.

Research Sample and Investigative Methods
The purposive sample consisted of 20 primary school teachers (n = fifteen female; five male) working in a variety of Catholic school settings, i.e. in urban and rural settings, mixed and co-educational schools, large and small schools, and inner city schools designated as 'disadvantaged'.

All the teachers involved had fewer than ten years teaching experience, the range being between one and eight years, and had been employed in at least two Catholic primary schools (range = between two and thirty). These schools were located largely in Southern Ireland with some in the Irish midlands. Four respondents also had experience of teaching in primary schools that were not under Catholic patronage, such as Church of Ireland schools, multi-denominational schools, community national schools and primary State schools in England.

The primary method of data collection used in this study was semi-structured in-depth interviews. For the purposes of the interviews participants[3] were placed in two equal groups of ten, based on the extent of their teaching experience: the first having taught for at least five years; the second between one and five years.

An interview schedule, comprising a relatively small number of open ended initial questions, was prepared as a guide for the participants. The theoretical framework for which was derived from the literature review using the structure of theory level questions to informant level questions. Thus, the theoretical framework of the study informed the broad typologies of questions designed to illuminate three main areas of experience: ethos (as a concept, with specific reference to Catholic schools, its general educational impact and its effect on school leadership);[4] the contemporary cultural context of Catholic schools; and the respondents' personal faith perspective on their educative role.

Exploring School Ethos
Many of the participants found ethos to be a difficult concept and expressed some concern about how helpful their responses would be, while others indicated it was not something on which they had reflected, apart from preparing a response to 'the standard ethos question' at job interviews. The example below, from a teacher of four years' experience, is a fairly typical response.

> '*I suppose ethos is kind of a hard one. Like, I even remember prepping for interviews coming out of college and that being one of the standard questions. You know you are going to get a question on ethos and you would kind of go 'what is ethos?' It is one of those hard, abstract terms. It's not the mission statement, it's more of a ... I think ethos is more who the school is for and what the school is all about really... It's kind of hard to put into words...I think it's what kind of atmosphere the schools want to foster or what kind of general vibe, that's sounds airy fairy, but what they are setting out to achieve really.'*

(Breda)

Despite evident difficulties in engaging with the concept, all the respondents were able to provide a description of what they thought the ideal ethos of a Catholic school might or should be. These responses, however, were varied. While collectively they could be regarded as adequately reflect the prescribed mission of a Catholic school, their variety suggests a more fragmented understanding, at least by this particular sample.

Eight distinct elements were cited as central defining features of the Catholic school ethos. In descending order (based on the number of citations) Catholic school ethos was described as determined primarily by Catholic liturgy and sacramental life; Catholic values; Religious

---

[3] The names of all participants have been changed in order to protect their identity and maintain anonymity.

[4] Note that this extract does not include references in the thesis to the impact of ethos on the leadership of Catholic schools [Ed].

Education; a holistic educative approach; the nature of school relationships; inclusiveness and the presence of clergy and/or religious.

The respondents were also asked to reflect on their opinion of the perceived difference between teaching in a Catholic school and a school with a different ethos. While those in the sample had experience of teaching in a number of Catholic schools, very few had experience of teaching in schools such as Church of Ireland or multi-denominational schools. As such this was a difficult question for the respondents and it was asked in a hypothetical sense.

The majority of the respondents felt that it would be different in the sense that there would not be any sacramental preparation of the pupils or bringing them to mass, but aside from this the generic values promoted by the school would be similar in each school setting.

> *'I wouldn't say that there would be a whole lot, because to be honest, values like understanding and caring ... like no matter what religion you are, they are going to be implemented anyway. But I suppose that comes more from the teacher's background as opposed to the Alive-O programme or whatever says you need to do this kind of thing.'* (Marian)
>
> *'I think that it's [the school ethos] trying to instil the values, you get that in subjects like SPHE, like if you're talking about bullying, treat someone like you would like to be treated, like that is a good lesson for anyone no matter what religion you are, so I think you can still be moral person without being a religious person.'* (Paula)

Nevertheless, perhaps typified by the example below, some they felt that they would find it difficult to be in a school setting where they would feel it might not be possible to mention their personal religious beliefs and expressed concerns about, possibly, inadvertently upsetting parents in a different type of school setting as they would not sure of the boundaries of its particular ethos.

> *'I would find it very difficult to leave my own Christian values apart from my job, because ultimately I went into teaching thinking that these are the things that I want to pass on to the children apart from promoting and helping them to develop academically, but you want a whole roundedness. And yes, obviously children who attend Educate Together schools are, you would hope, being developed in that sort of way as well. BUT* [respondent's emphasis] *I suppose it is so important to me and I feel so strongly about it that I feel it is only right that I follow and am true to myself and that I promote it as best as I can.'* (Aideen)

Catholic Ethos Descriptors - Liturgy, Prayer and Sacramental Preparation
The most consistent descriptor used by the respondents for explaining the ethos of a Catholic school was a reference to liturgy, prayer and sacramental preparation, both as an organic part

of every day school life, as well as celebrating on Church feast days and in the pupils' sacramental preparation.

> 'Well I think to have an intrinsic Catholic ethos would be to ... um ... you know... practising the word of God and making children aware of the word of God every single day. And then doing the rituals you know obviously praying during the day.'   (Paula)
> 'I suppose like that the Catholic ethos is strongest really at the important times of the Church year, at Christmas, at Easter, Lent. St. Brigid's Day, but, and obviously preparing for sacraments is a massive part of it, but I suppose most of the attention is given then and particularly with the sacraments.' (Aideen)

Pupils are involved in sacramental preparation, however, in Second Class and Sixth Class only; just two of the eight years they would spend in a Catholic primary school. Liam, who has had experience in a number of schools in rural and urban settings, provides some indication of a less intense overt religious focus in between times.

> 'Well from the schools I've been in, here we would have our prayers when we come in and in the evening, and maybe not every day. And to be honest, I wouldn't teach religion for the half hour every day.'   (Liam)

Others indicated they would not focus on teaching the formal religious education programme every day due to an overloaded curriculum, arguing that a routine of prayer in the classroom and the ethos of their schools ensured pupils were being encouraged to live their lives -

> '... in a positive way, in a wholesome way with regards morals and honesty, good behaviour more than anything ... rather than religion being pushed down someone's throat.'   (Dan)

Catholic Values
The second most common way[5] of describing the ethos of a Catholic school was in terms of the values that it seeks to promote. The following is fairly typical of many initial thoughts:

> 'I suppose the Catholic school the ethos is to promote the Catholic values, to be kind and to respect others and that's general like that I think in a Catholic school.'   (Maria)

Most respondents were anxious that their pupils showed kindness towards others. However, when encouraged to elaborate and reflect upon any distinctively Catholic characteristics in such behaviour many found it difficult to identify them with any clarity, or to link them explicitly to the stated mission and ethos of Catholic schools.

---

[5] Half of all respondents referred to the connection between values and ethos suggesting that the inculcation of values as an essential element of a Catholic school's ethos.

'Maybe that's what teachers want to instil regardless of if they are a Catholic school, yeah, so maybe that's what there always trying to be kind to one another, but I do find that you would, you would nearly ... Sometimes in Catholic schools, sometimes I find it is nearly more pointed, why it as asking the question 'why would you try to do that to somebody?' I do think that teachers in general would probably think about it as well, they would always try to in still that.' (Sheila)

'I think that's [consideration for others] there in multi-denominational schools as well so I don't think that it is strictly towards Catholic schools. But I suppose I do like the idea of the Catholic school because that is what I was reared with and I like the way religion is taught informally so you might have a little prayer in the morning or before lunch or if someone has died belong to someone you might say a little prayer for them just to let the child know that you are thinking of them and just small little things like that.' (Maria)

A minority of respondents, however, (often with a background in theology or having formal qualifications in Christian Education Leadership) were more confident in rooting their school's values to the Church's educative mission.

'I suppose ... what makes a Catholic school a Catholic school is the beliefs behind it. I mean that we are all made in the image and likeness of God and we are supposed to model that in our daily lives and in out teaching and it's not just during the Alive-O time that you would do that. It's the values and things like that; that you in still in them right throughout the day.' (Helen)

'... the relationships within the school are all modelled on that of Jesus Christ, His Life, Death and Resurrection. And there is a sense of Forgiveness is important, there is a redemptiveness about the school, that it is open and there is a search for truth in the school. And that all of these are lived out daily both by the management, teachers, principal, children and parents and they are all striving to live as Jesus did.' (Chris)

Religious/Holistic Education

The third highest descriptor used by respondents to explain the ethos of a Catholic school was to point to the formal religious education programme. While arguing its centrality of RE to the school most acknowledged its ethos to be much broader, incorporating values and attitudes promoted through all aspects of the life of the school.

'I have always said that ethos is so much more than the Alive-O programme being followed, more than communion being received, confession being received, confirmation being received, I mean you can't push religion into one half hour in a day and leave it at that. It has to manifest itself throughout the day in other aspects of the school.' (Dan)

In doing so, some respondents referred to developing the child in a holistic manner, accounting for all aspects of the child's development:

> 'I suppose to make the sure the whole child is taught rather than just the intellectual child, so that is probably what I would go about saying.' (Marian)

While the holistic development of the person is a central tenet of a Catholic philosophy of education, it is also one of the core principles of the Irish primary school curriculum. Thus all primary schools in Ireland, regardless of their patronage, would likely share this philosophy in the primary phase. As such, a respondent who makes a general statement about the holistic development of the child in relation to the ethos of a primary school may not necessarily be making a specific reference to that of a Catholic school. For example, there is in the following response some ambiguity as to whether it is referring to the ethos of a Catholic school or ethos in general.[6]

> 'Well for me the ethos is to try to develop the child holistically. The religious side of things has drifted for some parents and you have the option of Educate Together schools if parents are very strong about that kind of thing. From my own perspective if would be to develop the child holistically, and developing morals, good from bad, right from wrong.'   (Liam).

Other responses also mentioned developing the whole person as an element of the ethos of a Catholic school, though in the case below, while it is an aspiration, it is not clear whether it is an experienced reality. In contrast, some respondents made an explicit connection between the holistic development of the child and their lived experience of a Catholic school ethos.

> 'And [school is] a place where they try to promote Christian values maybe and a place where they are trying to develop the whole person. Well that would be the aspiration, so whether that happens or not I don't know...It probably does happen though I'd say when I think about it.'   (Rachel)
>
> 'The ethos I suppose is almost like the spirit of the school, like what the school wants from you, what kind of development they want from the children, not just intellectual, like all aspects of life, they would have spiritual growth and physical growth and religious and everything, it's not just intellectual based or school focussed and academic focussed. And, I suppose what I mean by the atmosphere is that you can feel it ... like I really love assemblies because you can really get a sense of the ethos there...because its lovely the whole school there and saying their prayers together and its lovely when the Infants can join in with their Father in Heaven and that. So I suppose ethos is about community as well, about sharing this one faith and uniting together.' (Jane)

---

[6] The addition of 'developing morals' in the response would suggest that the intention was to discuss a Catholic school ethos.

Relationships

A quarter of the teachers interviewed described the ethos of a Catholic school in terms of the formation of relationships within the school community. Some talked in a general sense without identifying anything specifically Catholic; others made only oblique references to Christian precepts of 'loving one's neighbour'. The two examples below are typical of the general tenor of responses that highlighted the relational element of ethos.

> *'I suppose within the schools you have to kind of see how the teachers would get on with each other, if there is conflict that can be seen and children would pick up on the negative vibes, so I suppose keeping a positive atmosphere within the school first of all and ensuring that the children are kind of happy in the school and if there is something wrong that they can feel that they can talk to somebody.'* (Marian)
>
> *'Well I think it is a place where everyone, it's a place where the teachers work together in the hope that all of the children in the school are treated equally and learn to treat other people as equals. I suppose that stems from the idea treat your neighbour as you would like them to treat you.'* (Jim)

Other Descriptors – Inclusion; Clergy Involvement

Inclusive education is a significant issue of public debate in primary education in Ireland.[7] However, only a small number of the research sample described the ethos of the Catholic school in terms of inclusivity. Where they did so, rather than considering how children from non-Catholic or non-religious backgrounds should/could be accommodated in Catholic primary schools, it was focused more on discussion of effective educational methods for children with special needs or non-Irish nationals, or ways to include all children at playtime or on a sports team.

Given that the inclusion of children of other faiths in Catholic primary schools is a major issue in the national educational debate it is perhaps surprising that only a small percentage of respondents made reference to the ethos of the Catholic school and inclusion. It raises questions about the extent to which young primary teachers in Ireland engage with the national education debates and policy developments in this area even though in recent years policy makers in Ireland have led a number of consultation processes and reports on inclusion.

The results of this research, however, suggest that the majority of the particular sample did not see a direct connection between the ethos of the Catholic school and the nature of educational inclusion. Slightly more of the research sample suggested that the ethos of a Catholic school was linked to the physical presence of a member of the clergy amongst the school community and the positive impact that this had, both on the children and as a bridge between home and Church.

---

[7] The major elements and themes of this debate are not included in these edited extracts but are extensively explored in the introductory chapters of the thesis [Ed].

'I suppose the parish curate would be a regular visitor to the school and there is a great sense of respect for the parish curate. He comes in very regularly and I think it is a fantastic element of the Catholic ethos.'   (Chris)

'I suppose the main thing is a kind of connection between the parents and the Church as well. It's great that schools use the parents and use the Church as much as they can. ... Our local priest always brings stories to them, a lot of them are altar serving with him and he knows their names and makes great reference to them when he does visit the school.'   (Paul)

Challenges to Sustaining and Developing the Ethos of the Catholic School

The members of the sample were asked to identify what they found to be the greatest challenges in being role models in 'living out' the ethos of the Catholic school. Three issues were frequently mentioned, though with different emphases, by most respondents: parental views about the character and purposes Catholic schools; changing societal attitudes towards the Catholic Church; and the role of the teacher in religious education.

Parental Attitudes and Life-Styles – Religious Practice

The greatest challenge identified by this sample concerned the parents and their attitudes towards Catholicism. Two-thirds of sample commented on the low level of Mass attendance by their pupils placing them (and their parents) in opposition to the values promoted by the school's ethos and encouraged by teachers, especially where they are involved in pupils' sacramental preparation.

Whereas teachers, at one time, would have been confident that pupils would be familiar with the words of common prayers and of Mass responses that was not the experience of many respondents.

'I suppose in the last few years the numbers going to Mass and attending church I suppose locally have dropped and that would affect the school. Like the school is trying to promote the Catholic values and attending Mass and then I suppose and then if you have parents going well I don't see the point in going anymore, well culture in that respect is changing.'   (Marian)

'And the children coming to school now and they don't know their prayers and they don't know the mass responses because are not being taken to Mass and it's left to us and they'll turn up on the day for communion and confirmation... I think that there is more of a responsibility on the teacher now to teach the sacrament, to teach the prayers, because the faith it isn't coming from home.'

Helen)

Religion Education Programme

Some respondents had recounted instances of being challenged by parents about the content of the Religious Education programme and being selective in their teaching in Religious Education to avoiding potential complaints from parents.

'I know myself I had a discussion with a parent who didn't want his daughter doing religion. And he was English and thought all the bible stores, as well as the Irish language were pointless, and he actually mentioned the fact that he was a carpenter and did I actually believe that a carpenter back in the olden days could build a boat that would try to carry species of every animal in the entire world. So I actually had a discussion with him and I do think that yes was a challenge.' (Paula)

'Even though it is a Catholic school you would almost feel in today's society ... they could almost still complain that you are promoting certain things. For example, I know that one man that I was talking to and he was telling me that he went into the school and was giving out that they were doing the Lenten story with the children. And I was like but it is a Catholic ethos school... And he said but I don't want... you know what it is, it's political correctness...but you wonder could the parents potentially be coming in and giving out, even though this is part of the Catholic ethos... I think that is very difficult for teachers.' (Aideen)

Some respondents suggested such attitudes were symptomatic of a lessening of deference towards authority figures - rather than specific concern with Catholic education - and a growing culture in which many parents automatically challenge the authority of the school and teachers.

'I don't think that there is the same respect for teachers as there used to be. Before it used to be the priest, the teacher and the guard... Whereas now they are coming into to kill the teacher, it's hard in that way. They don't hold the school in esteem anymore. They are more demanding. You know if you meet parents and you have concerns about their kids rather than respecting that you want the best for their child.' (Rachel)

Changing Attitudes Towards Organised Religion

Respondents also cited changing societal attitudes towards the Catholic Church due, in part, to recent child abuse scandals, an increasing diverse society and a more 'lax' attitude in general to the religious practice.

'I think people are, people's opinions definitely changed with everything that happened in the Church, but I'm not saying that's what changed culture, not just that alone. But like even like the change in media all in the last few years has completely changed culture as well and then there is recession as well, and all that's going on in the world.' (Anne)

In some instances, respondents argued that while parents may have become disillusioned with the institutional Church, they were not necessarily opposed to the proclaimed ethos of the Catholic school:

'I suppose you meet parents and the parents attitudes wouldn't be all that great towards, and it's not even about ethos or Catholic school ethos, but it is more about the Church. It's about the Church and the Church's fault. It's like why are you bringing them in there and teaching them about X, Y and Z.' (Breda)

However, this distinction was not common among respondents, who generally regarded a negative attitude towards the institutional Church as implying a negative attitude towards the religious nurturing and ethos of the Catholic school.

Teaching Religion

Half of the respondents suggested that one of the major challenges for the living out of the ethos of the Catholic school was connected with the teaching of religion, identifying as major factors, pupils with challenging attitudes towards religion, particularly in the senior classes of the school; a lack of knowledge on the part of teachers when responding to difficult questions; the need to adapt teaching styles because of pupils' low base line knowledge and the increasing presence of children from non-Catholic faith backgrounds in the Religious Education lesson. Some suggested there was a need to update the current Religious Education programme. Nevertheless, they were positive about engaging with such challenges.

'I just accept it, and I try to get it around to it much more every day and every week. I try to touch on as much of the Alive-O programme as I can, because you are aware that the children aren't experiencing as much outside school as they used to be when I was in school. And I think you have to do a bit more in school.' (Paul)

'Well I think, if you compared it to let's say, if a class had a low level of literacy, if they weren't reading at home, it would change the way you teach English, you would go back to a more basic level. And that happens then as well with religion. Now they are still displaying great attributes and all that would be kind of universal but ... in the actual faith element of it, it is ... I feel it is more basic now than when I was in school.' (Jim)

[The section above, taken from chapter four of the thesis, presented edited highlights from its findings. The following section, taken from chapter five, analyses the research findings using elements of Bourdieu's conceptual toolkit namely habitus, field and cultural capital to explore the multi-faceted and multi-dimensional concept of the Catholic school ethos derived from interviews with the respondents, Ed.]

Analysis of Data Findings

The data collected from the semi-structured interviews were analysed using the theoretical lens of *habitus* as embodiment, *habitus* and agency, *habitus* as a compilation of collective and individual trajectories and *habitus* as a complex interplay between past and present (Reay, 2004: 432-435). In addition, it will use the concept of spiritual capital to explore how teachers understand their role in relation to the ethos and mission of the Catholic school and the potential impact that it has on in sustaining and maintaining the mission of the Catholic school (Grace, 2010).

The Field: Catholic Primary Schools

In this study the Catholic primary school sector is conceptualised as a field. For Bourdieu (1992: 72-73), a field is 'a configuration of relations between positions objectively defined, in their existence and in the determinations they impose upon the occupants, agents or institutions.' A field is a bounded social space, as such the configuration of relations within a field are prescribed by a guiding set of principles but the medium of these relations is capital and habitus and these shape the practice within a field. Hence, a Catholic school is a field in that the ethos and mission have been externally defined but the practice within the Catholic school is shaped by the competing interests of capital and habitus of the occupants of the institution (Green, 2013: 14).

The findings suggest that the field - that is the Catholic school - does have an influence on the behaviour, attitudes and assumptions of a significant number of the sample in relation to how they interpret their role in relation to the school's ethos and mission. The respondents displayed an awareness of the objectively defined field of the Catholic school in terms of how they described the ethos and mission of the school, but there was evidence that these expectations did not transfer to other social spaces or fields that the respondents occupy. For example, two-thirds of the participants identified the greatest challenge they faced in living out the ethos of the Catholic school was low attendance at Mass by the pupils.

Yet, discussing their own personal faith perspective, only one-quarter expressed explicitly that their faith had an impact on their daily lives while a number indicated they did not practising their faith regularly or necessarily agree with [various aspects of] Church teaching. It is evident a significant number of the participants do not feel that it is relevant that they should comply with the expectations that they propose for/expect from parents, even though many of them argue that this is the greatest challenge for living out the ethos of the school. This indicates that some participants display a particular habitus in the field (that is, the Catholic school) which does not transfer to other fields. They have internalised a perception of what is appropriate action for individuals in a Catholic school which, in turn, shapes their attitudes towards parental practice, but outside of that context these perceptions and attitudes or habitus differ when applied to themselves. However, no awareness of this discrepancy was demonstrated by the respondents, suggesting the embodied habitus was held at an unconscious level. This form of individual collusion with the society of which they are a member, which Bourdieu labels 'fit', is like the sense of being at home in a family milieu, an 'ontological complicity' between embodied history and institutional roles (Atkin, 2003: 510).

This discrepancy raises questions about the impact that the expression of a habitus that encompasses 'a double perception of the self, successive allegiances and multiple identities' (Bourdieu, 1999: 511) has on the ethos of the Catholic school on a long term basis and whether teachers in a Catholic school should be expected to be living witnesses to the ethos and mission of the school. Further, while there has been a plethora of policy and position statements in relation to Catholic primary education in Ireland in recent years, the respondents did not evidence any awareness of these policies or any major engagement with the national debates that surround schools with a religious character.

Habitus and the Catholic School

Habitus refers to the deeply rooted assumptions, not explicitly reflected upon but held almost unconsciously, which everyone inherits (Bourdieu, 1977: 72) and which regulate both individual and collective action in the social world (Green, 2013: 7) Early childhood experience, both in the family and the school, play a critical role in the formation of these assumptions and dispositions. While it may be a product of individual history, these early socialisations are continually re-structured by individuals' encounters with the outside world. Thus, any particular habitus can be envisaged as a continuum; at one end, simply replicated by life's experiences or, at the other, which can be transformed into something very different from that initial milieu (Reay, 2004:435). If that is the case, this continuum of habitus exists in the teachers who participated in this study.

To some extent there was a shared habitus amongst the young teachers who participated in this study. Elements of this shared habitus were evident from the dispositions, attitudes and experiences that they displayed in the course of the interviews. This shared habitus was rooted in similar backgrounds in terms of their faith socialisation and experience. The vast majority of the sample recounted the positive impact of being brought up in devout Catholic families, even if they no longer practiced. Their habitus also encompassed the common experience in attending Catholic primary schools and, for most of the respondents, completing their education studies in a Catholic College. While the findings suggest that the majority displayed some elements of a shared habitus, for example, in their attitudes towards the teaching profession and towards the pupils in their schools, there was also evidence of differences with regard to their role in their particular Catholic schools. While one needs to proceed with caution with the use of categories, being aware of their limitations and open to the fluidity and continuum that exists between them, the data show that respondents could be categorised as falling into types of habitus; illustrated in the form of four teacher profiles.

The Fully Committed Teacher

The data show a quarter of the sample can be categorised as being fully committed to their role within their Catholic schools. During the interviews they discussed having a lived faith and how it impacts on their daily lives, referenced significant home and Catholic school experiences that affected their lives and religious faith and were actively involved at parish or diocesan level through Parish Pastoral Councils or Youth Ministry.

They enjoyed their work in a Catholic school and were articulate in describing its religious ethos, both in an idealised sense and its practical implementation. They demonstrated that they could explicitly describe the religious ethos of the Catholic school, had an awareness of the multiple dimensions of Christian faith,[8] could suggest how these might be realised in a

---

[8] See, for example, the discussion of ways in which religious faith can be actively promoted in schools through proclamation (*kerygma*), worship (*leitourgia*), fellowship (*koinonia*) and service (*diakonia*) in: Sullivan, J.

Catholic school and explain, to some extent, their role in language very similar to that found in the formal Church documents and exhortations on Catholic education.[9] It is clear that their habitus, formed from their early socialising experiences in Catholic homes and schools were being reproduced in the fields that they encountered in the adult and professional lives. Some respondents who fitted this profile, however, had not encountered fields that might restructure this habitus, for example, never having taught in schools with a religiously diverse pupil population. It is also noteworthy, particularly in relation to the broader conversation about Catholic education in Ireland, that while all the participants of this profile were identified as committed and confident about their role in the Catholic school, they were not familiar with recent developments or initiatives in Catholic education at a national level. On one level, this raises questions about how these policies and initiatives are communicated to teachers in primary schools and how their ongoing professional development needs are met. At another level it raises questions about field positions taken with regard to Catholic schools. It highlights the need to reflect on what has formed these positions and are they always positions that have encountered contemporary thinking on Catholic schools and Catholic education more broadly.

The Committed but Critical Teacher

The second category, or profile, is that of a teacher who is committed to their Catholic faith, but has adopted a critical stance towards aspects of the Catholic school and the teachings of the Catholic Church. While they spoke positively about the impact of their Catholic socialisation through their families and school experiences, and could articulate the aspirational ethos of the Catholic school, they did not use any explicitly religious language in doing so. In addition, they were cautious in their approach to evidencing or claiming how this aspirational ethos was manifested in the school on a daily basis.

These respondents debated the extent to which the ethos of their schools was reflective of the Catholic ethos or generated from the values and dispositions of the teachers in a particular school. The respondents from this profile were also highly critical of elements of the religious education programme used in Catholic schools. Yet, a number of the respondents in this profile were committed to their role in the Catholic school. They did state, however, that while they still went to Mass, this was not a regular practice. Nevertheless, the respondents in this profile were positively disposed towards promoting the ethos of the Catholic school and were particularly positive towards their involvement in the sacramental preparation of the pupils. On the other hand, they often perceived the authority and impact of the local clergy with regard to the school, its teachers and curriculum content in a generally negative way, suggesting that it resulted in a form of 'custodian' ethos (Hogan, 1984). This type of commentary on the role and relationship of the local clergy with the Catholic school was absent from the respondents in the other categories/profiles.

(2011) Text and Context: Mediating the Mission in Catholic Schools, in: Sullivan (ed) Communicating Faith, Washington D.C., The Catholic University of America, 106.

[9] See, for example, documents published by the Congregation for Catholic Education, 1977; 1988; 1004; 2013; 2014. See also documents published by under the authority of the Irish bishops, Catholic Schools Partnership, 2012a; 2012b.

While further research would be necessary on why these respondents in this case study held these dispositions and attitudes, it could be suggested that this reflects Bourdieu's explanation of the interplay of habitus and individual agency. Reay (2004: 433) proposes that habitus can generate a wide repertoire of possible actions, 'simultaneously enabling the individual to draw on transformative and constraining courses of action.' The respondents in this case study demonstrated how they were predisposed to certain ways of behaving, but simultaneously agency had a role to play in the reproduction of their habitus. Furthermore, their logic of practice may also have been influenced by encountering a field that transformed their habitus. A number of respondents who fit this profile noted experiences from their personal lives that might be perceived by some to conflict with the ethos of the Catholic school. Nevertheless, they felt that they were committed to their faith but not uncritical in their attitudes and dispositions. The role of individual agency was also evident in their interpretation of their approach to practice, in both their personal and professional lives.

This profile of respondent corroborated the theory of Hervieu-Léger (2000) that the 'chain of memory' of a religious tradition is challenged by the fragmentation and collective amnesia of society. These respondents could be identified as religious bricoleurs, using their 'symbolic repositories of meaning' to produce their own relationship to their religious tradition. This also echoes a recent study by Casson (2013: 64) which found that there was a fragmentary understanding of Catholic identity in a group of Catholic school students who did not retain a holistic or fixed view of what it is to be Catholic, but at the same time they did not reject a Catholic identity.

The Religiously Indifferent Teacher
The third profile of teacher that emerged from the data was what could be described as the indifferent teacher in the Catholic school. These respondents, self-identified Catholics, seemed never to have reflected on, or been overly concerned with, the ethos of the Catholic school in which they worked prior to becoming involved with this research. Though they had similar childhood socialisation in the Catholic faith from both family and school environments as others in the sample, some of these respondents made no comment, about their own faith practice; others, however, stated that they did not practice regularly.

They tended to regard the central purpose of Catholic schools to be about encouraging Mass attendance amongst the pupils; the only major aspect of school life that distinguished such schools from any other type. During interviews, they did not describe the ethos of the Catholic school beyond using the key words of prayer, sacraments and religious education. Nor did they use language that expressed any form of personal commitment to the ideal ethos of the Catholic school but tended to use abstract descriptors 'repeating a professional discourse as part of their training;' resulting in 'little usable data beyond the expression of institutional ideology in action' (Holstein & Gubrium, 2003: 385); what could be characterised as a superficial attachment to their school's ethos (Donnelly, 2000).

However, this does not, necessarily, imply they were actively opposed to the ethos of Catholic schooling; rather that they displayed a detached and indifferent attitude towards it; a form of complacency about their school's ethos and how it related to their educative role. It may be the case that they are simply unaware of the values that drive the initiatives that they implement in a school and as such they may not be aware of the competing philosophies and values that exist. Nevertheless, such teachers are always mediating the mission of the Catholic school in the context in which they operate. Therefore, such a context will shape a multi layered habitus, and teachers unknowingly synthesise values and apply to the various contexts in which they find themselves (Sullivan, 2011). Those in this category reflect, to some extent, the notion of Irish cultural Catholic proposed by Inglis when he argued:

> 'Most Irish Catholics are still born into the Church, baptised and socialised into its beliefs and practices. Between home and Catholic school, most children develop a Catholic habitus, a deeply embodied, almost automatic way of being spiritual and moral that becomes second nature and creates a Catholic sense of self and a way of behaving and interpreting the world.'
>
> (Inglis, 2007: 206)

It is recognised that extrapolation from this small sample is problematical. That it was possible, however, to identify this category of teacher working in Catholic schools suggests that while not all will subscribe to a recognised Catholic school ethos, it is important that there are sufficient who do, in order that such an ethos might be sustained and developed. As such, the existence of this category of teachers provides some empirical evidence to support assertions that a 'lack of critical mass, that is, having insufficient numbers of individuals in a Catholic institution who give concrete witness to the identity of the institution, is a major challenge for Catholic schools (Rymarz (2010: 300); and that 'diminishing spiritual capital is factor impacting on the mission fidelity of Catholic schools' (Grace, 2010: 124).

The 'Actor' Teacher

The fourth profile to emerge from the sample was that of the 'actor' displaying a multi-layered habitus comprising very different attitudes and views in relation to Catholic schools though their early childhood, family and school socialisation was consistent with that of all the other respondents. They were articulate in describing the ethos of the Catholic school yet they had reservations about the extent to which the formal ethos of the school impacted on the daily life of the school, often arguing that all schools are really the same in terms of the values that they promote. During interviews they were open about not practising their faith or sharing all the values promoted by the Catholic school. They also were critical of how contentious issues, such as human relationships and sex education were presented.

They would not, however, openly disclose such views to the principal or any member of the Catholic school community of which they were a part and tended to give their professional identity precedence over any personal considerations. For example, during interviews their language demonstrated some degree of care and vigilance in presenting a professional identity in school while hiding that which, they regarded, as being purely personal. Because they felt that they had to fulfil their professional duties first and foremost towards the schools in which they were teaching they tended to leave their personal identity at the door and played to the full the role model expected of them, masking their personal attitudes and values from the pupils.

Given the evident conflict between their personal and professional identities, these respondents could be described as being complicit with the ethos of the Catholic school but on the basis that none of them wanted to 'stand out or be the odd one out.' For them, the social space and culture of the Catholic school tended to constrain their 'natural' behaviour, and illustrates how the collective habitus of a social institution can impact on the individual habitus of all members. It also raises questions about how the ethos of the Catholic school can be maintained or developed if the majority of teachers in the school shared this position.

Summary and Conclusions

Acknowledging that education is always a contested space with a myriad of competing perspectives, this research sought to investigate how primary school educators understand their role in relation to the Church defined mission and ethos of the Catholic school, to explore the lived realities of young primary educators as they attempt to mediate that mission and, further to this exploration, establish what model of Catholic school ethos was emerging amidst the cultural context of contemporary Ireland, a context that is characterised by rapidly changing socio - cultural contexts; shifting educational paradigms; and political influences.

This was a small study attempting to explore the complex dynamic of relationships in the Catholic school from the perspective of the educator. The size of the sample (in the context of the number of Catholic schools that exist in Ireland) means, however, that it is limited in the extent to which the application of its findings can be made. Nonetheless, it provides critical empirical data in a field where there is a dearth of such studies and the realities presented may be indicative of the wider experience of primary educators in Catholic schools in Ireland.

It could be argued that living in this liminal age requires all involved in Catholic schools to have an awareness of the foundational philosophy that inspires their educational endeavour - the ethos and mission of the Catholic school - so the study explored the complex relationships that are intrinsic to these formative factors. Examining the educational and cultural contexts in which Catholic schools operated compounded the intricacy of the various influences that impact on the teachers' mediation of the ethos of the Catholic school: the foundational documents from the Catholic Church which illuminated the formal or espoused Catholic school ethos; the historical roots and evolvement of the Irish primary system to appreciate the complex relationship between Church and State at both an educational and socio-cultural level.

Employing a theoretical framework that acknowledged how these various influences come together in the practice of the educator and the contested nature of ethos; elements of Bourdieu's conceptual toolkit, namely habitus, field and cultural capital were applied to the data to excavate how teachers understand and ascribe meaning to their practice in this qualitative study.[10] The analysed data provided a significant insight into the lived realities of educators in Catholic primary schools as they try to mediate its mission.

The findings suggest that collectively the participants could express a coherent account of the formal ethos of the Catholic school, but at an individual level this account is much more fragmented in nature and there is a stark contrast in the language used by those who identified themselves as being committed Catholics and those who did not.

The majority of the participants did not demonstrate any overt awareness of the cultural, political and educational influences that shape their role in the Catholic school. There was indirectly, however, evidence that the liminal state in which Catholic schools operate was a cause of anxiety for some of the research sample at the micro level of the classroom. The rhetoric around the formal ethos of the Catholic school does not appear to have a great impact; with many respondents having difficulty identifying the implicit ethos of the Catholic school and only acknowledging the explicit aspects of the ethos of the Catholic school such as prayer, liturgies, sacramental preparation, visible icons and religious education.

Nevertheless, the respondents in this sample were positively disposed towards the ethos of the Catholic school; although emergent themes were evident in the 'field positions' that they adopted in their working lives. For some educators there was a lack of authentic connection with the ethos of the Catholic school to the extent that they could be described as fitting the field of the Catholic school rather than critically engaging with mediating the mission of the school. Consequently, from the potential of multiple lived realities, four separate teacher profiles emerged from the data provided by participants in this study - fully committed; committed but critical; indifferent; and 'the actor' – pointing to the tensions that exist between the theory and practice of the Catholic school.

While the four models of primary teacher may be helpful in clarifying positions that can emerge in Catholic primary schools, they also pointed to another layer of complexity when exploring issues of ethos and identity. For example, while the participants were open about the faith commitment to the ethos of the Catholic schools, some had not encountered any experiences that might challenge their assumptions and beliefs, nor were some aware of recent ecclesial developments that might impact on their role in the Catholic school. This, I suggest, has implications for the content and quality of initial teacher education and the ongoing professional development of educators with regard the ethos and mission of the Catholic school.

The findings also suggest that the recent plethora of policy and position statements from educational sector and the Church have had limited, if any, impact on young teachers.

---

[10] It is recognised that Bourdieu's concepts provide just one framework for accessing the unconscious elements of a teacher's identity and development. However, further research using a variety of methods of data collection, would be necessary to extend and substantiate the four emergent habitus of teachers found in the research sample. See, for example, Leitch 2006.

Furthermore, while the policy and position statements are helpful at the macro level, it is not enough just to have the rhetoric about the mission and ethos of Catholic schools, there needs to be an ongoing reflection and engagement with how this mission and values can be inculturated in the school community. This raises questions about communication and reception and how this might be enhanced going forward. It suggests that attention should be given to the ways in which educators can be facilitated in engaging with recent policies and initiatives.

The research sought to investigate the character of Catholic school ethos that was currently emerging in the contemporary Irish context. Given the spectrum of responses that were provided, it is difficult to make any definite claims. The recurrence of the centrality of liturgy, prayer and worship in the data, however, suggest that it is closer to that of the 'dualistic school' proposed by Arthur (1995: 227-228) than the ideal presented in official Church documents. Such schools operate a 'dual function' largely indistinguishable from any other school in the majority of their activities, but with a distinctive religious element added on. Consideration needs to be given to how school communities can be encouraged to reflect upon their ethos so that it is an intrinsic to the school as opposed to external cladding. The study, however, in an area with little empirical research, provides a significant insight through the four case studies into the lived realities of educators in Catholic primary schools as they try to mediate its mission. These findings are a helpful starting point for reflecting on and informing recommendations and future directions for Catholic primary schools in Ireland.

Recommendations

This was a small study attempting to explore the complex dynamic of relationships in the Catholic school from the perspective of the educator. While small in scale, the significance of the study is that is provides critical empirical data in a field where there is a dearth of such studies. Furthermore, the theoretical framework that sought to integrate the various educational, political, ecclesial and cultural influences on the teacher in the Catholic school and using the lens of Bourdieu's conceptual toolkit for analysis is an original approach to this context in the Irish Primary sector which, I suggest, will be a useful tool in any further research in the area. Given my small sample however, further investigation of the interplay of these complex positions would require a much larger ethnographic study, employing multi methods of data collection if it were to advance understanding of the problems and potential solutions to the dilemma.

Secondly, the four teacher typologies that emerged sharpens focus on the tensions that exist as to whether the respondents were mediating the mission of the Catholic school in a particular operating context or whether they were fitting to the field of the Catholic school because their perception of their professional identity enabled this ontological complicity. The rich data also have implications for professional practice in so much as they can provide a framework for critiquing the current diocesan structures providing ongoing support to educators in Catholic schools which, I would argue, relying on historically evolved that do not take adequate account of the contemporary context in which Catholic schools operate.

Thirdly, a review of initial teacher education programmes for Catholic educators should consider the balance between information and formation elements. This is particularly urgent given the fragmented understanding of ethos that emerged and the language that was employed by the participants in describing the ethos of the Catholic school.

Fourthly, the anxiety expressed by the young teachers in relation to teaching religion requires further exploration. A more specific needs analysis or diocesan focus groups would establish how future formation programmes might be designed to assist teachers in their role. A longitudinal study would be helpful in tracking if this made any impact in alleviating this anxiety.

References

Arthur, J. (1995) The Ebbing Tide: policy and principles of catholic education, Leominster, Gracewing.

Atkin, C. (2003) Rural Communities: human and symbolic capital development, Fields Apart Compare 33. 4. 507-518, London, Carfax.

Bourdieu, P. (1967) Systems of Education and Systems of Thoughts, paper presented to the Sixth World Conference of Sociology, (1966) and first published in International Social Studies Journal, 19. 3., in: E. Hopper (ed) (1971) Readings in the Theory of Educational Systems, London, Hutchinson & Co Ltd, 159-183.

Bourdieu, P. (1977) Outline of a Theory of Practice, Cambridge, Cambridge University Press.

Bourdieu, P. (1992) The Rules of Art, Cambridge, Polity Press.

Bourdieu, P. (1999) Structures, Habitus, Practices, in: A. Elliot (ed) (1999) The Blackwell Reader in Contemporary Social Theory, Oxford, Blackwell.

Casson, A. (2013) Fragmented Catholicity and Social Cohesion: faith schools in a plural society, Oxford, Peter Lang.

Catholic Schools Partnership (2012a) A Process for Understanding, Supporting and Taking Ownership of the Characteristic Spirit in a Catholic School (www.catholicschools.ie), [Accessed 20 May 2012].

Catholic Schools Partnership (2012b) Catholic Primary Schools: Looking to the Future (www.catholicschools.ie), [Accessed, 20 May 2012].

Congregation for Catholic Education (1977) The Catholic School, Homebush, NSW, St Pauls.

Congregation for Catholic Education (1988) The Religious Dimension of Education in a Catholic School, Homebush, NSW, St Pauls.

Congregation for Catholic Education (2004) The Catholic School at the Threshold of the Third Millenium, Dublin, Veritas.

Congregation for Catholic Education (2013) Educating to Intercultural Dialogue in Catholic Schools: living in harmony for a civilisation of love (www.vatican.va), [Accessed 6 June 2014].

Congregation for Catholic Education (2014) Educating Today and Tomorrow, (www.vatican.va), [Accessed 6 June 2014].

Department of Education, (1992) Education for a Changing World (Green Paper on Education), Dublin, The Stationery Office.

Department of Education, (1995) Charting Our Education Future (White Paper on Education), Dublin, The Stationery Office.

Department of Education (2014) Forum on Patronage and Pluralism in the Primary Sector: progress to date and future directions (www.education.ie), [Accessed 4 July 2014].

Donnelly, C. (2000) In pursuit of school ethos, British Journal of Educational Studies, 48. 2. 134-154.

Grace, G. (2002) Catholic Schools: mission, markets and morality, London, Routledge.

Grace, G. (2010) Renewing spiritual capital: an urgent priority for the future of catholic education internationally, International Studies in Catholic Education, 2. 2. 117-128.

Green, E. (2013) Research in New Christian Academies: perspectives from Bourdieu, in: M. Murphy (ed) (2013) Social Theory and Education Research, London, Sage.

Hervieu-Léger, D. (2000) Religion as a Chain of Memory, Cambridge, Polity Press.

Hogan, P. (1984) The question of school ethos, The Furrow 35. 11. 693-703.

Holstein, J. & Gubrium, J. (eds) (2003) Inside Interviewing: new lenses, new concerns, London, Sage.

Inglis, T. (2007) Catholic identity in contemporary Ireland: belief and belonging to tradition, Journal of Contemporary Religion, 22. 2. 205-220.

Irish Catholic Bishops' Conference (2007) Catholic Primary Schools: a policy for provision into the future, Dublin, Veritas.

Irish Catholic Bishops' Conference (2008) A Vision for Catholic Education in Ireland (Vision 08), Dublin: Veritas.

Leitch, R. (2006) Limitations of language: developing arts-based creative narratives in stories of teachers' identities, Teachers and Teaching: Theory and Practice, 12. 5. 549-569.

McGettrick, B. (2014) Being Open to Others, proceedings from the ACISE Conference, Liverpool Hope University, April 2014.

Reay, D. (2004) 'It's all becoming a habitus': beyond the habitual use of habitus in educational research, British Journal of Sociology of Education, 25. 4. 431-444.

Rymarz, R., (2010) Religious identity of Catholic schools: some challenges from a Canadian perspective, Journal of Belief and Values, 31. 3. 299-310.

Sullivan, J. (ed) (2011) Communicating Faith, Washington, Catholic University Press.